PRODUCING **HIT RECORDS**

by DAVID JOHN FARINELLA   SECRETS FROM THE STUDIO

SCHIRMER
TRADE
BOOKS

A Part of The **Music Sales** *Group*
New York/London/Paris/Sydney/Copenhagen/Berlin/Tokyo/Madrid

Schirmer Trade Books
A Division of Music Sales Corporation, New York

Exclusive Distributors:
Music Sales Corporation
257 Park Avenue South, New York, NY 10010 USA

Music Sales Limited
8/9 Frith Street, London W1D 3JB England

Music Sales Pty. Limited
120 Rothschild Street, Rosebery, Sydney, NSW 2018, Australia

Order No. SCH 10139
International Standard Book Number: 0.8256.7299.6

Printed in the United States of America

Cover Design: Josh Labouve
Cover photo: Corbis

Library of Congress Cataloging-in-Publication Data

Farinella, David John, 1967-
  Producing hit records : secrets from the studio / by David John Farinella.
    p. cm.
  ISBN 0-8256-7299-6 (pbk. : alk. paper)
  1. Sound recording industry—Vocational guidance. 2. Sound recordings—Production and direction. 3. Sound recording executives and producers—Biography. I. Title.

ML3790.F365 2006
781.49—dc22

                                    2005013954

CONTENTS

ACKNOWLEDGEMENTS

Of all things that make a strong story, I believe, the characters are the most important. I am thankful that the bounty of characters in the world of record producers and musicians is vast. It's to them, for their generosity in time and willingness to share the good, bad, and ugly of their craft, that I owe a tremendous debt of gratitude. To those who welcomed me into the studio while they recorded, those who took time out to chat with me over the phone in between sessions, and those who welcomed me into their homes: Thank you over and over again. I hope I did right by your generosity.

That said, this project might not have been possible without the support of my wife, Elizabeth. It is to her I owe the largest debt, because in our first year of marriage she put up with a new husband who was largely nocturnal, slightly pre-occupied, and occasionally absent. She made me laugh at all the right times and stood next to me during the tough times.

Likewise, there are a handful of people who deserve thanks for their support and heckling during this process. Steve Bigham, David "The King" Kuhner, Dave Smith, Rick Kutler, and the boys at the Nursery kept me grounded over the past two years. Certainly, a round of thank you's goes out to all branches of my family, who always asked in a concerned tone how the book was going. Done, I can answer now, with some relief.

I wouldn't have been in a position to write this book in the first place if it hadn't been for the editors that I worked with over the years who pushed me to ask better questions, write with care, and pay attention to deadlines and word counts…well, at least the first two. Also, thanks to Andrea Rotondo who offered (it seems so long ago) this project to me originally, helped me shape it into what it is now, and continually cheered me on from the other coast. Also, thanks to Barbara Schultz, who took time out between corralling her kids to polish my ideas and words into something a bit more cohesive.

At the same time, I need to express my thanks to the managers and publicists who assisted me in setting up the interviews that brought this book to life. Also, thanks to Lisa Pilcher, Shelley Young, and the team at TBL Transcriptions who saved me oodles of time.

In the last-but-not-least category, I do believe that I am incredibly lucky to have been surrounded by an art form that conveys such strong emotions, has pulled me through some of the darkest of days, and enhanced some of the best. Although I've spent much of my past two years working on this book (and a career writing about music), I have to begrudgingly agree with what Declan MacManus (aka, Elvis Costello) told *Esquire* magazine: "Songs are more powerful than books." Well, at least I tried.

—D.J.F.

ABOUT THE AUTHOR

David John Farinella has been writing about the inside of the music business since the beginning of his career, concentrating his attention on performers, songwriters, record producers, and occasionally the personality that fuses them all. Farinella got his start covering the San Francisco Bay Area music scene in 1990 and he quickly moved into the national media, contributing to such publications as *Billboard, Mix, Rolling Stone, Alternative Press, Performing Songwriter, Modern Drummer,* and a handful of memorable, yet defunct, music magazines. In addition to his regular magazine contributions, Farinella was an associate editor for *The Encyclopedia of Record Producers.* Although Farinella has interviewed some legendary performers, it is the story behind the story that has constantly fascinated him. Some of his most memorable professional moments have come in the studio as performers and producers put their hearts into the intricacies of a song.

1 THE MODERN DAY RECORD PRODUCER

During a spring Los Angeles night, the minute hand is sweeping its way through the nine o'clock hour as Ben Harper feeds lyrics to Blind Boys of Alabama singer Clarence Fountain over a microphone set up in the control room of Capitol Studio B. They are putting the finishing touches on the title track to the 2005 Grammy Award-winning release *There Will Be a Light*. The song, like most on this album, is a Harper original. So, over the course of two sets of five-day sessions Harper has bounced between the role of songwriter, collaborator, musician, band leader, vocal coach, and "producer."

In the middle of an afternoon, Matt Wallace paces the control room floor at Third Stone Studios as bassist Davey Faragher and drummer Brian MacLeod record a rhythm track that will provide the backbone for one of the songs featured on Caleb Kane's 2005 release *Go Mad*. Wallace listens intently as the rhythm section runs through another take and jots down a few thoughts in a two-inch binder that is jammed with notes from the recording dates. He asks a few questions of Kane, who is paying half-hearted attention, and then offers direction to the pair of session players.

On another day at another time, when asked how über-producer Rick Rubin works with the band, System of a Down's guitarist and chief songwriter Daron Malakian reaches for a book of Buddhist philosophy on non-violent resolution. "That's just something that Rick gave me, and this is how Rick influences me," he says. "That's Rick producing. I had a conversation with him recently and asked him what he's been up to with Weezer, who he's producing. He [said], 'Dude, we've just been having lunch and mentally producing.' Some people might think, 'What?' Actually, that's awesome. You don't understand how much that means to a songwriter. It's like Rick is really in tune with the song and the mentality it takes to bring out a vibe and a spirit and creating inspiration. Creating a good comfortable setting for you to go to him and have an idea and to take back his idea. He's a comfortable guy."

Meanwhile, another producer may be putting the finishing touches on a song that an artist is set to record. Another might be focused on a computer screen, editing bits of a performance together with a digital audio workstation. Then again, a producer might be breaking up a fight between band members, counseling a singer on a broken relationship, or conferring with a band manager about rampant drug abuse.

Fewer jobs in the world are harder to explain than "record producer." It's a job that's all encompassing and ill defined. Are they songwriters, musicians, engineers, accountants? Are they friends, cheerleaders, drill sergeants, therapists? A successful producer must sometimes be all of the above. But most importantly, a great producer knows what his or her role is at any given time, on any recording project.

And no matter the exact tasks that a producer performs during a set of sessions, his or her goals are always the same: To make it possible for a collection of songs to go from idea to release with the least stress possible for artist and record label; to work hand in hand with an artist so those songs will fulfill their promise to inspire, enrage, humor, or sadden. That job can be done in hundreds of ways, depending on the moment, on the musicians, on the music, or on that nebulous yet overused term "vibe."

The art of record production can seem like sonic voodoo to a casual fan, but the producers featured in this book know the ins and outs, the secrets and the tricks to running a successful recording session. The producers included here run the gamut of experience, from Platinum-selling and chart-topping releases, to indie cult favorites, to artists taking their first spin in the big chair. In candid, often brutally honest moments, each producer shares what it took to get into the business, how they continue to stay busy, how they work with songwriters and musicians, how they manage a budget, and how a session comes together once all the pieces are in place. In addition, a number of musicians and songwriters offer their own perspective on how to find the right producer, what they've found that works in the studio, and what happens when an artist makes the jump from the tracking room to the control room.

The goal of this book is not to enable a reader to be able to walk into a recording studio and produce a major-label release. Rather, this book is for anyone who is curious about what happens inside the studio when producer and artist get to work. The producers interviewed here also report on the issues they have faced on the road to their careers in music production. There are concrete steps that can be taken to join the ranks of record producers and pitfalls to be avoided.

Consider, for example, Don Was' recollections of his early recording dates on Bob Dylan's *Under the Red Sky* (1990). "At one point, Bob was telling me what he wants to do and I'm telling him why it won't work before we ever tried it," he recalls. "I had waited all my life to work with Bob Dylan—that was really my goal in life. I wanted to be Bob Dylan's bass player, and he was my biggest hero. Then, there I was finally in the studio with this guy, and he told me what he wanted to do, and I didn't even show enough respect to try it! I had predetermined that I wanted to go somewhere else, which was actually backwards to repeat something he had already done that I personally liked. When I [realized] what I was saying I wanted to vomit. So, now I try to be open to everything. My job is to facilitate. If someone has an idea, even if I am certain, I still try to go into it at least pretending to have an open mind, and I do everything I can to enable the experiment to work. When you work with good people, even if it fails nine times out of ten, that tenth time is going to be a real wow, and it's worth the other nine times. So, just being open and not having any preconceptions, judgments, or disabilities—that's really the most important thing."

Dennis Herring recognized that he was going to accept a different responsibility while working on Cracker's 1996 release *The Golden Age* before a note was recorded. "I felt going into it that the most defining thing I could do was pick the songs," he explains. "They gave me a ton of songs and let me pick. I'm glad they trusted me enough to do that. They're certainly a really good band, so I felt that if they were going to make a really great record, that would be based on the songs more than any other single thing. I felt like going into it that was going to be my defining moment.

"I suppose being a producer is always such a malleable job," he continues. "Different projects really call for different things. You can be in the midst of a project and find yourself the guy who is really in touch with the most spontaneous side of the record and you're the champion of that side. I can find myself on the other side, when I'm suddenly the champion of allowing enough reflection and being willing to stay on a song until it's great. It's all about loving the songs and having some kind of respect for the artist."

At the same time, some of today's record producers are finding that the creative interaction with an artist is a small percentage of the job they are hired to perform. The hard truth is that money—both controlling expenses during recording and making it on the back end—is driving the industry. Moreover, there are times when art is sacrificed for commerce. It's not news that the industry as a whole is reeling under financial pressures, and music producers are bearing a share of the brunt.

Take the experience that producer Mark Trombino—who helped Jimmy Eat World to multi-Platinum success with their 2001 release *Bleed American*—had after he turned in The Living End's *Modern Artillery* masters in 2004. "The record went over budget, only a little bit, and it had nothing to do with me," Trombino reports. "It had everything to do with things taking longer than we'd booked and the band wanting to do some things that we hadn't planned on. Everything was okayed by the label verbally, but when it came down to it, we were like $10,000 over. We're talking about such a small percentage of the overall budget, and yet Warner Bros. took it out of my back end. They made me pay for everything that I went over. It's the first time that happened to me and it just seems so wrong.

"I can understand if I was some crack-smoking producer that, instead of working in the studio, was out hiring strippers and had lines of coke on the fucking console, but I'm not that guy," he continues emphatically. "I'm a hard worker and I was not wasting time. It wasn't my fault."

While the producer responsibility clause is standard in any contract, this was the first time Trombino had seen it enforced. "I've had records go over budget, but I've never had it deducted from me," he admits. This case could influence how he works with the label in the future. "I guess, yeah, or not. I mean, it seems like I'm sort of powerless to do anything about it," he says. "I'd like to say, 'Fuck Warner Bros., I'll never work with you again,' but I gotta work."

Matt Wallace, who has worked with a range of acts that range from Maroon 5 to Faith No More, has observed an even more startling change. "The average budget, at least some years ago, was at least a quarter of a million [dollars]. But we did Maroon 5's for under a hundred [thousand dollars], Sugarcult was under a hundred, Squad Five-0 was under a hundred, so it's tight. The frustration is that it's hard to make a record for low dough if you want to do it just right and be able to go back and redo things," he says. "But then you talk to people in the R&B and rap part of the industry, and the money is flowing like a river. People are getting ungodly amounts of money. I read about a guy who got twenty-five grand just to come up with a beat. Twenty-five grand? I've done records for twenty-five grand, you know?"

This is a common refrain from today's producers, because of the well-documented changes that have affected the music industry: Shrinking audiences, MP3 piracy, a CD burner in every computer. Recording budgets aren't as high, because profits aren't as high, and the producer's job continues to be a catch-all for issues that are essential to artist and label alike. Dave Fridmann, who has worked with a range of artists, including The Flaming Lips, Wheat, and Longwave, defines the role of producer this way: "It's an overseeing kind of deal—to fill in the cracks wherever anything is falling through. That can mean having to do nearly everything, and that can mean having to do nearly nothing. But in the big picture, it's your fault if something goes wrong," he says with a laugh. "That's really what it's about. It's somebody sitting there saying, 'I promise to make sure this happens.'"

How They Do It

As you can see, music production is no cookie-cutter affair. From top to bottom, from rehearsals to the beginning of a session to the album release, each producer brings his or her unique approach to an assignment. That approach is, of course, influenced by past experiences—whether or not the producer was ever in a band, for instance—and what they are comfortable with today. To be sure, producers come in with different philosophies towards pre-production, song arrangement, recording, and utilizing technology to polish up a song. Some producers walk into a session with the idea of ruling with an iron fist. Others prefer a hands-off approach. Some producers prefer to work with bands, building up an entire collection of songs that bolsters their image. Others would rather take a singer and craft an entire album around an individual voice, utilizing session players and multiple songwriters.

While Walter Afanasieff was under exclusive contract to Sony Records, he was asked to go into the studio with bands such as Train and Aerosmith, as well as the solo artists he is most famous for producing: Mariah Carey and Celine Dion. He discovered fairly quickly where his strengths lie. "I didn't do anything for Train other than realize that we weren't meant for each other. I realized I'm not a band producer," he explains. "I like working by myself, and the best [situation] for me is a singer/artist who is going to write the song with me. That's my niche, but me walking into a room with five guys in the band where there are five different egos, five different ways of doing it, five different instruments playing five different ways, five different levels of out-of-tune, five different levels of out-of-time, and five different levels of how they want the song written…It was just a different scene for me. I bow to the guys who can go in year after year [and work with bands], like Brendan O'Brien. I think that's an awesome thing to be able to produce bands. I've always wanted to."

On the other hand, Dave Jerden says, "I don't play producer for the artists [themselves], because I played in bands and I understand bands," he says. "That's number one. Number two, a combination I always look for is the singer/guitar player combination. It works for Aerosmith. It works for the Rolling Stones. It worked for Jane's Addiction, and it worked for Alice in Chains. There is always a tension there, when you have that dynamic. When a band comes into the studio [and] everybody's 'love, love, love,' sometimes that doesn't make for a great record. The tension that's happening really makes it work."

"I say to [bandmembers], 'You're the artist, be the artist. Don't think of me as a record producer; don't even call me a record producer. Think of me as just another person in the band.' I don't have like fifty-one percent of the vote and everybody else has forty-nine percent," he continues. "I have an equal voting share, so everything's going to be done through a collaboration. My experience is those records come out the best."

Mark Trombino had worked almost exclusively with bands in the emo-punk genre, but had wanted to get into the studio with acts where he could be more creative and stretch his sound palette. He got that chance while working with songwriter Val Emmich, who re-recorded his self-released debut *Slow Down Kid* for Epic Records in 2004. "It was the first singer/songwriter type thing that I'm getting to do," Trombino says, "although he does have a band. I've asked him to leave them at home. When the project was presented to me, Val was the singer/songwriter, and I was going to build the record from the ground up. I've always wanted to do that, and then suddenly he had a band and his band wanted to come out. I thought that would be cool, but then eventually I thought, 'No, that's not why I took this record. I don't want to do another band record.'"

Country music's Tony Brown has a wealth of experience working with singer/songwriters. "There are singer/songwriters that I'm already totally aware of their abilities and I have an opinion about certain songs, but then there are artists that I didn't know wrote at all. They go, 'You know, I've got a song that I wrote a couple of years ago that I've never had the nerve to play for anyone. You mind if I play it for you?' And I go, 'By all means.' It will turn me on to the inside of them that I didn't know. There have been times that I've encouraged an artist to write more because I loved the direction of the song."

WHY THE RIGHT PRODUCER IS IMPORTANT

One of the great gifts of today's digital technology is that artists are free to create, record, mix, master, and distribute their own music without the financial overhead that was required in years past. More often than not, the artists who opt to take that route will produce themselves. Although more material has been released without the assistance of a producer in recent years, many self-produced artists realize at some point that they would benefit from the interaction, the objectivity, and the technological expertise a producer can offer.

Yet, hiring a producer does not guarantee that everything will run smoothly, and finding the right person for the job is crucial. When the Counting Crows were getting ready to record *Recovering the Satellites,* the 1996 follow-up to their smash debut *August and Everything After,* they considered a number of producers before hiring Gil Norton. "It seemed like a few of the guys we talked to, all they could talk about was sound. 'We're gonna do this to get this guitar sound.' Man, we don't give a shit about that," recalls Crows guitarist Dave Bryson. "I don't think what makes great records is great guitar sounds. What makes great records is the lyrics, and songs, and everybody being on the same page. Gil's first phone conversation with Adam [Duritz, the band's songwriter and singer] was completely talking about this image he had for this song and this lyric, and how we were missing the point. Adam was like, 'He was right, he totally got it.'

That was a huge part of Gil, and he was that way the whole time. He was always working toward the song."

Whereas Norton was hands-on throughout the recording of *Satellites,* the Counting Crows had a different experience during the T-Bone Burnett-produced *August* sessions, where the producer was a less frequent visitor. There are some bands and artists who flourish under that type of laissez-faire approach— System of a Down with Rick Rubin, for instance, or artist Joe Henry while he was working with Burnett on the 1990 release *Shuffletown.* Henry welcomed Burnett's approach after what he remembers as a dismal experience with producer Anton Fier (of Golden Palominos) during his 1989 major-label debut *Murder of Crows.* "Once I started working with Anton, it became evident to me really quickly that the record label [A&M] had a lot more invested in their relationship with him than with me," Henry recalls. "So, essentially, what was happening was he was making a Golden Palominos record conceptually, using my voice and my songs. I was absolutely the lowest man on the totem pole. The record that we made had nothing to do with the record that I wanted to make, and it was a really hard lesson for me."

Perhaps because Henry wasn't sure of the rules in a studio, Fier exerted his will over the songs, the players, and the eventual outcome of the release. "You know how much struggle you put into just getting into the studio? You don't know that you can just say no," Henry says. "You don't know that you can stop and say, 'You know what? Let's all go home. I'm going to have a conversation with my label, because this is not what I want to do.' And anyone who ever writes to me for advice, that's the only advice I know how to give: You can say no, you can go home. Don't ever put yourself in a position of listening to somebody else's opinion to do the work that you didn't want to do."

"It was a really hard period of time for me, but it really influenced where I went," Henry continues, "because the next record I made was still for A&M. It was called *Shuffletown,* and it was the first time I met T-Bone Burnett, who is still kind of a godfather to me. The idea of that record, which was live-to-two-track recording, was just building this huge possibility, and it was still possible for somebody else to meddle in what I was doing. T-Bone stepped in and he was this great buffer. He went to A&M and said, 'Don't worry about it, I'll help him.' They just disappeared and he wasn't around until we were actually rolling tape. I put the band together and rehearsed them, as I wanted. T-Bone was there as a human shield that protected me from A&M."

THE GENDER FACTOR

As you read this book, a startling truth will be unveiled, and that is the lack of women who sit in the big chair during a recording session. The vast majority of label executives and artists don't necessarily avoid hiring women for these assignments, and there are a handful of women who are very in-demand for their productions—Sylvia Massy Shivy, Linda Perry, and Trina Shoemaker are three—but the numbers definitely tilt toward male producers. "I don't think that there is discrimination against women in the industry," Massy Shivy reports. "I think that the job demands a lot, and most women figure out early on that that's not what they want to do.

"I don't know what happened to me," she adds with a laugh. "But the hours are like twelve hours a day. You may not get paid for two years, or more, and you have very little social life out of the studio. The creative side is fantastic and I think everyone wants to do it, but I think both men *and* women get so discouraged after a certain amount of time of starving, doing shit jobs, working on music that they don't like, and dealing with some of the egos involved that they bow out.

"I think women have different drives than men, as far as biological drives," she continues. "I mean, if you get to working on your career for ten years, you're going to lose the opportunity to have a family. So, I think women have different things in mind when they choose their careers, and I think it's just too much, to do this, for most women. But, geez, I think this is the greatest job in the world."

2 WHO THEY ARE

The forty-plus producers featured in this book have worked in a variety of popular music genres—from rock to country, pop to metal. They have helped shape quintessential, genre-defining releases. They have shepherded underground critical faves. They have masterminded tracks that have pushed artists to the top of the *Billboard* charts and multiple Grammy awards.

Some of these producers have transcended the traditionally anonymous roles played by their peers. Rick Rubin, for example, has become a reluctant celebrity. Nashville's Tony Brown has gone from playing in Elvis Presley's band to producing such country stalwarts as Vince Gill, Reba McEntire, and Wynonna Judd to serving as record label president. Dave Jerden guided such genre-defining classics as Jane's Addiction's *Ritual de lo Habitual* and *Dirt* from Alice in Chains. Sylvia Massy Shivy, who is also a talented engineer, made a name for herself with such seminal releases as Tool's *Undertow*.

Likewise, the musicians quoted here span a number of genres: Rock, punk, folk, soul, and gospel. Many, such as Ben Harper, Chris Vrenna, Joe Henry, and Solomon Burke have spent time on both sides of the glass, whether producing their own work or that of other artists.

Even as they span a diverse range of styles, these producers have many qualities in common, especially great passion for the music they produce. Each brings a unique strategy to a recording session. That might include avoiding all pre-production to let things happen in the studio, or it might mean months of pre-production to hone songs before stepping foot in the recording arena. Some might be on the scene for every note played; others might only touch base at key points during the sessions. Opinions can vary widely enough that trade magazines dedicate entire issues to the topic.

Likewise, the paths these individuals took to become producers are as different as the approaches they take in the studio. Some have risen from runner to apprentice to engineer before producing a session. Others made their marks as musicians before switching to the other side of the glass. These days, another class has started out with computers and digital recording software before receiving the production mantle.

One common characteristic of the producers interviewed in this book is that none of them is overwhelmingly interested in critical acclaim or Platinum-sellers. Sure, there is a drive for success, but the relationships these producers have built with artists and the strength of the songs seem to rule the day. This is most evident when you look at the careers of such producers as Tony Brown and Walter Afanasieff, who have worked on back-to-back-to-back releases from the same artists with continued success. The trust they have built with these artists is an essential ingredient to that success.

In the following pages, dozens of producers will share stories about how they got their start, the tricks and techniques they use to help turn an artist's musical vision into an inspiring reality, and what they foresee in the future of music production.

WALTER AFANASIEFF

Born into a musical family, Walter Afanasieff started his musical career playing keyboards with jazz/fusion violinist Jean-Luc Ponty, and then he kicked it up a notch as a founding member of The Warriors. The Brazilian-born Afanasieff moved from the stage to the studio under the tutelage of 1980s hit-maker Narada Michael Walden, with whom he worked on releases by the likes of Whitney Houston, Lionel Ritchie, and Barbra Streisand. In the early 1990s, Afanasieff started to work exclusively with Sony Music, a relationship that lasted for thirteen years. While there his touch was heard on such smash-hit songs as the Grammy Award-winning "My Heart Will Go On" by Celine Dion, Mariah Carey's Number One single "Love Takes Time," and Josh Groban's genre-crossing releases *Closer* and *Josh Groban*.

MICHAEL BARBIERO

Michael Barbiero has made a career of having a "can-do" attitude in the recording studio, having started out remixing tracks for Whitney Houston, Simply Red, and Mick Jagger; moving into the engineering end of things with producer Steve Thompson as they worked with the Rolling Stones, Tesla, Blues Traveler, and Gov't Mule; and then producing his own sessions for Ziggy Marley, Chris Whitley, and Cowboy Mouth.

HOWARD BENSON

Before Howard Benson jumped into the producer's chair, he was pulling double-duty as an aerospace engineer during the day and a rock 'n' roll keyboardist at night! After four years of that schedule, he started producing demos for then-unknown L.A. bands. He learned enough to capture a number of production credits (in the rock, metal, and jazz genres), and then he caught on at Keith Olsen's Goodnight L.A. Studios. Shortly after that, he took a label gig as an A&R rep while still producing a handful of bands that included Seed, Zebrahead, and P.O.D. Benson is known for producing meticulous vocal tracks.

TONY BROWN

Tony Brown's unique perspective on eliciting great performances stems from the diversity of his experience—from playing with gospel groups in his youth to becoming part of Elvis Presley's backing band, to producing more than one hundred Number One country songs, to becoming label president. On the business side, Brown has worked as an A&R rep and label president at RCA, MCA Nashville, and Universal South, the label he co-founded in 2002 and co-owns with former Arista Nashville chief Tim DuBois. In the studio, Brown's touch can be heard on releases by legendary artists such as Reba McEntire, Vince Gill, George Strait, Emmylou Harris, and Marty Stuart.

DAVE BRYSON

Before Dave Bryson became one of the founding members of the Counting Crows, he ran a small recording studio in Emeryville, California, by the name of Dancing Dog Studios. Bryson's experience gave him a leg up when it came time for the band to pick producers or equip the studios that the Crows outfitted while they recorded their albums.

SOLOMON BURKE

He is called by many names—The Bishop of Soul being the most prevalent. Solomon Burke's vast catalogue of gospel and R&B releases spans generations. Over the course of his career, Burke has kept a hand in the production of his releases, until he worked with Joe Henry on the 2002 album *Don't Give Up on Me*.

T-BONE BURNETT

It's hard to imagine the T-Bone Burnett (born John Henry Burnett), the man who has worked on such seminal releases as *King of America* from Elvis Costello, *August* and *Everything After* from the Counting Crows and the *O Brother, Where Art Thou?* soundtrack, got his start working with speed metal bands in Fort Worth, Texas. Yet, that's exactly where Burnett launched a career that's taken him across a bevy of genres as a musician, producer, and record label president.

ED CHERNEY

By starting out as a runner/gopher at Paragon Studios in Chicago and then moving up the ladder to assistant engineer to engineer/mixer to producer, Ed Cherney has experienced every aspect of studio work. Just as his responsibilities have varied over his twenty-five-plus-year career, his credits run the genre gamut from The Ohio Players to Bonnie Raitt to Iggy Pop to Carly Simon. His experience includes more than a decade as the first-call engineer on all Don Was' productions. In fact, his work with Was on Bonnie Raitt's 1994 release *Longing in Their Hearts* earned him the Engineer of the Year Grammy Award.

MIKE DAVENPORT

Mike Davenport has been the bass player for the four-piece pop punk outfit The Ataris since the band's inception in the mid-1990s. Over the course of four records, including the 2003 major label debut *So Long, Astoria,* the band has consistently improved on their craft and built a fervent fan base. Davenport has also branched out to artist management and production.

SULLY ERNA

On Godsmack's first three releases, the band's songwriter and singer Sully Erna shared production responsibilities with Mudrock (*Godsmack* and *Awake*) and David Bottrill (*Faceless*) before he assumed the mantle on their fourth offering, *Other Side.* For a musician who has taken an active role in his band's music and sound (he also gets engineering credits on the albums), taking on the producer's role was a natural evolution.

MAYA FORD

Bass player Maya Ford, formerly known as Donna F., is part of the rock quartet The Donnas. Before the band released their 2002 major-label debut, *Spend the Night,* they had four indie albums to their credit, as well as a handful of national and international tours. *Gold Medal,* the 2004 follow-up, was produced by Butch Walker.

J.D. FOSTER

As a musician, J.D. Foster has played alongside some great talents, including Dwight Yoakam, Marc Ribot, and Syd Straw, which gave him a head start when it came time to jump to the other side of the glass. After Foster tired of the road life, he got busy in the studio, moving from Austin, Texas, to the West Coast and then the East Coast, looking for the right situation. As a musician/producer, Foster often gets the call from artists, like Richard Buckner, who are looking for a songwriting partner in the studio.

DAVE FRIDMANN

Being a record producer, as Dave Fridmann explains it, is his fallback job. When he first started out in the music business he was angling for a rock band gig, but he started to take classes in engineering and found out he loved the studio environment. After all, he points out, as a producer you can make many records a year, but as a musician, you might only make one record every two years. The exchange has worked out, as he has been in the studio with such off-kilter outfits as The Flaming Lips, Mercury Rev, and Sparklehorse, along with acts that are a touch more mainstream: Longwave, Phantom Planet, and Wheat.

MITCHELL FROOM

Mitchell Froom dipped his toes in the music pool as a musician back in the mid-Eighties, providing the score for the film *Café Flesh*. He dove in headfirst, though, manning the board for an assortment of bands that included Los Lobos, Crowded House, Richard Thompson, and Suzanne Vega. His partnership with engineer/producer Tchad Blake netted some of the most innovative music of the 1990s.

DON GEHMAN

When he first started out in the music business as a live sound mixer, Don Gehman was focused on getting a band's sound from the stage to the audience. It was only later, when Stephen Stills pulled him into the studio, that Gehman saw the studio side of the industry. He caught on quickly and was a staff engineer for a number of years at Criteria Studios in Miami, Fla., before producing acts as varied as John Mellencamp, Nanci Griffith, Hootie & the Blowfish, and R.E.M.

LOU GIORDANO

After earning an electrical engineering degree from MIT, Lou Giordano started his musical engineering career at the cult recording studio Fort Apache in Boston. While that might seem like a mighty leap, for Giordano it made perfect sense considering it made him fearless when he got in the studio. Giordano was smack in the middle of Boston's indie surge of the early 1990s, as the Blake Babies, The Lemonheads, and Hüsker Dü were making their marks. Giordano has since moved on to such mainstream successes as the Goo Goo Dolls' *Boy Named Goo* and The Ataris' *So Long, Astoria*.

RYAN GREENE

If it was not for his older brother, who attended recording school in Los Angeles, Ryan Greene might not be the producer he is today. Along with the engineering lessons he learned from his brother and a live sound-mixing gig, Greene got a job at MCA Music Publishing, where he watched some of the day's top songwriters—Glen Ballard and Diane Warren among them—work in the studio, before he moved on to EMI Music Publishing as the chief engineer. From there, he entered the hip-hop world and then the punk-rock scene after Brett Gurewitz saw him working. Gurewitz asked him to produce the punk-rock stars NOFX, and Greene carried the lessons of harmony and melody that he learned in his early days into those sessions.

BRETT GUREWITZ

The old adage of sticking to what you know has served Brett Gurewitz well in his production and music career; since becoming one of punk's godfathers, he has remained a steadying force in the genre. Gurewitz served as Bad Religion's songwriter, guitarist, and producer during the band's heyday, while also working in the studio with such acts as L7, NOFX, The Offspring, and Pennywise as both engineer and producer.

BEN HARPER

Since Ben Harper came onto the major-label scene in 1994 with the release of *Welcome to the Cruel World,* he has built up a fervent following of music fans and earned critical acclaim as well as the respect of his peers. In addition to the production work he has performed on his own releases, Harper has been asked to produce tracks for indie and major-label artists alike in a multitude of genres. In 2002, he produced the track "Brain Washers" for the Blackalicious 2002 album *Blazing Arrow,* and in 2004 he went into the studio with the Grammy Award-winning gospel group The Blind Boys of Alabama. In between those projects, Harper produced his own *Diamonds on the Inside* release.

JOE HENRY

During the recording sessions for Joe Henry's 1990 album *Shuffletown* release, his producer T-Bone Burnett encouraged him to pick up a new skill—producing. It was not because Burnett did not believe in him as an artist; it was because he believed Henry had the ears of a producer. While in the Burnett camp, Henry worked with Bruce Cockburn, Spinal Tap, and A.J. Croce before going solo in the producer's chair in 1999 with Shivaree's debut. Since then, he has continued to release his own albums while producing such artists as Teddy Thompson, Solomon Burke, Aimee Mann, and Ani DiFranco.

MIKE HERRERA

MxPx went from playing high school gigs around their Bremerton, Washington, home base to a major-label deal to global tours over the course of a decade. Herrera, who is the band's songwriter, has turned his songs over to a pair of the best-known producers working today: Jerry Finn for the 2000 release *The Ever Passing Moment,* and Dave Jerden for the 2003 offering *Before Everything & After.*

Dennis Herring

In a career that has spanned close to twenty-five years, Dennis Herring has bounced from the outer limits of Timbuk 3 and Camper Van Beethoven to the musical center with the Counting Crows and Bruce Hornsby. He began his career as a session guitarist, working with Glen Ballard and Phil Ramone in Los Angeles. Through those experiences, Herring laid the groundwork for a career that finds him catering to musicians looking to make an artistic statement.

Ross Hogarth

First and foremost, Ross Hogarth considers himself an engineer who happens to produce and mix many of the artists he works with in the studio. Working as a quadruple threat—he also plays guitar—has enabled him to bounce between artists like Ziggy Marley, Melissa Etheridge, Devildriver, and John Fogerty, all within the same year. Hogarth has also worked in the studio with Celine Dion, Gov't Mule, Belinda Carlisle, Nickelback, and R.E.M. He started down this path as a guitar and drum tech, and the relationships he built back then with musicians such as David Lindley, Kenny Aronoff, and Jim Keltner continue to this day.

Mark Howard

As the engineer of choice in Daniel Lanois' camp, Mark Howard had the opportunity to witness the creation of some of the most striking albums of the last two decades. Howard's engineering talents can be heard on releases from Bob Dylan, U2, and Peter Gabriel—all Lanois productions. After going solo as a producer (his first production gig was on The Tragically Hip's *Day for Night* in 1994), Howard has worked on a bevy of stunning releases, including Lucinda Williams' *World Without Tears*, Tom Waits' *Real Gone*, and Vic Chesnutt's *Silver Lake*.

Dave Jerden

He was in the producer's chair for some of the most influential albums of all time: Jane's Addiction's *Ritual de lo Habitual*, Alice in Chains' *Dirt*, Social Distortion's eponymous break-through release, and *Mother's Milk* from Red Hot Chili Peppers. Jerden has influenced a generation of artists through his work on The Offspring's uber-popular releases *Ixnay on the Hombre* and *Americana* while working out of Eldorado Studios in Burbank, California. Jerden's introduction to the studio came via his bass-playing father, and he built a reputation as an engineer before he took on his first production.

Nick Launay

During the height of England's raucous punk rock days, Nick Launay was front and center, smashing around the scene and being seduced by the energy of it all. One of his first studio jobs was taking the hit songs of the day and editing them down to two minutes, thirty seconds for K-Tel Top 20 compilations. After a series of assistant and engineering jobs in his native England, Launay moved to Australia, where he produced breakthrough albums for Midnight Oil, The Church, INXS, and Silverchair. In the early part of this decade, Launay had success with Nick Cave, American Hi-Fi, and The Living End.

DAVE LETO

As a member of the rock 'n' roll outfit Rye Coalition, Dave Leto has had the opportunity to work with a pair of standout producers—Steve Albini on their 2002 release *On Top,* and Dave Grohl for their offering *Secret Heat.* Leto admits with a laugh that the band was hoping to get Phil Spector to produce their latest from jail. In this book, Leto offers his perspective on choosing and working with producers.

DAVID LOWERY

It was with the cult favorite Camper Van Beethoven that David Lowery first became known, but since then he has made his mark both as a frontman with Cracker and as a producer for such artists as the Counting Crows, Guster, and Sparklehorse. As an artist Lowery has produced some of his own band's tracks, and has entrusted their music to such producers as Dennis Herring and Don Smith.

DARON MALAKIAN

When System of a Down went into the studio to record their break-out *Toxicity* album, Daron Malakian added co-producer to a list of responsibilities that already included songwriter and guitarist. Malakian worked hand-in-hand with the band's other producer, Rick Rubin, to come up with an album that topped many Best Of lists in 2001. In addition to his work with System, Malakian has gone on to produce albums for Amen and Bad Acid Trip.

LONGINEU PARSONS III

Talk about a varied musical career, drummer Longineu Parsons III got his start playing in his father's jazz fusion band Tribal Disorder (learning on Max Roach's drum kit) in front of worldwide audiences before he got together with four friends to form the pop punk outfit Yellowcard in 1997. Yellowcard broke through with the 2003 release *Ocean Avenue* and the songs "Way Away," "Ocean Avenue," and "Only One."

LINDA PERRY

It might be a tricky switch from alternative rock star to Grammy Award-nominated producer and sought-after co-writer, but it would be hard to tell by Linda Perry's experience. After fronting 4 Non Blondes, who scored a hit with the track "What's Up?" in the early 1990s, Perry moved on to a solo career before launching a dramatically successful production career. One of her first turns in the producer's chair came with Pink as the two collaborated on the 2001 *Missundaztood* release and the Top Ten single "Get the Party Started."

J.P. PLUNIER
Working hand in hand with Ben Harper, who he managed as well as produced, J.P. Plunier got his toes wet in the music industry in the early '90s. It wasn't his first exposure, nor was it his last. While continuing to work with Harper, Plunier started Everloving Records and has also worked with Jack Johnson on his 2001 break out *Brushfire Fairytales,* Ritmo Y Canto, and Wan Santo Condo.

JOHN PORTER
John Porter could be considered a genre-busting producer, because his credits range from Los Lonely Boys to Ryan Adams to Bryan Ferry to B.B. King to The Smiths. He was blurring those boundaries early on, in his musician days, when he went from the blues of Long John Baldry to the progressive pop of Roxy Music. Being a stringed-instrument player—he is credited with playing guitar, bass, Dobro, and mandolin on a variety of albums—has enabled Porter to be both a sideman and musical arranger in the studio.

GARTH RICHARDSON
Growing up, Garth Richardson used to follow his father, a renowned producer in his own right, to the studio where he learned just about everything from engineering to cleaning up after the bands left for the day. He is now known mostly for his work with such hard-rock acts as Rage Against the Machine, Mudvayne, and Kittie, as well as alternative acts such as Catherine Wheel and the Melvins. Richardson also played the French horn in youth orchestras, and that musical background enables him to assist bands with arranging and song-writing, while his engineering background helps him get the tones he needs in the studio.

BOB ROCK
The goal at the beginning of his career, Bob Rock says, was to be standing on the rock star side of the music business instead of the producer side of things. An assistant engineer job at Little Mountain, a studio in Vancouver, opened the doors to the world of recording, and Rock jumped in with a handful of indie rock bands scattered around the city. Rock moved up the chain, engineering a number of records with the late Bruce Fairbairn before assuming the producer's chair. His best-known work has been done with Metallica, Cher, and Simple Plan.

MICHAEL ROSEN

If not for the ragged-looking Capitol Studios engineer who came into the 7-11 where Michael Rosen was working during high school, who knows where Rosen would be now? The engineer invited Rosen to observe in the studio, and the rest is history: Enthralled by the vibe of the studio, Rosen was inspired to pursue a degree in electronics and broadcasting at San Francisco State University, and then nagged his way into a job at the Automat studios in San Francisco. At the time, Automat was "the" studio in San Francisco, the place where Narada Michael Walden was working with Aretha Franklin and Whitney Houston, and David Rubinson was producing Herbie Hancock and Santana. Eventually, Rosen moved on to engineer and produce an eclectic range of artists that includes Rancid, Testament, Santana (he won an engineering Grammy for his work on the 2002 *Shaman* release), and Tesla.

RICK RUBIN

With credits running across widely divergent styles—country, metal, rap, rock, pop—Rick Rubin defies being pigeonholed. Where that type of approach might have hurt other producers, Rubin has flourished. Success found Rubin with his first production gig, the rap act T. La Rock, when he was a student at New York University, and he enjoyed continued success with his work with the Beastie Boys, Slayer, Run-D.M.C., Tom Petty, Johnny Cash, and System of a Down. Rubin has also made an impact on the music business as the head of the American Recordings label.

SYLVIA MASSY SHIVY

It might be a long jump from college radio disc jockey to Platinum-selling producer, but for someone like Sylvia Massy Shivy it makes perfect sense. Shivy learned the ins and outs of studio work as an engineer in Los Angeles, where she worked with Rick Rubin on such seminal releases as *Unchained* from Johnny Cash, System of a Down's self-titled debut, and Donovan's 1996 album *Sutras*. However, what kicked off Shivy's production career was the debut from Tool, the Platinum-selling *Undertow*.

CRAIG STREET

Craig Street's introduction to the world of production came when he was called to work on Cassandra Wilson's *Blue Light 'Til Dawn*, which was released in 1993. Since then Street has gotten the call from a range of artists, including k.d. lang, Norah Jones, The Dirty Dozen Brass Band, and the Gipsy Kings. As much as he's known for working with some stunning voices, Street is not too shy to take risks with the artists he works with by having them cover songs that might be out of their comfort zone. Wilson covered Van Morrison's "Tupelo Honey"; he had

Holly Cole rework a number of Tom Waits songs; and the classically trained vocalist Jubilant Sykes sang the Bob Dylan number "Ring Them Bells."

STEVE THOMPSON

Along with partner Michael Barbiero, Steve Thompson had a hand in some of the most popular releases of the mid-Eighties. Thompson, who concentrated on the production end of the work, got into the music business as a club disc jockey during the disco-laden 1970s. That background gave him the ability to find a song's hook and make it the prominent part of any arrangement.

MARK TROMBINO

While a student at San Diego State University, Mark Trombino stumbled into a bevy of engineering and production gigs, while he was busy recording his own band. It was an accidental shift, he says, even as he was continuing to play drums in the influential punk band Drive Like Jehu. Bouncing between San Diego and Los Angeles, Trombino continued to perfect his studio strategies, which culminated in sessions with Blink-182 (*Dude Ranch*) and Jimmy Eat World (*Static Prevails*). During the late 1990s and early 2000s, Trombino was known as the hot hand when it came to the emo side of punk rock. That reputation was cemented with Jimmy Eat World's self-titled release in 2001 (though it was originally released under the name *Bleed American*), and continued to grow as he worked with Gob, Midtown, and Finch.

CHRIS VRENNA

As the drummer in Nine Inch Nails, Chris Vrenna learned his craft from the innovative voice and talents of Trent Reznor. Not only did the duo work closely on the Nails' sessions, they combined forces on a number of Reznor productions. After he left the band in the mid-Nineties, the drummer turned his attention to remixes and producing such acts as Cold, Adema, P.J. Olsson, and Rasputina. In the midst of those gigs, Vrenna continued to compose music for films and video games, as well as for his own band, Tweaker.

RUFUS WAINWRIGHT

Drawing from influences as varied as theatrical pop, opera, and orchestral music, Rufus Wainwright has built a career out of eclecticism and critical acclaim. By his own admission, Wainwright had not found a producer to share his vision until his work with Marius deVries on the 2003 release *Want One* and the subsequent *Want Two* album.

BUTCH WALKER

Before producing albums for The Donnas, Avril Lavigne, Midtown, and Sevendust, Butch Walker made his mark as a singer/songwriter with his band Marvelous 3 and a pair of solo releases. While he continued to take a two-pronged approach as a songwriter and producer, Walker's work with both The Donnas and Lavigne met with both commercial and critical success. In fact, two of the songs he worked on with Lavigne, "Don't Tell Me" and "My Happy Ending" were Top Forty hits in 2004.

MATT WALLACE

Matt Wallace describes himself as "the nerdy guy in the band" and because of his knowledge he moved into the producer's chair easily. His musical background has made him an asset to bands Faith No More, The Replacements, and Maroon 5, as well as to solo performers John Hiatt, Sheryl Crow, and Caleb Kane. In addition to his engineering and production credits, Wallace is a sought-after mixer. His mixing credits include the break-out hit "Meet Virginia" for Train, the live tracks for a Rolling Stones HBO special, and the R.E.M. song "Revolution," which was included on the *Batman & Robin* soundtrack.

DON WAS

From his early days as a musician to his production dates with the Rolling Stones, Bob Dylan, and Bonnie Raitt, Don Was has influenced more than one generation of producers and artists. Throughout the 1980s and 1990s, it seemed as if every recording that climbed the *Billboard* charts or won a Grammy Award had the Don Was stamp. All that success culminated in the 1995 Producer of the Year Grammy Award, and he continues to be one of the most sought-after producers working today.

BRAD WOOD

When Chicago's alternative music scene was at its most frantic, Brad Wood was in the midst of it all. He engineered Liz Phair's *Exile in Guyville* album in 1993, as well as Veruca Salt's 1994 release *American Thighs*. He also supplied his talents to influential bands such as Tortoise, The Smashing Pumpkins, and Sunny Day Real Estate. While in Chicago, the producer operated a recording studio, which enabled him to work with a number of new artists that broke through to the mainstream. After moving to Los Angeles, Wood contributed both his production and musical talents to Pete Yorn's break-out offering *musicforthemorningafter* and the follow-up, *Day I Forgot*.

3 THE EVOLUTION OF TODAY'S PRODUCERS

The old adage in the production business is that on any given day a producer needs to be a psychologist, songwriter, marriage counselor, engineer, career adviser, best friend, adversary… Indeed, it's as if a record producer walks into any session with a knowing smile, because there never seems to be an end to this tricky juggling act. That's why a producer's qualifications don't have nearly as much to do with specific skills as they do with the producer's personal talents. After all, there are producers who have no musical training, but understand chords and scales. There are those who have no education in audio or electronics, but they can tell you exactly what compressor, or limiter, or microphone preamp they need to get just the right sound. Moreover, there are still others who can barely play an instrument or engineer a session, but have the right combination of vibe and ego to get through.

As John Porter explains, "Anybody can [produce], and every set of circumstances is different. I don't have a rigid plan, because it's not about that. It's about [the artist] making a record. It's their record. I'm supposed to try to get the best out of them. So, [my job is] whatever is required. Sometimes, it might be just making a cup of tea. Really, quite often the best track was the easiest one to make, and that's partly because the artist comes in with a vision of what they want to do. It's good, they know it, and they're going to do it. All you can do is screw it up. Basically, [the producer] is there to facilitate whatever [the artist] needs to help them to express themselves. If that requires that I twiddle the knobs, then I'll twiddle the knobs. If it requires that I do some arrangements, I will do the arrangements. Or if it's just make a coffee and stay out of the way, I'll make a cup of coffee and stay out of the way."

Nick Launay observes that being a record producer is akin to being a film director. "As a director, you would read the script and then you have to inter-pret it," he explains. "We have to interpret the songs in a way you think they are going to be received the best, or understood the best by the listener, and you have to get the best performance out of the artists at that time in their lives. And, just like a director decides how the overall movie is going to look, you have to decide how the overall album is going to sound."

Sylvia Massy Shivy says with a laugh, "I think I make a great cheerleader, but I also have to be the counselor, and the co-writer, and the babysitter. I think, I hope, every producer has a little bit of everything in their repertoire. I think the producer is someone that gets along with people."

THE SONGWRITING PRODUCERS

One of the first responsibilities a record producer takes on is polishing the songs that are set to be recorded. Perhaps this type of assignment is best handled by the producers who double as artists (or vice versa), such as Ben Harper, David Lowery, Joe Henry, Linda Perry, Chris Vrenna, or Daron Malakian. After all, not only are they concerned with the songs that will be recorded for the project they are producing, they are constantly writing their own songs. It would seem logi-cal that artists would look for someone who has those types of skills at the ready.

In fact, many who have hopscotched between the two sides of the glass have contributed to the albums that they have produced. Joe Henry had an immense impact on Solomon Burke's 2002 Grammy Award-winning release *Don't Give Up on Me* by helping to pick the songs and guiding the band through the musical bed for Burke's vocals. David Lowery has picked up a guitar and played alongside Sparklehorse's Mark Linkous while the duo worked up the band's 1996 debut *Vivadixiesubmarinetransmissionplot.* Ben Harper provided the majority of lyrics and music for his production of the album *There Will Be a Light,* by three time Grammy Award-winning act The Blind Boys of Alabama. (For more on the impact of the songwriting/artist producer, see Chapter Four, Artists as Producers.)

Daron Malakian, who has served as System of a Down's chief songwriter and as co-producer on the band's two most recent albums, did not feel qualified to offer any production suggestions on the band's 1998 eponymous debut. "I was very intimidated on the first one, because I had just met Rick [Rubin, the band's producer]," he recalls. "I really didn't say much on the first record, except I wrote a lot of music and had input here and there. I didn't want to step on Rick's toes, man. I was brand-new, and I had a lot to prove at that point. I felt that to gain that respect, you have got to work for it and prove yourself. You can't just sit there and say, 'I sold a million records. I want to produce.' I just think that's bullshit."

So, Malakian kept his eyes and ears open and his mouth shut. He learned some valuable lessons. "[I learned] how great it is to record things organically. Rick is a huge inspiration to me in many, many ways," he says. "It comes down to this: The biggest part of production is the song. There is no way production sounds good if the song is not good. [For example], we love all these great punk-rock records that sound like crap. Why do we love these records? Because the songs are great. So, sometimes it doesn't even matter how it sounds. If it's this beautiful, heartfelt song, it's going to come through, and that's what I work on. When I am in a situation with any band, whether it's my band or any band I work with, it's all about pre-production and putting songs together. The flow of the songs is more important than all the knobs you twist and all the effects you might add. It's finding a comfortable flow and then recording it in the best way you think sounds organic, too. I like that organic vibe, and that's something that I picked up on the first record."

There is no doubt that a producer with songwriting talents can contribute to an album's success. Yet, that does not have to mean that they get in there and grab a guitar or take the drumsticks to get the point across. Launay, who does not consider himself a musician, says, "I'm pretty good at explaining things. I know how to talk to them to get them to play different chords, and I know what I'm hearing. I know what majors and minors are and I know that if they're doing an odd chord that's not quite working that there are other chords to be had. I'll just say, 'Look, that chord there isn't really doing much, play me other options and then work it out.' I'll do that rather than grabbing the guitar from them and doing it, which is really intimidating for a young band.

"I fully intended, when I actually started producing and being employed by record companies to be a producer, to learn an instrument," Launay continues, "but it never became necessary. I actually realized the benefit of not being a musician, because I listen to things from a different perspective, which is as a listener. I don't get obsessed with, 'Oh, that's a favorite chord of mine, and I love to put it in every song.' I don't think that way. I am purely all about listening to what the band wants to do and trying to make what they want come to life, because that's what they don't know how to do and that's my job."

Not only does Launay get called in to work with young bands, he reports, "I tend to work with bands who are very creative, who get a little bit lost in their creativity and they need some focus." That is also where his lack of musical training becomes an asset. "I'm more like your average music fan who buys a lot of records and listens intensely to things and loves it for what it is," he says, "but then I also have the knowledge of how to make it. So, I tend to be the person who comes in with a fresh ear and says, 'That bit is crap, that bit is great.'"

FROM ENGINEER TO PRODUCER

Launay came to the production game by working his way up from tea man to assistant engineer at Townhouse Studios in West London, where he worked with engineer Alan Douglas. His first gig was with The Jam while they recorded their 1980 release *Sound Affects*. Then, he started working with Hugh Padgham and Steve Lillywhite. "I was very inquisitive, and I used to drive Alan nuts with my questions," Launay recalls. "I was very hyper, still am, but imagine what I was like when I was nineteen or twenty. I was like, 'How do we get that drum sound? What does this compressor do? Why is this compressor better than that one?' He was busy with the producer work, and he kept saying, 'Ask me later.' When I was working with Hugh, was much more relaxed and much more open. His way of recording was actually pretty simple. He had a great drum sound, so I learned how to get that drum sound from him."

At that point, Padgham took the young Launay under his wing and had him assist on albums for Phil Collins, XTC, Genesis, and Kate Bush. This was during Padgham's heyday, and he was doing a couple albums a week and working on another during the weekend. "Hugh couldn't do everything he was offered, and the next thing that came up was Kate Bush. Kate wanted to do more, so he [suggested] that she use me, and I found myself engineering for Kate. She was producing, and I was engineering. That was for *The Dreaming* album."

As *The Dreaming* sessions were going on, Launay did a weekend session as an assistant with Public Image Ltd. where his hyper-questioning nature paid off. Turns out the engineer on the session wasn't sure how to operate the Solid State Logic (SSL) console or get the delay sound that PiL's John Lydon wanted, and he continually asked Launay for suggestions. "I knew exactly what John wanted, and this guy just couldn't get it right, so John said, 'Come up and sit at the console. You're running backwards and forwards like a yo-yo, and you're making me dizzy.' So I did. Then the engineer got up to go to the bathroom, and John got up and locked the door behind him. He said, 'All right, let's make some music.'" Launay finished engineering and mixed the Lydon-produced release. "When that [record] came out, John said to the press that I co-produced it because I had done so much work and I put so many ideas of my own into it. I was never credited like that on the record, but that's what he said in the press. So, then I had Gang of Four ringing up, and The Slits and they wanted to work with me because this Public Image Ltd. record sounded really radical. I ended up producing those bands on the weekend or at night, any time I could get cheap studio time at the Townhouse. During the day, I was engineering something like Phil Collins as an assistant to Hugh, and then Birthday Party at night."

While Launay shot up the ranks fairly quickly, at the time he wasn't sure he was ready for the jump. "It just happened," he admits. "If John hadn't mentioned in the press that I'd co-produced, then who knows? I was at the right place at the right time. I really do think everybody gets breaks in their lives. They get big breaks sometimes, and they don't even know it; they just go by and nothing happens. Sometimes you do realize it and follow up on it and it happens. That's what happened to me; I got really lucky, and I was really enthusiastic. I was putting in stupid hours and I was hyper, hyper, hyper. I loved the music and I knew what these bands wanted to do, because I had seen them live. I guess I had the luxury of going into a really good recording studio with this great drum room. I knew how to get those drum sounds, because I'd watched Hugh do it. So, it was a combination of all these things that just fell into place. It was quite a magical time, and I still get offered work based on those records I did during that time, because those records were very influential records."

Michael Rosen, who has bounced between engineering and producing credits over the course of his twenty-plus year career, got his start learning the studio ropes at the Automat Studios in San Francisco under the tutelage of Narada Michael Walden and David Rubinson. During those days, Rosen learned everything, from how to technically set up a studio to how to create the right vibe to the importance of strong songwriting. He sees a lot of this training lacking in today's music scene. "I'm teaching a class," he explains. "I tell them, 'I know that none of you are going to work in a studio. You all probably have your own Pro Tools rigs, and you'll do this at home, but I'm going to teach you the way it's supposed to be done.' It's too bad that this is the way it's done now. I mean, that's why the records are so shitty. When you started back in the day, you learned everything. When you're cleaning toilets you go, 'What am I doing? This sucks, man. I went to school for five years to clean toilets and make sure engineers have clean pencils and tapes in the studio?' But when you get up there and you're the producer and you go to that pen jar and there are no pens…You flip out, and it ruins your day.

"They just don't [teach the importance of paying dues] now. They say, 'Oh, I'm not an engineer, I'm a producer. I've got a couple of [Shure] 57s and a Mackie [console]. Let's go.' It's like, 'No, you're not a producer. You're a guy that's got a couple of 57s and a Mackie.' Maybe that's why the record business sucks. These are not people who learned how to make songs and produce records. Now anyone can do it."

Ed Cherney, who started as a gopher at Paragon Studios in Chicago before moving up the ladder from apprentice engineer to assistant to engineer, echoes Rosen's philosophy and experience. These days, he has added producer and mixing credits to his list of responsibilities. Just how much did all that experience help? "It's kept me working for twenty-five years," he says with a laugh. "I knew the medium from the bottom up. I knew what it was from mono to two-track to three-track. I saw that progression, and a lot of times kids come up and there is some software on a computer and that's all they know. If someone says that we need to record a drum kit, they say, 'Gee, how do you do that?' Everything [for them] is sampled, or they have to create a special effect, instead of knowing how to make something flange, how to make the air and the space move by moving microphones and creating the effect. I learned those techniques and learned how to record all kinds of different music in an acoustic space.

"To their detriment, kids now don't get a chance to serve an apprenticeship, to sit behind guys that really know stuff," he continues. "The crux of it is, you're manipulating software, and that's a lot of instant gratification. That's the way of the world, and I don't know if it's necessarily bad, but it's nice to know the history of everything."

When Trombino started out in the control room, all he was doing was engineering, yet he got production credits because he was helping bands with more than just recording. "It was during that time, too, when it wasn't really cool to be a producer," Trombino says "You know, like Steve Albini. It was more about being a 'recordist.'"

Cracker and Camper Van Beethoven frontman David Lowery gave a producer's credit to engineer John Morand, who did much more than twirl knobs and set up microphones during the recording sessions for Cracker's *Forever* release, which Lowery produced. "At some point he ended up doing all the stuff that a producer does. He was going beyond the role of engineer, and when you are doing things that are beyond the role of an engineer you should get the credit for it," Lowery explains. "He would do all the vocal edits, all the vocal comps, and he would do all the time and sort of feel things, because I just didn't want to do that on my own records."

For Lowery and his Cracker bandmates, having someone else in the studio gave them all crucial perspective. "You begin to crawl through your own ass if you start editing your own vocals and you start deciding what's the best take. We'd sit there and listen to stuff, but we'd been in the studio for a long time. So, an engineer who can handle the producing role is really good for us, because he can make the decisions about what takes we're using, what edits we're doing, and it's going to be just fine. It's going to be way better than what I would come up with, being on the inside."

FROM THE ROAD TO THE STUDIO

There are those magical moments in the recording studio when musicians give birth to a song, yet it is when those same musicians play that song in front of an audience that it comes to life. Live sound mixers are in a unique position to watch as audiences and musicians respond to each other. Likewise, these front-of-house engineers have to respond almost instantly to problems that arise, which can run the gamut from faulty gear to failing instruments to singers who might need a bit of technical assistance to hit all the appropriate notes. For many active producers working these days, including Ryan Greene, Don Gehman, Ross Hogarth, and Mark Howard, this was the perfect training ground for the stresses and joys of the studio environment.

Although Greene had been working as a staff engineer in Los Angeles, he says he learned some valuable lessons during his live-sound gigs around town. "When you're doing live sound, you really learn frequencies," he explains. "If something is ringing in the system, you don't have a lot of time; you have to know." He and other members of the live-sound crew would play a game as the band was sound checking, called "Name That Frequency," where they would try to guess what frequency was being altered by another engineer. "It was stupid, but I really learned a lot. It was almost ear-training in a weird sort of way."

In addition to the sonic challenges that live mixing affords, according to Mark Howard, working in that environment also gives you a head start when it comes to tackling technical problems in the studio. "In the live world you show up, you've got a P.A., and you set it up. 'Why doesn't this work? The show is going to start in ten minutes…' It's all about fast thinking and knowing and troubleshooting, and I think that kind of technical thinking works in the studio, because you plug in and if it doesn't work then you've got to think. A lot of studio guys don't have that kind of training, and they kind of work at their pace and it's slow. For me every time I go to record it's like you're onstage, and that's the opening of the show and you better have your fader up and you better have your level when that guy starts to sing. You can't mess it up or there can't be no signal, because that might have been your take.

"You have a small window of opportunity to get performances out of people," he adds. "I steal performances out of people, because if you don't get them and you start to labor, then you're not going to get that soul. I rely on that kind of stuff for vocals. If I looked at the percentage of all vocals or overdubs, I think a lot of the great stuff comes from that very first time through. They are thinking, 'Okay, this is my first pass.' They'll try a bunch of stuff and you'll get an amazing take, but once they start to refine it they lose a lot of the character."

For example, Howard points to the guitar tracking sessions with Marc Ribot on Tom Waits' 2004 album *Real Gone*. "He's an amazing guitar player," Howard reports. "The guy is phenomenal. The first pass, the guy just plays a bunch of crazy stuff and it's wild, but once he starts to refine it he loses that. It's perfect and it's amazing, but the excitement of it is kind of tamed. So, that's what happens; the more you sing the song, the more you refine it. For some things that's great, but when you are going for performances and you want attitude and you want all that stuff, it's going to happen in one, two, or three takes."

Ross Hogarth moved from the road to the studio while he was working with guitarist David Lindley as a guitar tech. "David was working on a solo album, and Jackson Browne, who he had been with for years and years, was producing it. Jackson's engineer was working on the stuff and then they had something else to do, so David was basically left with me and an assistant who was more trained than me, but I was more trained then David, so I was plopped into the chair to basically run the tape machine," Hogarth recalls. "It was a very strange position, but it was a lot of fun and very exciting. I hadn't yet made the total transition [and] I was still sort of considered a road guy, so I went out of town and did some more gigs. Then I got a gig with Don Gehman on a record that he was producing with a guitar player (*Who Am I?* by Todd Sharp) that I had worked on the road tuning. It was a great place to be, you know; it's where I wanted to be."

Gehman had a special affinity for Hogarth's position, because he had gone from working on the road with Stephen Stills as a live-sound mixer to the studio. "I was really burned out on this three-hundred-one-nighters-a-year [schedule]," Gehman recalls. "Stephen saw that my heart was really into music and not so much in this travel thing, and he offered me an opportunity to help finish a record that he was working on at the time (the 1975 release *Stills*). So, I did it and he thought I was good and had the right personality, and he set me up at a place called Criteria Recording Studios in Miami, which at the time was like Atlantic South—Tom Dowd, Jerry Wexler, and Arif Mardin were all there. The Bee Gees came in. The Eagles. It was just a great place to be for most of the Seventies, and it was where I kind of cut my teeth on how to produce records."

Not only did working at Criteria give Gehman an understanding of how to work in a studio versus the road, it put him at the right place at the right time. John Mellencamp, who was then working under the stage name John Cougar, had been brought to Criteria to work with the legendary producer Tom Dowd, but Dowd was busy with a Rod Stewart project. "Tom thought that maybe the Albert Brothers [Howard and Ron], who were another set of producers there, might do well with him," Gehman says. "So, they made a record with [Mellencamp] where I did most of the work, and out of that situation John came back to me to co-produce records with him. That's really where people began to really know me as a record producer." The first Gehman-Mellencamp production was the 1982 offering *American Fool*, an album that featured the break-out songs "Hurts So Good" and "Jack and Diane."

FROM RECORD COMPANY TO PRODUCER AND BACK

Back in the early days of the commercial music industry, going from the record company to the studio may have been a common career path—record company reps who have an aptitude for music or engineering find themselves in the studio shepherding musicians through sessions. Of course, this was in the era of songwriting factories a la the Brill Building, where songwriters worked under contract to create songs for new and established artists, who worked in company-owned recording studios, so the studio was seen as an extension of the company rather than an independent business.

The modern-day example of a record producer who got his start on the company side of the business is Tony Brown, who made his name in the music industry as a player, touring with gospel groups like the Blackwood Brothers, the Stamps Quartet, and the Oakridge Boys (while they were singing gospel) before moving on to play with Elvis Presley, Emmylou Harris, Rosanne Cash, and Rodney Crowell. After leaving Harris' band, he took a job at the RCA Nashville affiliate Free Flight Records in Los Angeles. "I was a pop A&R guy for about a year-and-a-half and really missed being on the road," he reports. "So, I went back on the road for another couple of years with Rosanne Cash and Rodney Crowell. After that, I was going, 'I've had the ultimate experience in bands; now I'm ready to do something else.' I had reached the pinnacle, in my opinion, of being a sideman."

There were some other reasons, as well. "You can only make a bigger salary," he points out. "I wanted participation, and you had to be an artist, songwriter, or producer. I opted for the producer side of it. I aimed for that. Through the years, all my networking that I did with the people I worked with eventually helped me get a job with RCA." For a while, Brown doubled as an A&R rep and a record producer, which was just fine by him. "I wanted to be an A&R person that produced and worked for a record company, because I wanted the security of working for a record company," he explains. "Plus, I wanted to be able to sit in the room when the marketing plan went down, when the promotion plan went down, and when they did the album cover. I wanted to be involved in all aspects of the recording process." There was also another issue for Brown. "There was definitely a financial benefit to being a producer/executive," he admits.

In the early part of this decade, some producers jumped from record producer to label head. The office of record company president at major labels Virgin, Capitol, and Arista was occupied by producers Matt Serletic, Andy Slater, and, for a time, L.A. Reid, respectively. As Brown points out, this may be a nod back to an earlier time. "Reprise Records A&R, back with Russ Titelman, Ted Templemen, Mo Ostin, and Lenny Waronker was the model, to me, that defined creativity at its best," he recalls. "They covered every angle of pop music. They got away from it when they let Mo go and all the other guys went, too. There were no more creative people at the label, and it got to where the bean-counters were in charge, or it appeared that way."

Brown sees things turning the other way now. "I think what's happening is that the labels are saying, 'We've got to put creative people in charge, or the artists won't come to us,'" he says. "[Artists] are more apt to be attracted to Matt Serletic [record producer and Virgin Records Chairman and CEO] talking to them about their music then they are with somebody that's non-musical. I think these pop labels are trying to use these pop producers as magnets to attract the best talent." The return to form, Brown believes, is the way labels are saying that musicians can come talk to their presidents, because they understand. After all, that was the type of environment that Brown found when he joined Jimmy Bowen at MCA, where Emory Gordy was also a staff producer. It is also similar to what he has tried to do as a co-owner of Universal South, a country label he started with partner Tim DuBois.

This is a positive change for music, he says. "I think the only down side is if they get a bit un-objective about anything except what they produce," Brown admits. "But I don't think that L.A. Reid or Matt Serletic would take their position lightly. For one thing, I think once they get in there, there's so much to be done that they won't have time to put everything in their stack."

A couple of years after T-Bone Burnett produced the wildly successful *O Brother, Where Art Thou?* soundtrack, in 2002, he opened a boutique label, DMZ, under the Columbia Records banner. According to Burnett, the label is operating under different rules. "We're specialized in that we don't have a quota," he says. "So, we're only going to do things that we think are really, really good. We don't have an A&R staff, so we're going to allow people to make records without meddling."

Burnett's vast experience in the industry, as a musician and producer, is one of the main assets he brings into this label. "Well, I feel that I've made every possible mistake that you could make, and I hope to be able to help the young bands that we start working with," he says. "I just hope we can help everyone not to make those mistakes, not to do the dumb things that cause you to stall out or go in some other direction [that] you didn't really want to be in. I mean, sometimes that's not possible. We all have extraordinary mechanisms for defeating ourselves if we're not careful, you know. All us musicians, I would say, do. But, I hope to be able to just help keep things going in a strong, creative direction and not get hung up thinking about things that are counter to the creative process."

Although the *O Brother* soundtrack was one of Burnett's biggest successes, he is a producer known for working across many genres. For example, the soundtrack he produced for the film *Divine Secrets of the Ya-Ya Sisterhood* included songs by Lauryn Hill, Macy Gray, Taj Mahal, and Bob Dylan. Likewise, the *Cold Mountain* soundtrack featured songs from the alt-rock hero and The White Stripes leader Jack White. DMZ will take a similarly eclectic approach. "Categories don't mean anything to me at all," he says. "It either sounds good or it doesn't sound good. It either has something involving, or it has something that keeps a distance between the artist and the audience. I'm interested in music that is pointed toward the audience, rather than music that is pointed toward the artist."

"We've just come through a twenty-year period of the arrow pointing toward the artist," Burnett continues. "It's all been about the artist. 'Look how I look. Where's the camera? Look how I can play like I'm singing this song. Love me, send me money, and make me a big star so I can be on television some more.' It's been about that since the early Eighties. I guess it took a big hop with MTV, which is all about mugging, and I guess whoever mugged the best sold the most.

I think the events of 2001 rendered that philosophy idiotic, and I think it's time, once again, for the artist to begin to be generous to the audience. I mean, generosity is the hallmark of an artist." He pauses a second and then adds, "The record business took over music. When I was producing [more] records, these kids would talk about the marketing more than the music. That's frightening."

GOING FROM REMIXER TO PRODUCER

In traditional music production, many producers don't go into a session with the idea of leaving his or her own stamp on the recording. The goal, it seems, is invisibility. On the flip side there are the legions of remix producers who are ready when record companies or artists want a fresh track that can be serviced to a club or a radio station, or for inclusion in a soundtrack. Certainly, the ranks of the remix producers have swelled above and beyond the hip-hop and dance markets, where they first established their dynamic presence. Today, when a metal band is looking for a more industrial sound, they turn to a remix producer. When pop singers want to cross over into different waters, or established acts want to reach a new generation, they use a remix producer. It is not that "conventional" producers could not handle the change; it is that these remix producers have built this type of work into an art form.

When Garth Richardson was just starting out in L.A., he was looking for anything to do to keep active. That included engineering dates where he was paid five dollars an hour, and dance remix gigs that were done overnight and ended when the studio's owner pulled into the parking lot in the morning. "I would do anything," he says. "And you know what? I never made a single penny. It was all about getting my foot in the door and having people know who I was."

Before Chris Vrenna started out as a remix producer, he'd already paid some dues as the drummer for the industrial rock band Nine Inch Nails and as an engineer/assistant producer for a number of Trent Reznor-produced albums, including Marilyn Manson's 1994 *Portrait of an American Family* and the 1996 offering *Antichrist Superstar*. From Vrenna's perspective, the line between producer and remix producer has been blurred over the years. "There have been a lot of debates about it, because a lot of times for a remix we will require additional production," he explains. "I may add or subtract some things, and there are some remixers who are almost like songwriters, when you're writing all new parts within a whole different genre. I almost think a lot of times more work goes into that than the original production, because, let's say, if the band is a four-piece rock band, you help them on their song arrangement, you get their tone, you figure out what kind of approach they want to take, and you do it. But when I'm doing a remix, it's not like I have the band in front of me and I can say, 'Play that now as if you were a heavy metal band.'"

The one time that Vrenna had the opportunity to direct a band for a remix was when U2 was asked to rework the song "Elevation" for the *Tomb Raider* soundtrack. "I guess they had four or five different people doing remixes. I got a random phone call one day [and the person said], 'Hey, U2 loves your mix and they want to work with you. However, all those new parts that you added? The band wants it to be them. They want to be the ones to do it all. What's your schedule like? Can you go into the studio with them for two days?' I said, 'You tell me when, I will be there. I don't care if I'm getting married that day, I'll be there.'" Along with the entire U2 crew and guitarist The Edge, the song was re-recorded. "It's the only time in the history of a remix that the band has got a remix and then used it as the basis to re-do the song themselves," Vrenna says proudly. On a lot of the remixes I've done, the band doesn't even know it's being done. There was one artist in particular and the label wanted to get her on KROQ [a leading alternative radio station in Los Angeles], so we did this heavier version of one of her songs. The label loved it, radio loved it and she said, 'No way. That's not who I am as an artist, and if the only way I can get on the radio is to be represented by something that isn't me, then I'd rather just not get on the radio.' She shelved the whole thing." The artist who said no was Poe, and the song was "Haunted," which originally appeared on the 2000 release of the same name.

"It was really sad in a way," Vrenna admits. "I was really bummed that she felt that way, because I thought I really did her justice. My approach is always to push them sonically as far as you can to fulfill the whole reason the label is hiring you, but you can take something too far to where it's not believable." This is the lesson that he learned during his remix days that he takes into his production dates now. "That's my rule; be believable. It's something that's always been my barometer. I want the artist to say, 'Wow, that's cool, but it's still believable.'"

IN THE FINAL ANALYSIS

Clearly the roads to the big chair in the studio are as varied as the methods those producers use when they get there. Today's record producers have worked their way into sessions by starting as a gophers, live sound mixers, artists, label execs, remix producers…Through each of these experiences, they have learned what it takes to be successful in the studio, which is vastly different from what it takes to have a hit song, a Platinum album, or even a Grammy Award on the mantle. Being successful in the studio, for these producers, boils down to satisfied artists who can walk away with a collection of songs that best represents who they are. Over and over, the producers featured in this book confirmed that nothing is more satisfying than an artist taking a deep breath after a session and saying, "This is exactly what I heard." Certainly, getting to that point is sometimes an arduous process, and yet just as often, those words come after the producer takes a step back and lets the artist have the space to be creative.

There is no hard and fast rule, yet having a combination of types of experience before hopping into the producer's chair seems to be helpful. Vrenna has been a musician, engineer, remix producer, and producer over his career. "I'm not an engineer, but I know enough about engineering techniques that I can engineer myself if I have to, and sometimes I want to," he explains. "I know just enough about actual music to be able to offer a few things. It's funny, though, because you get guys that are so schooled in music, but they don't have any feel. It's like Nirvana, that guy (Kurt Cobain) probably couldn't read anything, but he could write a God damn good song.

"There are so many hats you wear as a producer," he continues. "You have to know about music, and you have to have good creative sound ideas, and there's a bit of engineering in there. There's even programming and coming up with fresh ideas to help expand the record, and you have to be a psychiatrist. I've had a few friends tell me that the first thing I needed to be a producer was a psych degree, because there are so many personalities. Musicians are a special breed of people. You're not just selling widgets—you're selling their soul, their creativity, their thoughts and feelings. People get personal about that stuff, as they should, and you gotta balance all those personalities, and sometimes substance abuse problems and business issues, label issues. You have to have a good business sense: You're given a specific budget, and you have a time frame, and you have to plan for [any] contingency. So, you have those things to think about. It's just so many small things that all kind of add up into one big person."

And that one big person needs to know his or her strengths and weaknesses, explains Don Was. "It doesn't make sense for me to be the songwriter, be the singer, arrange all the instruments, and tell everybody what to play," he says. "It is imperative that I know how to do it in case there's a problem. If we hit a dead end on something, I should be able to suggest a way out of it, and I can get involved if necessary. I could, although I have never once had to do this in twenty-five years, grab the guitar out of the guitar player's hands and say, 'No, like this.' It's good to know that you can get out of a situation and that people can look at you and know the boat is not going to sink. There is certain comfort in knowing that it could only get so bad. But, that's just my own style."

At the end of it all, the key is finding the best way to convey the song. "For me, it's all about passion," says Matt Wallace. "I think making records can be boiled down to a very, very simple kind of statement and that is: We're really just selling emotions. If we could do away with all the sound and lyrics and you could buy a disc to convey emotion, I think we'd do it. But because emotions are so deep and broad and sometimes so mysterious, the only way we can deal with them is to either dance, paint, or sing about them. I tell that to all bands, 'Hey, we're just selling the emotion, so whatever we do has to support or reiterate that emotion.'"

4 ARTISTS AS PRODUCERS

The ultimate goal of any recording session is for the artist to leave with a collection of songs that best represent that artist at that moment in time. So, a producer who understands the emotional upheaval that a songwriter goes through in the studio might be the best choice. Perhaps that person is also a musician who knows that feeling of inspiration when a song comes on; a musician who recognizes what it takes to communicate the idea to bandmates; a musician, finally, who understands how to grow the germ of an idea into a fully realized musical movement.

But, how does an artist become a producer? Perhaps the years and years of listening to a voice coming over the talk-back mic drive artists to the other side of the glass. Perhaps they feel that they have a better idea of how a session should go. Perhaps they feel that helping other artists' ideas come to fruition, rather than chasing their own dreams, would better serve their talents. Perhaps the artists who become producers are simply ready for a new challenge. Most likely, an artist lands in the producer's chair because of a combination of factors, plus any number of happy accidents. While many producers admit to having just a basic musical talent—Garth Richardson jokes that he can't play the guitar or piano because he suffers from poor coordination and that he's a lackluster drummer and bass player—the producers featured in this chapter have established themselves first and foremost as artists.

These days, there's certainly a bevy of artists making a name for themselves on the other side of the glass. Jack White's work with Loretta Lynn on the 2004 release *Van Lear Rose* was a critical and fan favorite, and earned the album a Grammy Award for Best Country Album. Ben Harper entered the studio to work with the multiple Grammy Award-winning gospel outfit The Blind Boys of

Alabama. Jerry Harrison, former keyboardist in Talking Heads, has gone on to work with a diverse pool of acts, including No Doubt, Live, and Kenny Wayne Shepherd. Dave Grohl has gone from Nirvana drummer to Foo Fighter frontman to acclaimed record producer for such artists as Queens of the Stone Age and Rye Coalition.

THE ART OF CO-PRODUCTION

There are also a number of artists who have taken co-production credits on band releases. System of a Down's Daron Malakian has worked hand-in-hand with Rick Rubin on the band's releases. Joe Henry shared responsibilities with Patrick McCarthy (*Trampoline*) before producing a pair of his recent releases. Godsmack's Sully Erna has earned production credits on three of the band's four releases, sharing them with Andrew "Mudrock" Murdock (on their 1997 self-titled debut and the 2000 follow-up *Awake*) and David Bottrill (for the 2003 release *Faceless.*) On Godsmack's 2004 release *Other Side,* Erna stepped up to helm the sessions himself.

Having Erna take control of Godsmack's productions has worked for the band. According to the singer/songwriter, the band has encouraged him along the way. "They are very comfortable with me producing," he explains. "As a matter of fact, they always encourage me to produce the next record, because they feel that I am there so much and most of the ideas that go down are usually mine. It saves us money, and they want to put some dough back in their pockets. It's always just kind of been the way it's been, and the guys are really comfortable with that. They trust my judgment; they've never not liked what the final results were."

Turns out that Erna had established that position from the beginning of the band. "Even through the Murdock days, it really was me that produced those records," he says. "I don't like to sound egotistical—that's not my intention—it's just that I'm really the one that's in there telling them what to do, and telling them how I want certain things to sound, and how I want certain levels set. To me that's producing." It seems to be an extension of the role he plays as the band's singer and one of their chief songwriters. "I've always got my nose in everything," he says with a laugh. "I can't help it. I guess I am a control freak to a certain point, and I just know what I want. I hear things in my head very clearly, and sometimes I guess I don't really need someone to produce, but more or less engineer. The thing I don't know how to do very well is turn the knobs, but I can hear what I want, so I am able to voice that as long as I have a great engineer behind the desk to actually dial in the sound that I'm looking for."

While he enjoys the work, Erna can see how important it is to have another pair of ears that are outside the band in the session. "It's nice to have that other person there that can kick in that extra flavor that you would have just went, 'I never would have thought of that.' Sometimes they would zig when you would zag, and it's a cool thing." He says that, while they had that relationship when Murdock was producing the band, they relied on Bottrill to work as a pure producer.

The Bottrill-Godsmack team worked together for the first time when the band was asked for a song to go on *The Scorpion King* soundtrack. The film's director, Chuck Russell, was interested in using "Voodoo," the single from their debut, but Erna had another song in the pipeline he felt would work better. Russell agreed, and the band hit the studio. "I started thinking it was time to shift gears and try someone new. I really loved the production on the Tool records, and I loved the Peter Gabriel stuff [Bottrill] had done, but we started to bounce around different people like Bob Rock and Sylvia Massy Shivy, who had put out records that had nice clean, crisp productions that were punchy. Bottrill was available. I sent him the music, and he liked it. It was kind of a test run for us, to see how he was, and if he had a good personality, and if our ideas jibed. It worked out so well, and [the song] went on to become our biggest single yet. It was like fourteen weeks at Number One, so we definitely felt it was worth giving him a shot at the full length."

Giving Bottrill the reins in the studio for those sessions was crucial to the musical success of *Faceless*. "He opened us up a lot. He really worked the band over and over and over again to get the parts perfect. He was a vocal Nazi. I mean I was doing thirty to forty takes for one song, to the point where I was ready to choke him with a phone cord, but I listen back and I go, 'Well, you know, he got a great performance out of me,' and I can't argue with that. So it was really kind of nice to bring some new blood into the band," Erna says. "Now I understand that variety is the spice of life. You don't know what you are going to get until you try new things, and with him, I would have never known that he was able to open us up the way he did. He really expanded the band—our sound, our harmonies, our capabilities—you know things that I probably wouldn't have tried on my own. It was nice to have someone else there to say, 'It's okay—let's not sound the same on every record. It's okay to try something different, and if you think it sounds weird because it's different then it's a good thing.' Well, hopefully it's a good thing, because who wants to sound the same all the time? We are always trying to reinvent the band to a certain degree to just come up with that thing that sounds a little bit different."

"Unfortunately the record came out in the worst time in the history of music," Erna continues. "Music just went through the biggest crash ever. I mean, bands got washed away left and right, and music was at its ultimate low for touring, for retail, for everything. I mean this whole crossover with piracy and the Internet, digital formatting and digital imprints, and all this shit that's happening really fucked the industry. We dropped what we felt was our best record at the time right during this point, and were out there with the biggest production we had ever built, and we couldn't fill up an arena. Then we realized that everyone was getting affected by this at different levels, but we were still able to sell a million records. So, for whatever it's worth, that step we took with David was strong enough to help us survive that thing that everyone else got kind of washed away on."

Given that experience, Erna is encouraged to open the door to either Bottrill or another producer. "The experience that we had with him was just a great experience and nothing failed. More or less what we have learned from working with him is that we need to work with more people," he says. "How much can you work with one person? They only have a certain bag of tricks, and maybe now we'll move on to work with somebody else. Again, the band, they are challenging me to produce the next CD, but I don't try to make those plans ahead of time. I base that decision on how the writing goes. If I feel the songs are solid, and they are in place, and it is what is, and I don't think it needs to be too jazzy or fancy, then I'll take the steering wheel and I will produce it. But if I think the song needs help, the arrangement needs help, maybe there is something missing in choruses or verses or it's not feeling as melodic as I want it to feel, that's when I want to reach out to somebody because they can hear the raw foundation of the song and bring what they bring to it."

THE RISKS OF PRODUCING A LEGEND

The benefits of working with an artist/producer are easy to see: Assistance with composition and arranging, compassion with the struggles that happen in the studio, and the camaraderie of working with another artist. Each of those talents came into play when Joe Henry was busy with Solomon Burke's Grammy Award-winning 2002 release *Don't Give Up on Me*. Not only was Henry responsible for putting the band together to record the album in four days, he helped guide Burke's vocal approach, and he and Andy Kaulkin, Burke's A&R rep picked all the songs for the soul singer from an impressive assortment. Ultimately, the duo picked songs from Bob Dylan, Elvis Costello, Brian Wilson, Dan Penn, Van Morrison, and Henry. While Kaulkin had already been pursuing a number of artists, when Henry came aboard he brought his own opinions and experience. "I sat down and listened to stuff as it came in and kind of pushed things to fruition," Henry explains. "I was wading through stuff as it came in to see what could have made a record. Once Andy and I had in a bag what we thought made sense, then Solomon heard everything and he had his opinions, but he was incredibly trusting and very open [to the fact] that we were doing something different."

That kind of approach gave Burke peace of mind as he was driving to the studio to record his vocals. "I met Joe once, and he's a very great guy," Burke reports. "He's a likeable young man, southern young man with a lot of spirit and a lot of soul. I came into the studio, I listened to his musicians that he had organized for this session, and started singing. That was it. There were no rehearsals or none of that. On these sessions I did no changes, I did no producing. I just did the singing."

For an artist who has had a hand in many of his productions, this was a refreshing change. "It was a lot of pressure off of me," Burke says, "to not be responsible for what the music sounded like or how it was going to go. [This time] it was like, 'This is the song? This is the way you want it? Okay, here it comes. You put the flour out there, I'm going to make the cake. Sorry, guys, if you don't like upside-down cake,'" he adds with a laugh. "The next one is going to be chocolate. So, we played bakery, and up popped the goodies."

Henry's musical background enabled him to take the Burke sessions in a new direction. "From the beginning, I said pretty plainly [that], if I was going to be involved, I had no interest in making a retro soul record," Henry says. "I was trying to be referential to an old sound or an old idea, [but] I don't want any horn sections, I don't want it to be something that's overly grand and ornate. What I really wanted was to do something that was as stripped down as it could be, so that every nuance, every trail off of his voice was full-frame. The idea of having new songs from some very outrageous sources, songs that nobody has ever heard before was very intriguing."

Burke was impressed that Henry would take the risk of working with him. "It took a lot of guts, because there were a lot of different producers who would not produce me," he says. "Why would you produce someone sixty-two years old that's been in the business for fifty years? What happens if you fail? What if you don't come up with a record? Where do you go from there? So, it was a sure shot and a smart move for him, because he knew just how to stay on the wire and to be there and get what he wanted, and he heard it. It's a little different for me, because I'm accustomed to hearing more music, more horns, and more this and that. But sometimes less is best."

Beyond songwriting assistance, Henry was called on to direct the musicians he hired to play the sessions. That level of communication was crucial in this instance, because the team recorded the entire album in four days, live to tape. "I think the best moments on the record were one or two takes," Henry recalls. "Working very quickly just became a thing, and there are takes when I can listen back and I can hear the process of Solomon taking hold of the song, because it was very new to him, very fresh to him, as opposed to [when] he wrote a lot of things that he recorded in the Fifties and Sixties, or came into a session where everybody had charts and it was just a matter of literally getting a take because everybody had it charted out." The Nick Lowe-penned song, "Other Side of the Coin," is a prime example of that process. "I think we did three or four takes of that, and they were all wildly different in character and tone," Henry recalls. "The first take was very much like an old Nat King Cole Trio song, very much like a jazz ballad, very skeletal, which I really loved, but we decided very quickly that it needed to have more of a backbeat than that for Solomon to dig into it. But it was a great example of how, over a couple of takes, it was not a matter of people having a good moment as musicians or he as a singer, but just deciding on where does the song live and how does it best serve the whole of the record."

"The Judgment," Elvis Costello and Cait O'Riordan's contribution to the album, gave Henry the opportunity to work with Burke, the band, and Costello, who came into the studio. It was big-time pressure for Henry. "I knew that [song] was going to be the tough one, because structurally it's odd," he states. "There's a hanging bar. It's very orchestral that way. To me, it's kind of like a Roy Orbison song in that it's operatic and the dynamic is grand in that way, and the structure is odd. That one took the most work to wrestle to the ground. I think a number of us, myself chief among them, kind of sagged at that moment. It was like, this is not just falling into our laps. But Solomon was strangely undaunted by the audience and by the fact that Elvis was there, and by the fact that we really had to roll up our sleeves to find it.

"I certainly had a moment where, as a producer, I thought, 'I really need to have a solution here.' That's a sobering moment," he continues. Turns out that having Costello there, and available to explain to Burke the feel of the song, was the solution they needed. "It was a really terrific moment; it ended up being one of my favorite moments of the process, because Elvis is such a fan and he's never been in the room when someone was recording his song before, which I didn't know. Elvis talked to him about the phrasing and the odd structure of the song, and that's how we got a leg up on it."

Burke has his own special memories of that day. "I'm really overwhelmed by [Costello]. He's just an unbelievable talent, and for him to personally fly in and supervise the song, is just unbelievable," the singer recalls. "For him to be there and then stay there until two o'clock in the morning...Superstars don't do that. That was just an amazing situation. I was very honored to know that him and his [then] wife even wrote the song for me. He was very caring and very easy and very wonderful to talk to, and I kept wanting to say, 'I need your autograph. I need your autograph.' I was very excited about it. When you know an artist's legacy and their performance and their works and the things that they've done, especially in their country and your country, it means an awful lot."

Though not as musically difficult, the recording of the song "None of Us Are Free" with The Blind Boys of Alabama was equally daunting for star power and vocal arrangements. It was Henry's second test, as Burke was learning the song, Henry was working with the Blind Boys' musical director on the arrangements, and the band was figuring out the music. "It was intense, and probably more than the Elvis song, I felt in the hot seat to make sure that all these balls stayed up in the air," Henry recalls. "When the song happened, it was chilling, because I kind of felt like we were shooting blind. At a certain moment, I leaned into Solomon's vocal mic and counted off the song as a joke to see where everybody was, and the song just kind of happened. I didn't know if everybody had headphones on, I didn't know if everybody could hear me. I just thought everybody was in their own world.

"I just called the room to order and counted off the song, and everybody just fell in," Henry continues. "It was really shocking. It kind of blew me back. I felt air leave my body because everybody was in, everybody was there. We did two takes of the song and that was it; everybody just kind of left. I don't ever remember people asking if it was a take, if it wasn't a take. The Blind Boys just kind of got up, Solomon left, and that was the end of the session."

For any producer, there is no better feeling. "It was remarkable. It was the end of the fourth day. Solomon was done working, he got up and thanked everybody, and he left. We sat around, had a little bit of Scotch and listened to some things back and said, 'Wow, there really is something.' It was a really intense four days. It's kind of a blur when it's happening, and then you kind of come out of it a day later, and you go, 'I think it happened.'"

PRODUCING ON-THE-FLY

Ben Harper's songwriting ability came into play when he went into the studio with the hip-hop act Blackalicious to work on the song "Brain Washers." "The song was written in the studio," he recalls. "I mean, we were writing lyrics, and we were putting out ideas. It was freestyle in the studio. I was harmonizing, stacking vocals, playing guitars, coming up with different drum samples and different rhythm ideas. Gab (Gift of Gab, the act's vocalist) was writing lyrics. It was full-on commando style. We started at noon and walked out at five in the morning with the track."

Rather than this type of schedule lending confusion, Harper believes it worked out for the best. "Limitations can force opportunity," he says, "and if you're ready to discipline yourself to not give up, to obtain the best of the track, then you can get the track. You have to be motivated and inspired by music, period. For me, the intentions have to be musically pure in that you're there to serve the song, not to make a song that will hopefully serve you. I've never stepped into any musical environment with any other consciousness but to serve the song."

That mentality served him well while in the studio with the Blind Boys, especially while they were recording Clarence Fountain's vocals for the title track. After a couple of passes at the vocal, executive producer Chris Goldsmith turned to Harper and said, "I'd like to hear him come out and be a little reserved one time." Harper thought about it for a second and responded, "Do you want that because it's Clarence, or because it's good for the song?" While the question hung, the duo asked Fountain to give it one more shot. "It's my indulgence," Goldsmith admitted. The more reserved vocal made it onto the track. "I look at it like, do you want some heavy slide riffs, because I can do it, or do you want it because you really feel that's what's going to bring out that moment of the song and the song as a whole?" Harper explains. "Knowing that from a player's perspective gives me that from a producer's perspective. You've got to look at it from that perspective, instead of what Clarence can do physically, because we all know that."

A STUDY OF PINK

There are scores of examples where songwriter/producers have helped artists realize their ideas by working with them before the recording process begins. One of the most dramatic over the past five years was probably the combination of Linda Perry's songwriting and studio experience with Pink's vocal talents, which resulted in Pink's smash album *Missundaztood*. Not only did these sessions provide the producer with a new avenue of creativity—she went on to work with Courtney Love and Christina Aguilera after the successful Pink sessions—it also helped cement Perry's ideas about technology, using real instruments, and working in the studio.

Perry's production career started while she was living in San Francisco and still a member of 4 Non Blondes, the band that broke out in 1992 with the album *Bigger Better Faster More?* and the smash hit "What's Up?" She produced the band's contribution (a cover of "Misty Mountain Hop") to a Led Zeppelin tribute album. After leaving 4 Non Blondes, she set up Rockstar Records and began producing San Francisco bands, such as Stone Fox. Yet, her other-side-of-the-glass knowledge spiked when she worked with producer Bill Bottrell during the sessions for her 1996 solo album *In Flight*. "He is just a genius to me. I learned everything from him," she reports. "He was really supportive of getting me to sit at the board and learn to trust my ear. Even if maybe technically I might be doing something wrong, it doesn't matter if it sounds good to my ear."

But even with her newfound knowledge, Perry was initially reluctant to take on the Pink project. "She called me and left me a ten-minute hysterical, frantic, crazy message," Perry recalls. "I could barely understand what she was talking about. So, I called her back, and she was like, 'I've been looking for you and I found your phone number. I want you to write a song with me and produce it, and I would love for you to sing with me as well.' The only response I could have is, 'You know I'm not hip?'"

The two had eight days together where they wrote four songs. "Everything seemed to be clicking. I have a home studio, and I was getting really great sounds, and the demos that I did sounded so good that that's everything that made it on the record," Perry reports. "She took four songs to her company, and they were basically, 'Whatever you are doing with this girl just continue to do it.'" Less than two months later, sixteen songs were written.

"Eventually" was the first song they wrote together, but it was "Get the Party Started" that became the hit. Perry had written the song a week before Pink phoned, while she was learning how to program drums. "I came up with the beat, and then I got the bass and guitar," Perry explains. The hip-hop party ditty was so outside of what Perry was known for that she and her manager had no clue what to do with it until Pink called. "She loved the song, and the [record] company loved it as well. I put her voice on there, and she was mimicking the vibe that I had on the demo version. I had really distorted my vocals and she's like, 'I want to get that distorted vocal sound that you got.' So, I dialed up the same sounds that I did for the demo and she nailed it right on the spot."

During these sessions Perry relied on the lessons she learned while working with Bottrell. "If I'm riding my Fairchild [compressor] too hot, technically that's wrong, but the overdrive is creating a vibe and it feels good. With every song I try to create a vibe," she says. "Sometimes I got her off the [Neumann] U-47 and put her on a bullet microphone or a harmonica mic and put it through my Echoplex. I would never dial up the same sound with her. Every song to me had a certain sound that I needed to find and if it was programming it on the [Akai] MPC for the drums or finding a loop that fit, everything was different. It was cool."

Instrument-wise, Perry has an eclectic collection, including a Trident, Akai MPC, and a bevy of guitars, basses, and amps. "The Trident is as high tech as I get," she reports with a laugh. "It's got some cool drum sounds in it, but I use the MPC to program drums, and I always seem to pick more of the live drum sounds over the 808 sounds that everybody uses. It wasn't until I got the Trident that I started realizing that everything in music sounds exactly the same—everybody is using the exact same programs." What sets Perry apart from the crowd is the fact that she plays a real bass—typically a 1967 Fender P-Bass with an Ampeg flip-top B-13 that she runs through a Bass Pod's sub-bass sound. "I just compress the sound out of it on the LA-2A and I get this fat, fat bass sound. Also, the thing is that it's my bass that's giving me that sound. I think that's what people forget, that the instrument is actually the most important part of it all."

Using real instruments and amps has shocked a few engineers she has worked with, Perry says. "I was recording one time, and I said [to the engineer], 'I'm going to plug in my AC-30.' I look over at the guy, and he's got the AC-30 up on the Pro Tools." She then asked the engineer, "'Tell me, why would we do that when I have an AC-30 right here? The real thing with all the static-y noise and the crunch and the crackles?' He just had this blank look on his face. I said, 'Okay, well all you gotta do is stick a microphone over here, and we'll be good to go.'"

Perry does not move into Pro Tools until she is ready to edit. "If Pink didn't sing the song in three takes, that's all she had. To me, if you need to sing a song more than three times, then you need to go figure out what you need to do with your voice," she explains. "I go into some studios, and they've got the Pro Tools rig and eighty tracks for the person to sing. To me, it's like, 'You know what? If that person needs that many tracks to sing a song, then they need to learn how to sing.'"

Or else, she believes, they need to learn how to write songs. "I think what happens is people try to make songs out of Pro Tools. I write the song before it goes anywhere. I don't have a choice, because I don't have Pro Tools, so I have to write the song. I can't cut and paste anything. Everybody right now is like, 'Oh, let's cut and paste. Let's put the bridge here, let's put this here.' Okay, here's an idea, sing. So, they're missing the depth in the song, and most producers I don't think know how to get depth out of a performer. I'm not dissing on any-body, because I think there's so many great people, [but] I think it's the per-former's fault, too, for being so generic."

It's that instrument-and-performance-first philosophy that pushes Perry away from the pack as she works with artists such as Pink and Christina Aguilera. For instance, Perry points to a session she was in with rap producer Rockwilder (Busta Rhymes, Jay-Z, Redman) where she brought in a Moog, Echoplex, and a handful of guitars and basses. "I look over at Rock's area, and he's got all his computers and all that stuff," she recalls. "He looks over at my area, and here's all my analog stuff. It was a beautiful pair-up. The guys were like, 'I don't think I've seen anybody play a real guitar in any of these sessions.' It's pretty funny, because it makes all the sense in the world why everything sounds the way it does right now. It's because it's all sampled and programmed from the Trident, and it all sounds the same.

"My job right now—I'm going to pretend it's really my job because I'd love to have it—is to bring a fresh idea into this really generic, cleaned, polished music that's happening right now and actually give some of these girls some balls—give the music some depth, and give the listener some actual real emo-tion," she continues. "It's cool, too, to be a chick and be doing this because there's not a lot of chick producers. I'm an up-front kind of person and like I said, I just think I'm good at it and I don't think anybody's really looking at me as a chick coming into this male-dominated producer thing. They're just letting me by, and I'm doing my job, and everybody's really digging it."

GOING SOLO IN THE STUDIO

Just as many artists co-produce their own recordings or produce other artists, there are also quite a few who are going all the way and producing their own sessions. The reasons for taking on that responsibility are numerous: They want to save money, they feel they don't need another producer, they're satisfying their own ego, etc. Without question, however, artists who wish to produce their own albums today need to have a willing band (or set of session players), an understanding label, and an extremely trustworthy engineer.

Some modern-day examples of artists who have undertaken their own productions include Third Eye Blind frontman Stephan Jenkins, Joe Henry, David Lowery, and Ben Harper, who turned producing responsibilities over to his manager, J.P. Plunier, for his first four releases, and then took over the producer's chair for the 2003 release *Diamonds on the Inside*.

It seems that the key for these artists-cum-producers is learning every detail that they can while working with other producers. "By the time *Diamonds* came I knew the parts, I knew the pieces, I knew the type of boards, the types of mic pre's, the types of rooms, the types of instruments, the types of amplifiers, the types of players, and the types of engineers," explains Harper. He also had the good fortune of working with bassist Juan Nelson, percussionist Leon Mobley, and drummer Oliver Charles, who make up the majority of his touring band, the Innocent Criminals. Harper says they were all supportive of him producing the *Diamonds* sessions. "It was totally one hundred percent excitement, enthusiasm, and positivity from all the players involved," Harper says. "The first time I stepped out was the Blackalicious track, and those guys gave me a professional nod of enthusiasm that was totally genuine and sincere. I remember Leon saying, 'Man, that's where you should be; you should be doing that.'"

At the same time, Harper faced directing Juan Nelson, who had been his friend and bandmate since 1994, when the singer launched his first tour to support his debut, *Welcome to the Cruel World*. "Juan and I have a very specific relationship, and it's only similar to that of my brothers. He and I are both very emotional people and we are both very musically opinionated. We're both very open as long as you're liking what I'm saying," Harper explains with a laugh. "So, there's been some tension, and I think he will attest to it, but we've never walked out on one another and we've always stuck it out in the moments where it's uncomfortable. None of us takes easily to being molded. Not me."

The two have shared musical ideas, he adds, that neither thought would work. Yet, it comes together, sometimes to Harper's surprise. "He'll [suggest things] to me sometimes and it's like, 'Ouch, ouch, ouch…No, no. Oh, you're right.' You can't really get a square peg in a round hole, but you can put a round peg in a square hole, you know what I mean? That's always challenging, but we've done it. I mean, and if we've done it for ten solid years, I think we can do it, you know, as long as we want."

It is almost as if it would be easier to bring in a session player at times. "It would always be easier to do that, but then you get a session player-sounding album, and if there is one thing I can say, none of my albums are that," Harper says. "You can say whatever you want, but they ain't session player albums; these are all friends of mine who I have known for over a decade."

Another artist/producer who has worked with a handful of musicians for a long period is Joe Henry, who produced his own *Tiny Voices* right after co-producing *Scar* with Craig Street. His experience has been quite different from Harper's. "It couldn't be easier to direct [my band], because we've done so much work together that there's enough respect there," he says. "They know because they're there that I love and respect them, and I don't find myself having to, like, baby-sit anybody."

There are times, however, when that familiarity breeds less than inspiring music and Henry knows it. He also knows how to break out of it. To illustrate the way he works with musicians on a self-production, he points to the work he and the musicians (drummer Jay Bellerose, bassist Jennifer Condos, and keyboardist Dave Palmer) did on the song "Your Side of My World," which appeared on his 2003 album *Tiny Voices*. "I'd done a demo of it with Jenny, Jay, and Dave at my house, and it kind of came off sounding like something that might have been like a demo for *Beggar's Banquet*. It [sounded] more like classic rock. I mean, it didn't mean to, it was just the way we played it, and the way we were set up it just had more structure like a rock song." The trio went into the studio, played it a couple of times in the same style, and Henry was not happy. "I was just completely annoyed by it, and I was obviously going to throw this song out; it was boring me to tears. We left it for the next day. We ran through it a few times, and Jenny and Jay were going, 'I think it sounds really good.' I'm like, 'You know, but...yeah it sounds really good, it sounds fine, but who cares. It's not taking me anywhere, you know? I'm embarrassed by it.'"

So, Henry threw on his production hat in order to help the band hear it a new way. He called Bellerose and told him to bring in a different kick drum and to play only that and a hi-hat. "I told him to think like he was in a parade and he was just a parade drummer," Henry recalls. "I didn't want to hear a rock beat. The idea was just off the top of my head. I told Dave to play a piano intro that we could fade up on. I was just trying to create a different mood with the band just starting to play. We had to think of this as more like orchestration than like a rock band. I think we did two takes that way, and then Ron Miles started to treat the trumpet in a different way because those needed to come to the fore and not be about guitars or anything like that. So, it was produced in a manner that could have easily not worked, but in that case, it worked to get us to thinking in terms of it being [more like] some kind of strange, dream-like, orchestral idea than a rock band. But it's frequently just a matter of, how can you trick somebody into starting over, like restarting a computer."

It is a trick that Henry learned during his stint as an engineer for producer T-Bone Burnett. "He'll listen to something and go, 'Hey, that's great, but check this out. I just found this little Jimmy Reed thing, and you just gotta hear it, man. This is so deep.' He'll play that and not even refer back to what you've just been working on for hours that he's been listening to," Henry recalls. "Like, 'Hey, yeah, that's cool, but check this out.' You know that what he's doing is [saying], 'Leave this. Get out of it,' and then maybe he'll go back to another song before he'd ever come back to that one. Or somehow, listening to Jimmy Reed will lead to another conversation where he'll go, 'You know what, let's just go play that one again, but just you two go play it.' It might not ever end up like that, but it's just something to help you find a different handle on the song. And sometimes it can just knock you off balance enough to get away from your pre-conceived notions."

Chris Vrenna learned that same lesson, albeit a bit differently while he was co-producing his own band, Tweaker, for their 2004 release *2 a.m. Wakeup Call* with Clint Walsh. "It's pretty hard to produce myself, which is why I'm so glad I have Clint in my life now," Vrenna says. "The first record, I didn't really have a partner, and two heads are definitely better than one. The problem I think I had with the first record was that I was more concerned about production and how weird I could make sounds be, and I didn't pay enough attention to just starting it off as songs first. It's hard, because I get so emotionally attached to stuff, and then sometimes I'm either worried about production and I'm forget-ting about songwriting or vice versa. So, Clint will be behind me going, 'Dude, doesn't this…' and I'm like working on the delay return on a vocal for like an hour or whatever."

Not only did he bring in another pair of ears for this album, he changed how he approached the recording schedule so he would avoid the navel gazing he admits he suffered from on the Tweaker debut. "I wanted to break it into writ-ing an album, and then going back and producing an album, where I didn't have to think about both at the same time," he explains. "So we wrote a batch of about twenty songs and then took three weeks off. Then we came back, wrote for another three weeks, and then picked the songs. Clint and I picked the songs, and we got opinions from all our friends and my wife Carrie, then we pared it down to the twelve we knew we wanted to do." The duo spent a cou-ple of days on each song, making sure the performances were right. "Then we added all the fill-ins, the noises, the drones, and all those little ear-candy pro-duction things. We did those totally separate, so we already knew what the song was going to be.

"It wasn't like trying to figure out what the chords were going to be and what kind of sound did we want to play them with," Vrenna continues. "For me, that really helped a lot, just separating the two aspects. [It was like] pretending we were a band first with demos going to a producer saying, 'We want to sound weird, how do we do that?' Then [we] put on the producer's hat and said 'Man, those chords are really great. The song is bad. Where's the next one? The arrangements are great; okay, let's go make it sound fantastic, let's give it dimension and all that.' That's the way we decided to do it, and I think it worked out pretty well, too. It kept my head together at least. Whether or not anybody likes the record is a different story."

Breaking the sessions into segments and bringing in an outside voice was crucial to the sessions for Cracker's 2002 *Forever* album, which were produced by David Lowery. "It's successful to self-produce, but you have to go about it in a totally different way. What you do is, you record for a very long period of time," Lowery explains. "You can't record it all because you don't have the same perspective. Some people, I think, are more successful at it than others. I'm probably in the middle. Like, I can look back at *Forever* and go, 'Oh, we should have done this to that song, this to that song, and this song should have been on the record and not that.' But it's not bad. I think we got all the right things in the right place, but we'd just do three or four songs at a time and get some basic tracks, then take a couple of weeks off. I'd listen to it a couple of nights and change the words around, maybe change the arrangements, just worked on it bit by bit, piecemeal. We never recorded for more than, like, seven or eight days in a row, ever. I enjoyed doing that. But you have to spend a lot of time. It had to have been done over a period of a year, at least."

THE KEY TO SUCCESS? PERSPECTIVE

Sure, heading into the studio as your own boss can be a rewarding experience, but you also take the ultimate risk of losing all perspective. The danger of slipping into self-obsession, or endlessly searching for perfection is always present, especially for a musician whose dream of releasing his or her music to the world is about to come true. That is not to say that it is impossible to self-produce; the key is to find perspective and maintain it.

Ben Harper only stepped up to produce his own release after four albums that were produced by somebody else. While he was working on *There Will Be a Light,* an album made up mostly of his own songs, he commented, "I'm so deep in, but I've had enough experience now to have attained a heightened level of objectivity."

His point is that it can be done, but it is difficult. Even a Producer of the Year Grammy Award-winner agrees: "A songwriter could write a song and be as lost as the songwriter in the song and not really cater to it in as many ways as a producer who didn't write the songs," explains Walter Afanasieff. "You've got to be careful with that. In the event I have to cut a song that somebody else wrote, I'll get a demo from the songwriter who has already put the spirit of the song into it. Sometimes they put it in with certain elements that have to be honored, to keep the song the way songwriter intended it to be. A lot of times, a producer will disregard those elements of the demo, and often he will lose the meaning and the spirit of the song by doing that. Yet, in another sense, the songwriter who is not a producer gives up the right to their song being produced by somebody. So, it's a two-way street, but I think a songwriter/producer is the best way of coming out with the most proper version of the song, if you will.

"Usually, we take it for granted, but it's hard," he continues. "If I was going to write a song for Celine [Dion], or if I was going to write a song for Faith Hill, or if I'm going to turn around and write a song for Toni Braxton, they are so different—each one of those artists, and my skills as a songwriter to write that particular artist's song, and yet to turn around and produce it in that particular way. So, all of these skills are having to be kind of honored, and it's difficult."

System of a Down's Daron Malakian echoes those sentiments, pointing out that he starts to think about production as he's writing a song, but he wouldn't do without either his band's or Rick Rubin's point of view. "Everything comes out at the same time—the production, the structure, the songs, the vocals, the lyrics, the sound, the vibe, the way it should sound on the album, everything," he says. "The best songs come out that way." Then, sometimes a year after the original idea arrives, he will take the song to the band and listen to their input. He is not protective. "No, I can't be. I'm working with a team. I do respect what everyone says, and at the end of the day, it does come out better because of the input. I only care about the song. I don't give a fuck about my ego. I really want that song to be bad-ass. It's like you want the best for your kids, you know? And if someone else is going to come around and give some opinion that is going to be the better for your kids, you'll take that opinion.

He says the band relies heavily on Rick Rubin's point of view. "It's not just about sound and all that," he says. "We really need someone to tell us which of these songs are the greatest, [or] which songs are good but need work. I'm so inside of it all. I have to have that guy. I'm an awful judge, terrible judge on System's music. I'm like the last person you should ask if the song is good or bad," he says with a laugh. "I guess [artists who self-produce are] the kind of artist that doesn't like other opinions, though some artists do that and make great albums. It's all in how you are comfortable expressing yourself, and I wouldn't feel confident enough relying on myself to judge which ones are the best songs to get on the record."

PLAYING WHILE PRODUCING

Perhaps it is obvious that an artist/producer can offer more to a session than songwriting and musical help; they can play their instrument during the recording dates. Don Was, whose main instrument is bass, has had the experience of playing on albums he has produced, and not playing. "Sometimes playing on a record is a really good thing. I would play bass on all the records if people wanted me to," he says. "The risk you run is, if you don't play bass to the artist's satisfaction, it trickles over into your ability to produce. I don't want to compromise myself by not playing bass well, especially by forcing myself on the thing. I never play unless someone asks me, and even then, only when I think I can handle it. Sometimes I really want to and I won't do it because they haven't asked me. Someone really needs to be paying attention to the whole."

As an example, Was points to a recent session that he produced and played on for Jessi Colter. "I played string bass and found myself getting distracted. I found myself listening too much to the bass during playback," he says. "So, I took the bass out because I should have been concentrating on the vocals. It didn't matter what the bass was doing; if the vocal was good, I could always go back and fix the bass. So, it's a bit of a balancing act.

"You don't really understand the innermost workings of a band until you play music with them," Was continues. "There's something about playing music where people reveal themselves. People learn over a period of time how to finesse a situation, verbally and with some manners, and you can cover up serious neurotic tendencies. You can't do it in music or I don't know anyone who can do it in music. Everything is revealed when you play music; you can tell whether someone listens or doesn't listen. You can tell if they are generous, if they are considerate; you know all the basic things about them.

"I didn't understand the Rolling Stones fully until I played bass with them, and then I became aware of a whole other dynamic," he continues. "It's like suddenly the picture went from black and white to Technicolor. I could see that first of all, they dig each other and they have fun. Man, they're jocular. They listen and answer. It is like a four-way conversation all the time, and it is just like great friends on a street corner trading barbs or whatever. They're just hanging out and throwing stuff at each other that you then send off or build on top of and send back, and no one is hogging the space. There is none of that—it's just generous, gentle play. And that's why they have this wonderful relaxed feel, and they know the nuances of each other's playing because they have been together so long. So, once I got in the middle of that and understood what was going on, it helped me even deal with the personalities, because I could see that where I thought there was tension, there was actually love there."

5 GETTING INTO THE GAME

How does an aspiring producer get started? "Open a recording studio," Brad Wood exclaims. "That's it, that's it. That's the foot in the door, and then work like a dog, you know, just make as many records as possible. For me, literally, it was almost like quantity over quality at some point. You have to internalize the process of setting up mics and getting ready *bang-bang-bang*. Then you stop thinking about the technical aspect, and you start listening to the music more. At least for me, that's how it worked. And if I would have spent three months making a record right when I started, I don't know that I would have gotten as good as I think I got as fast as I did."

Wood opened Idful Studio in the late Eighties, when the Chicago indie music scene was just beginning to boom. "I worked with a lot of bands, and the kind of bands that I worked with, especially at that time, would make records in a few days. So, it might be three days to make an album, and I would sometimes make two albums a week. I averaged like fifty-some albums a year for a number of years. But they were really quick, like track all the music in one day, cut the vocals and do the overdubs in one day, and then mix it on the third, and they're done. I think that's a really great way to do it. Own your own studio if you want to be a record producer; it's the easiest way to get it done, and if you're the boss there's no one to tell you that you're not a record producer. Just hang your shingle out. It's easier than ever to do it now and that's good, because the playing field is leveled from a technical aspect."

While Wood speaks from experience, getting into the game of production can still be a frightening prospect. The key, it seems, is to be willing to take the first risk. "I really didn't know anything about what I was doing, [but] I wasn't technically daunted by anything," says Lou Giordano, who earned a degree in electrical engineering from MIT before he started to work at Radiobeat Studios in Boston. "I went into [Radiobeat] with a band called SS Decontrol, and the studio owner of Radiobeat hated the music but he admired our enthusiasm and he taught me to run all of the equipment so that he wouldn't have to do it. So, it was just baptism by fire. There I was, and I kind of fought my way through that and I soon became a staff engineer there, and so that means you do anything that walks in the door just to keep the income coming."

Giordano's technical background helped him in a roundabout way. "I guess it's helped me to approach the larger task and the big picture in kind of a methodical way, and to just think things through kind of carefully, rather than just going about it from the seat of the pants."

Not everyone has that sort of technical pedigree, however. Garth Richardson got his start in the studio business working as a part-time janitor at the Nimbus 9 studio where his father, Jack Richardson, worked. (Ironically, Garth was nominated for the Jack Richardson Producer of the Year Award at the 2003 Juno Awards.) "I had to come down to my Dad's studio when I was in Grade 7 and clean and vacuum the floors, and then I'd stay until four or five in the morning watching Bob [Ezrin] do Peter Gabriel's first solo album or Pink Floyd's *The Wall* and then go back to school the next day to sleep."

The time working with his father and the cadre of producers that surrounded him at Nimbus 9 taught Richardson some valuable lessons, which helped him to get his foot in the door at first, as well as keep him busy today. "It basically taught me really good values, to care, and about what a song was," he explains. "So, working with him and watching him make records taught me to care."

Although Richardson got his start thanks to his father, he also worked extremely hard and took the risk of moving to L.A. with producer Michael Wagener in the mid-Eighties to make his own name. His risk paid off, as Richardson went from engineer status to producer. In short order, he received the opportunity to work on Rage Against the Machine's eponymous debut, an album that helped change the face of rock music in the early Nineties.

Michael Rosen got his break thanks to persistence. After getting his college degree, he decided that the Automat Studios in San Francisco, where Narada Michael Walden was creating some of the most memorable music of the Eighties, was where he wanted to work. "I walked by the studio every day on my way to my regular gig," Rosen remembers. "I said to myself, 'I went to school for all these years to do this.' I just picked the studio that I wanted to work at and bugged [studio manager] Michelle Zarin every day for two months until she hired me."

And, of course, there are the producers who stepped to the other side of the glass for the first time while recording an album with their own band. "I had a punk-rock band and I made my own records," Rick Rubin says of his start.

"Then I started making rap records from the beginning. I'm not an engineer, and I have no technical ability whatsoever."

Mark Trombino shares that experience, since he started tweaking things in the studio while recording his own band at the University of California at San Diego. "That band was very cool, and I did our stuff because I was frustrated with the people that we worked with," he says. "I never felt like we got what I thought we could get, so I just started doing it. We were doing seven-inch [singles] and demos. For me, it was like a matter of the stars properly lining up. San Diego at the time was pretty cool and happening. There was a record label [Cargo Records] there that was putting out decent records. There were a lot of cool bands at the time, and I was able to find a studio [on campus] that was basically empty and I could kind of take over. So, I started by doing it, calling myself a producer and convincing people that I knew what I was doing, and doing it, and learning on their records."

Sylvia Massy Shivy came at it through working as a college radio DJ. "Those people know how to party," Shivy says with a laugh. "We went to all the clubs and we got to hang out with the cool bands. It was a great place to be in college, but ultimately when I did radio commercially for a living, I realized it's not about the music at all, it's about commercials. So, that's when I decided to move from radio into the recording of the music and making records."

After a bit of work as an engineer in San Francisco, Shivy moved to Los Angeles and looked for work at a recording studio while doing a day job at Tower Records. The traditional ways of finding work were not working for her, so Shivy got creative. "I had the best résumé, I had experience, I had been producing records already, but I couldn't get a job anywhere in the land of studios," she explains. "I had to find a way to set myself apart, so you know that newspaper the *Weekly World News?* I made a paper with a headline that read, 'Elvis Has Risen From the Dead.' I wrote that he had taken me hostage and that the only way that I could be saved from the evil Elvis was for someone to give me a job. I stapled that to my résumé and sent that out, again, to the same studios that I had been trying to get a job at and suddenly I got, like, five calls." Her first gig after being hired was with Phil Ramone, who was producing Barbra Streisand's 1985 release *The Broadway Album* at Lion Share Studios.

Shivy still believes it is important for aspiring producers to set themselves apart somehow. "Probably more so now, because I think the studio business has really tightened up. I don't think it's necessary to have the schooling that a lot of up-and-comers have," she says. "I never went to school for it, but I did do a lot of time observing and experimenting and working for free."

"I think [to get started in production] you need to have made some records, either as an artist or a musician or as an engineer," David Lowery says. "There's not one way to do a record, but there are definitely certain time-tested ways to do a record." That starts, he says, with pre-production, where songs are picked and arrangements finalized before going into the studio to record. "Then you concentrate on getting great takes and a great sound for the song, with a great vocal take and a great mix." Another method, and the way Cracker operates, is to set up somewhere to write songs without a real idea of where things are going. "That's the way we do stuff," he explains. "We'll just start with a few songs, to give us something to start with and then we may just jam and play some other things, and some ideas get laid down that might later turn into songs. I might take certain pieces of a song home and work on them by myself, then do vocals and play other parts and bring them back. We do things piecemeal.

"I think you just have to be sort of familiar with one of the ways of doing stuff that's going to work for your situation," he continues. "I don't think you really have to know anything about engineering, because I know people who are really great producers who do not really engineer at all. They've learned over the years, like, 'Oh, for this kind of vocal, we should use this kind of mic in this way,' but I don't think you really have to know anything about engineering. There are plenty of engineers who don't know a lick of music."

In addition, Lowery does not believe producers or engineers have to know how to operate Digidesign's Pro Tools or any other digital audio workstation. "Actually, in a way, it's a hindrance because working in Pro Tools is such a specific way of working, and I don't think it works for all bands," he says. "I think that's one of the problems. It makes a certain kind of record." Hand in hand with that, Lowery would rather turn to someone who is street-smart rather than Berklee School of Music smart. "I would weigh really heavily on the street-smarts side, because we are dealing with pop music."

On the other hand, Richardson sees how engineering experience helped him during his early producing dates and believes that a technical background is key. "I think that a record producer should know everything that is going on," he says. "He should know how a gate works, and how a plate reverb works, and what mic does what, because you tend to have to say, 'This sound is not right. Maybe you should try this or you should do that.' Then, all of a sudden the sound comes in."

John Porter, who started out as a musician, believes that having some sort of musical background helps in the studio. "I don't think you have to be a musician—anybody can produce a record, and anybody quite often has, but if you want to make more than one [album] or if it's your career, then it helps if you have some clue as to how those building blocks are best placed in relation to each other," he says. "So, yeah, it does help. I think it helps a lot, and the fact I can actually sit down and do it myself cuts through a lot of crap. I remember when I was playing a session, somebody actually said to me, 'Can you play it more like a banana?' This was quite a well-known producer. I was doing a guitar part, and the chances of me seeing what he wanted as a banana…It was so abstract. I can actually sit down and say, 'Well, look, play this part here, and play three of these on these alternative bars.' It just cuts through a lot of crap."

MOVING UP THE RANKS

It is not as if producers are the top of the food chain and engineers are secondary citizens, yet there are countless examples of engineers who have gone on to sit in the producer's chair. Call it the natural evolution of the studio dwellers, because engineers are exposed to the widest diversity of musicians, producers, and sessions, and must develop the ability to adapt to whatever type of experience faces them. As Garth Richardson, who started in the studio cleaning his father's recording rooms and lounge, moved to an assistant engineer position with producer Michael Wagener and then to producing a bevy of acts on his own, says, "You really do have to know from the bottom to the top."

The bottom that he speaks of is the men and women in the studio who clean the rooms; the top is made up of the owners of the studio and producers who walk the halls. It is a sentiment echoed by Nick Launay, since he went from editing British hit songs for compilation albums, to tea boy, to assistant engineer, to engineer, to producer during his stint at Townhouse Studios in England. Both Richardson and Launay repeatedly assert that their bottom-to-top education in the studio shaped their current production philosophies, and continues to give them the confidence to enter the studio with bands that challenge them musically and technically.

Howard Benson, who earned his production stripes doing demos for any band that he could find, believes the rules have changed for beginning players. "When I started, you could hang out at studios in the middle of the night and work," he recalls. "They let you do that. You can't do that much anymore. You're either a producer or trying to come up through the ranks, and it can be kind of hard. It used to be that you automatically came up; you know you were like a second engineer, first engineer, and then a producer. Now, you can be a second engineer and stay there for the rest of your life."

Rather than move up the ladder from engineering to producing, Benson went from producing demos for a number of Los Angeles-based bands to the 1986 *Revenge* release from TSOL. "I was lucky [because] I got free studio time, and I was able to produce a bunch of demos, then I was like at a Denny's and met this guy who was managing a band called TSOL. This band was almost ready to be dropped in the meantime, and we kind of had a discussion over our greasy fries. I didn't even know who TSOL was, by the way; at that point I was totally into R&B and dance music. That kind of Orange County punk rock was completely alien to me, and yet I said okay, because it would be my first production and I was able to get in there and do the album. Basically [*Revenge*] was produced by somebody else and they just didn't think it was good enough, so I went in there and spent a few days fixing the album, and I was able to get my first producer credit. It was an amazing thing, because you're working and working and working and never think you're going to turn an album over and see your name on it. But, finally I was able to get that credit, and that credit led to another credit, and I did a jazz album [Greg Smith's *No Baggage*] with the same record company, Intima Records, for like five thousand dollars. It was a cheap, quick record, but it built my career. You start looking at your résumé, and instead of nothing, there's one thing, then two things and you get your name out there as long as you keep moving.

"My thing at that time was I was going to produce anything. I didn't care what it was, anything just to kind of learn the craft," he continues. He worked on *Hit and Run,* TSOL's 1987 follow-up, which went on to sell 25,000 copies. "At that time, that was considered a lot for me," he reports. "One thing led to another, but that was the beginning for me. I started actually a lot different than most producers; I came right at it from the artist's point of view. I didn't really come up from the studio. I didn't second-engineer, I didn't get coffee, none of that. I just walked into the studio with a band and started producing. In some ways that was healthy, and in some ways it wasn't."

Benson goes on to explain that, because of his lack of early experience, he was disorganized when he went into the studio with a band. "I didn't have a plan or an idea of how to make records," he admits. "Every time I went in, I'd start an album differently." After about five years of producing by the seat of his pants—which can have its own rewards and tends to open the doors for some inspiring music—he was fired from a project, and producer Keith Olsen was brought in. Rather than running away, Benson made friends with Olsen. "He was one of the most successful rock producers of all times. He was a great guy, and he was unbelievably cool to me. I said to him, 'Look, I know I am not part of this record anymore, but do you mind if I hang out? I'll do whatever you want.' I mean, here I am a real record producer and all of sudden I saying, 'I'll get coffee for you.' I did that because I knew I needed to learn, I needed to take it to a different level, and I needed to watch him and learn everything he did."

After a year of working with Olsen, Benson went out on his own again and brought his mentor along. "I brought him in to co-produce with me, as a payback for him being cool to me, because his career was starting to wane at that point," Benson says. "It really, really helped me to watch him produce vocals. I mean, that's how I kind of all of sudden started becoming more successful; I started focusing more and more of my time on vocals. That is where he spent most of his time, and I learned more about harmonies and arrangement and things like that from him, and I started doing records in a very specific way, after I met him, and that was what really started my career."

What propelled Michael Rosen up the ladder was paying attention to what other producers—Narada Michael Walden and David Rubinson, among others—at the Automat were doing. "I kind of tripped out on how [the producers] were doing what they were doing, as well as the engineer, but mostly how that guy was getting that person to do what he wanted him to do without pissing him off, or putting together the song part of it," he says. "I got lucky, I worked with some good producers and some good engineers." Around that same time, Rosen was asked to produce *Souls of Black,* for Testament, a San Francisco Bay-area heavy metal band. "That record turned out well, so another band said, 'Oh, you worked on that record? How about if you produce our record?'"

The year was 1990, and Rosen found himself in the studio with a couple of different bands all within the same genre, including Vicious Rumors and Flotsam & Jetsam. It was odd to step into the producer's chair during those first dates. "It was sort of surreal," he says. "I mean, at one point, you don't realize you're doing it, and you go, 'Wow, I'm actually producing this band's record.' On the other hand, it was amazing. I loved it. It was like a puzzle, like an audio puzzle. I looked at [the album] like a movie: I needed a good beginning, a reason for telling this story, a good middle, a good end. That's the part that I really groove on—putting it together properly. It was like being out of your body. I mean, it was something you wanted to do, and you were doing it. It doesn't get any better than that."

THE IMPORTANCE OF A MENTOR

There is no doubt that any number of today's aspiring producers have the talent to jump into the big chair immediately, yet the responsibility of managing a budget, working with technology, arranging songs, balancing musicians' personalities, and delivering an album can be daunting. Even an engineer can't imagine many of the situations that may arise for a producer. That is why many of today's top producers relied on mentors for guidance early in their careers. It is especially important, given the transient nature of the studio business (not to mention the music business), to find that one person who can offer meaningful experience and solutions to problems.

Howard Benson surely considered Keith Olsen a mentor. After all, it was Olsen who taught him how to set studio schedules and work on vocals, and helped him figure out how best to arrange songs. The ever-inquisitive Nick Launay relied on Alan Douglas, Hugh Padgham, and Steve Lillywhite in his early days. While Mark Howard was engineering sessions for Daniel Lanois, he learned how the producer got the sounds he was best known for and has utilized the lessons he learned from Lanois on his productions with Lucinda Williams and Vic Chesnutt.

Of all the producers that Sylvia Massy Shivy worked with in her early days, she learned an important lesson from Rick Rubin. "I think what I learned from him in particular is you don't have to be the nuts and bolts person," she reports. "You can be the overseer and put together a brilliant crew that will carry your vision into the studio. You don't actually have to be the person to call the shots, but if you put the right people in the right situation, you'll get a great product. I learned that, and he's got a soft, gentle approach, which I really admire." Shivy picked up that type of vibe on the Rubin-produced albums by System of a Down, Smashing Pumpkins, Tom Petty and the Heartbreakers, and Johnny Cash. "He participated to different degrees in all of those sessions—some of them he was there the whole time, some he was there not so much. But, it all has his production sound and results. They're all great records, and they all deserve to have his name on them."

While a member of Nine Inch Nails, Chris Vrenna spent time in the studio with the band's main brain, Trent Reznor, as well as producer Flood (né Mark Ellis), who worked on NIN's *Pretty Hate Machine* and *The Downward Spiral* releases. "I kind of based my entire style after Flood," Vrenna says. "You should never know the producer was ever there. The producer should be an invisible layer to bring out the best of whatever band the producer is working with, but still being that band. You cannot hear *Mellon Collie and the Infinite Sadness* [the 1995 release from The Smashing Pumpkins], and compare that to Depeche Mode's *Violator,* and then compare that to a P.J. Harvey [album], and then compare that to Nine Inch Nails. There are some producers out there, and I won't name names, but no matter what type of band it is, they only know how to do one thing and they're uncomfortable doing anything other than that, so what they do is they try to cram the square peg in the round hole, and then you get these, I think, just horribly generic-sounding things. The thing about Flood was that he would just let the artists do what they were going to do.

"It's not like Flood has one sound and he brings in his bank of drum samples and everything gets sampled and sliced," Vrenna continues. "So, I have always tried to do it that way: Let the band be the band, and give the band the freedom to feel totally trusting in you and that they can try anything in front of you. If half of it's crap, you're not going to make fun of them, or you're not going to tell them that they suck or that was bad. There has to be this level of trust, and when I work with a band, I become like the fifth member, you know, or the fourth member, depending. I get really emotionally attached as well, and I'll argue for stuff that I totally think is the right decision when a decision needs to be made but it's not simply my way or the highway. That's kind of the main thing I've learned from Flood—just let it happen, let the band be the band."

Vrenna was likewise influenced by his time playing and performing with Trent Reznor. "He's such a great songwriter, great keyboard player, and a very creative individual. When we were in the studio, it was just the two of us usually.

Sometimes, Flood was in there, sometimes we had [engineer] Sean Beavan in there, but if [Trent] has to sing the track, then I was the one recording it. We just came up together because I've known the dude for so long," he says. "I bought a Linn drum off of him in high school—that's how I met him. So, it was just cool having a best friend that has the same sort of musical taste, and you know our tastes are definitely left of center, that's for sure."

GETTING THE GIGS

It's one thing to get your foot in the door; it's quite another to stay busy. Producers who turn their first album in and then rest are akin to musicians who finish an album with the thought that the hard work is done. It is quite the opposite. For producers, the hard work includes meeting new bands, labels, and managers. It includes looking for new acts. It includes, sometimes, taking the next project that becomes available for whatever money and almost under any circumstances. After all, for better or worse, music business success is measured by the latest credit, not necessarily the greatest.

One way to guarantee consistent work is to find a music community that is comfortable, and then work hard. Dave Fridmann, for instance, bounced between Mercury Rev and the Flaming Lips throughout the Nineties. Those albums—there were close to a dozen during that decade—made him the indie "It" producer and bolstered his reputation so much that he didn't have to spend much time chasing work. "I've only really ever chased after, like, one or two things. In general, people just find me and call, and if it's the right thing, we end up doing it," he says. One of the people he remembers chasing is Adam Sandler. "Just because I think he's so funny. It never worked out, and that's fine. But most of the time, I feel like anybody I would want to work with like that, I would end up just being too weird about anyway, so it probably wouldn't work. It seems better when people just find me. I know how people [find work]—they go to the clubs, they see bands, and if they like them, they talk to them and do that kind of thing. What's weird is, I just haven't really done that. I don't know why. Maybe I'm dumb. But I've always been sort of busy enough with things that I wanted to do that I haven't worried about it."

Ryan Greene is another producer who found a community and stuck with it, but Greene's camp is the punk-rock community. His first exposure came with the 1994 NOFX release *Punk in Drublic* and his credit list has grown since then, including such punk stalwarts as Lagwagon, No Use for a Name, and Swingin' Utters. His first work with NOFX was not an easy set of sessions, especially when it came to the mixing dates. "Fat Mike and I had different mixing styles. He wanted it super dry, and I wanted things a little more natural with a rounded sound. [He said,] 'This is how punk rock is supposed to sound.' I said okay, as I was ducking away from the NS-10s [monitors] because they were just so bright. I thought when that record came out my days were over, and it was their biggest-selling record," he reports with a laugh. "So, there you go. It was just one of those things, and from that point on it's been pretty much nonstop."

Yet, being "known" in one community is just not enough most of the time. With that in mind, Greene established a Website (*ryangreene.com*) that includes a discography, samples, reviews, and contact info. Likewise, Ross Hogarth set up his own site (*www.hoaxproductions.com*). As discussed before, there are also a number of resources out there where producers can list their services so that artists and labels looking for producers can find them. In other words, one key to finding work and continuing to be busy is to be accessible, whether that means creating a personal Web page, getting listed in a resource guide, or making a round of calls to labels and managers who might be looking for producers.

"For the most part, I get jobs the way I've always gotten jobs, which is that people approach me," Craig Street says. "It's probably split fifty-fifty between either artists or their representatives, or record companies approaching me. Sometimes a record company will call me up and say, "I've got a job," or a manager; sometimes an artist will call me directly."

"Mostly you get gigs from other projects," explains Michael Rosen. "A band likes what you did or heard something you worked on."

Or, as Hogarth explains, referrals come from musicians that have been in on other sessions. "Generally, it's word of mouth," he says, "and I have to stick my hand up in the air and say thank you to my really good, close, and excellent friend Kenny Aronoff, who I go back to having helped build John Mellencamp's studio in the mid-Eighties. I worked out of John's studio and did records with John, did records that John found and wanted to produce, and then records that I would co-produce with John's guitar player Mike Wanchic. Kenny played on all of those, and then I engineered a ton of records that Kenny played on. He and I have a really long-running relationship as engineer-drummer and engineer-producer-drummer, so he refers me to jobs. Or he might be the drummer on a gig, and that artist will say, 'Well we're considering this person or this person' and if my name is in that loop, I'll get the big vote of confidence from Kenny, which makes a huge difference."

Hogarth also gets nods of approval from Jim Keltner, David Lindley, and Jackson Browne. "These are people that I worked for very early on in my career as a guitar tech and a drum tech, or when I was doing stuff on the road as a sound man and a road manager and production manager. Those people have stuck by me, because I was a trusted employee, and they have been very helpful. A lot of musicians are really helpful to me; there was a lot of word of mouth with A&R guys. I think generally this business works off of reputation that you hopefully can maintain and build on," he continues. "I guess I've made some records that my name is on and that might have referred me to a gig, but a lot of times those are kind of weird." As an example, he points to the 1998 Jewel offering *Spirit,* which he engineered and mixed. "If you do that kind of record, then all these girl artists want you to work with them, and you may not actually want to do that. So, that's kind of interesting. It's possible that good gigs come out of those situations, but they are usually a bit more cookie-cutter, like someone wanting to do something exactly the same as something that they like, and that can get old really quick.

"I think a lot of [keeping busy] just happens to be maintaining relationships and friendships," he continues. "If you've done good work for someone, and you've done it with a smile and have a good attitude and generally the way I believe that business should be done, hopefully your reputation will precede you in any other conversation that you have no control over down the road, when someone is looking for someone and maybe your name comes up."

ESTABLISHING RELATIONSHIPS

According to the majority of producers interviewed, Hogarth is on the right track when establishing relationships with bands and musicians. Although record companies are the ones paying the bills (initially anyway), the lack of consistency in label management staff has made building relationships with labels futile at best. In fact, look at the bios of many of the major label presidents. How many of them have been working for the same company for five years? Not many. How about A&R staffs? Just as dicey.

"Everyone I've known at the labels and had relationships with are gone," says Mark Howard. "So, you're always building new relationships with people. When I started, working for Lost Highway, Frank Callari was the head of A&R and general manager; he was the guy I talked to, and he's gone. I don't know anyone at Lost Highway anymore. I think it's the managers of the artists that are the strong ones; once you get a relationship with them, you will have recurring records with those people. Record companies are changing so quickly, and the people that you had relationships with are gone, or people that you like have moved on somewhere else."

J.P. Plunier, who has managed Ben Harper's career since the early days, knows from personal experience: "Since Ben has been at Virgin, since 1993, there have been thirteen people who have been head of the company, let alone the number of revolving product managers and A&R people. That never makes it easy, and you almost have to be autonomous to survive that, because if you look at every other band that got signed back then they're all long-gone."

From the beginning of his career, Mark Trombino has been trying to build rapport with the bands in his genre while remaining open to labels and managers. "I know some people in labels, and managers, but all my work comes from bands," he says. "It comes from a record I did, some band that I worked with, or friends of friends." On the day of his interview, ironically, Trombino was between meetings at two different record companies. "You caught me on a weird day where I'm actually meeting some A&R people, but I never do that."

Of course, as Trombino's experience illustrates, producers cannot exclude labels from their list of associates. "It's everybody," Garth Richardson states. "This scary thing is, you don't know who is going to be who. When I was working with Michael Wagener, this guy was hanging out and he smelled; his jeans were dirty, and he had food on his T-shirt. So, I go up to Michael and say, 'Who is that? He stinks.' He said, 'Shut up. That's the guy that invented the Water Pik.' He was worth billions and billions of dollars. So, you have to become basically buddy-buddy, and you have to be very cordial with everyone."

In Sylvia Massy Shivy's experience that started back when she was working at the information desk at Tower Records in Los Angeles. "The real important thing was that I did hook up with local groups that I was able to get jobs from later," she explains, "and working at the record store was a real great resource for musicians 'cause it seems like musicians, you know, have to have day gigs and that's where they work. So, it was my fellow employees that wound up being in Green Jello [later, Green Jelly, whose 1993 debut, *Cereal Killer Soundtrack,* she produced] and Tool and those types of bands.

"I'd recommend working somewhere in the industry to anyone just starting out, whether it's sales or radio or marketing," she continues. "It seems also like the people that you meet early on are going to be the same people you work with later. So, never piss anyone off. Make friends with everybody, because you'll be seeing them again for the rest of your career. Everybody and anybody, because they all rotate, you know? Anyone from a label that's working in the mailroom when you first meet them may be the president of the label in six years. You never know." This is not idle speculation on her part: "When I worked at Tower, a gentleman named Simon Potts came in and he had just moved here from the U.K.," she recalls. "I became friends with him, and he wound up being the president of Capitol Records for a while."

Benson is on the same page when it comes to treating everyone equally. "I think that the best producers have to have relationships with just pretty much everybody," he says. "[But] you can't be a pushover. You need to have good solid relationships with people that think you're fair and doing great for the project." The key, in Benson's opinion, is the song. "People's feelings are always going to get hurt, but as long as you keep your eye on the song, you'll always see work. That's the thing I found out, is that it is all about the song. Everybody can talk about all kinds of stuff and all the politics and blah, blah, blah, but a good song and a great vocal kind of cures everybody's problems. So, as long as you keep that in your head and stay focused, you will always, always, do well."

GOT MANAGEMENT?

Another way that many of today's working producers have found projects and career assistance is through a management company. Not only can a manager help chase work, he or she can handle the recording budget; be a buffer between label, management, and producer; and take care of accounting issues. To be sure, having a manager is not for everyone. Some argue against paying a fifteen to twenty percent commission for work that they can do themselves. Others could not do without the help.

One of the first questions an aspiring producer must ask when considering management is what the producer hopes to get out of it. For instance, Ross Hogarth does not look for his managers to find him work. "I don't believe that management companies are employment offices," he says. "It would be nice if they were, but generally they aren't."

On the flip side, Mark Howard works with Sandy Robertson at Los Angeles-based World's End Producer Management. "I had a manager on the East Coast who was getting me work, but I was working mostly off my reputation," he says. "When I got married and had two kids I thought, 'Okay, if I'm going to work for six months [on an album] then I'm going to need some help, so I got Sandy and he turned things around for me. I've done some pretty weird acts that he throws me in." For instance, Howard found himself in the studio with a Japanese funk band and an interpreter. "I did six songs for that album, and it sold millions," he recalls. "Sandy also got me together with Eddie Vedder and we did a track for the *I Am Sam* soundtrack. So, he brings some cool things to the table. My work with Tom Waits [Howard engineered the 2004 *Real Gone* release] and Lucinda Williams [he produced, engineered, and mixed 2003's *World Without Tears*] comes from the grapevine. He doesn't go out and get me that work. There are a lot of mixing jobs he brings to me, which I like to do because it fills in the gaps. So it helps, but you have to weigh the good against the bad. I think you definitely need somebody to represent you."

Based on his experience, Michael Rosen is not so sure a producer needs a manager. After all, when he was using the management services of Cahn-Man [who also managed Green Day's early career] it did not work out for him. "The only plus to it, from what I can tell, is this: When you're in the middle of a project, it's a bitch to look for your next project," he says. "I mean, when you're like six weeks into a big album, it's hard to look for work and they kept feeding me leads. But my first manager told me, 'We can't get you the gig. We can put you in touch with the people. We can get you the interview. We can get you the connections. But you have to get the gig. You have to meet with the band, connect with them.' So, I said, 'Well, then, what the fuck am I paying you twenty percent for? I'll find out how to get a hold of that band.' I'm pretty good at meetings, you know. Either I'm going to get the gig or not. I didn't need them to take twenty percent just to say, 'Hey, I heard that such-and-such is doing a record.'

"I think the whole producer/engineer manager thing is a crock of shit," Rosen continues. "I think it's like owning the race track, you know? I don't think they honestly can sit down and listen to a track and go, 'You know who would be perfect for that? Ben Grosse.' They don't actually artistically know if you would be right for that; they just want to own every pony in the race and take their fifteen percent and move on about their business."

"I don't think there's anyone who could manage you better than yourself," says Matt Wallace, "if you have the time and the energy, and if you aren't an asshole and don't put people off. I think I was a great manager for myself. I got The Replacements only because I called the label consistently. I knew they were initially working with Scott Litt and that didn't work out, so I kept calling. Then they worked for two weeks with Tony Berg, and I kept calling." A friend of Wallace's then called him and said it was time for him to call again. "This was over a period of two, three months, and I got the gig because I kept calling and calling. I don't think there's any manager who's going to do that."

That said, Wallace is managed today by Frank McDonough of McDonough Management. "Now I just really want to make records," Wallace says. "I don't want to deal with the financial stuff. I don't want to deal with the billing. I've got a wife and kids, and I don't have the time for that kind of stuff."

That is the same relationship that Dave Jerden has with his manager, Gary Gunton. "This is going to sound really bad, but I never know what the budget is and I don't care," Jerden says. "My manager works all that out, and he tells me what the parameters are. He'll usually say it's not going to be big-budget, or it is a big budget. In fact, he never tells me it's a big budget. But he'll tell me when it's a small budget. He'll tell me things like, 'On this record, watch the Drum Doctor.' That means it's not a real big budget. All the business stuff, talk of money anything like that, he does all that and I don't even really want to know because I don't want him to make that a consideration for me really. I always just do what I do and I don't even know if I'm going over budget or not; my manager just doesn't bug me on that. He just wants me to do what I do best and just call the shots the way I think they should be called, and then if it goes over budget or whatever he'll deal with that."

SPECIALTY PRODUCERS

On the artistic side of things, releasing a song that can crossover to a number of different radio formats, creating a multi-genre and multigenerational fan-base, is the Holy Grail. Likewise, for a producer, the goal is to have crossover success, in order to avoid the pigeonhole that could confine them to one genre for an entire career. This is not to say that producers pick jobs with reckless abandon just to mix things up; rather, it seems as if they are looking for ways to challenge themselves constantly and avoid musical stagnation.

In the year 2004, Don Was bounced between production assignments with The Rolling Stones, Kris Kristofferson, and Solomon Burke, to name a few, as well as some live dates with Led Zeppelin. That is in addition to the film score work he had completed. Part of his philosophy, he explains, is to remain creative. "There's a huge difference between creation and re-creation," he says. "If you go with the tried and true, you're basically repeating things you've done before, and you are using a completely different part of the brain and doing boring shit basically. Whereas, if you are constantly tossed down a well and forced to climb out, that's when you must be a wily individual and rely on your wits to get you out of there. That's when good things happen."

John Porter shares the sentiment, and an incredibly varied credit list that runs the gamut from Roxy Music to Los Lonely Boys to B.B. King to Ryan Adams. "It's partly by default, partly by design, I guess," he says. "I like all kinds of music. I like music to be soulful, but I don't mean that it has to be soul music. If whoever is doing it is submerged in it and really believes in it, then I can believe in it, too. It's all music to me, and it doesn't matter where you go in the world, it's really the same. If left to my own devices, I probably would [produce] jazz or what used to be R&B. That's where my tastes lie, but I love working with young kids, as well, and that's worked for me and against me.

"If you just do one thing," Porter continues, "then people hire you to do that one thing. I've been told that I've worked on too many different things and that I wouldn't get a guitar or a rock 'n' roll album because I've done a lot of blues records. But it's the same for everybody. Whatever you do, people pigeonhole you. When I played with Roxy Music or worked with The Smiths, everybody thought that the only bands I wanted to work with were bands that wore makeup."

Another producer who has bounced between genres is Rick Rubin, who started in the rap world before moving into rock, alternative rock, metal, and country. "I like doing different kinds of things," he says nonchalantly, "and I always have. When I started making rock records after making rap records, I was unanimously told, 'You shouldn't be making heavy-metal records because you make rap records.' And then, 'You shouldn't be making rock records because you're a heavy-metal producer.' I've been labeled a lot of things over the years. I just try to make records I like."

Rubin is not the only one who benefited from his varied career, since Sylvia Massy Shivy worked alongside him during many of those sessions. On her own, though, Shivy has made her mark with metal releases. "I think all producers are in danger of being pigeonholed, and anybody could be victimized by that," she says. "I'm trying really hard not to be pigeonholed. I try to branch out as much as possible into different genres. I think the Johnny Cash thing was a great thing to do, and I'm trying some hard funk right now, which is great." She is also working with some more art-rock, punk rock, and retro rock-sounding bands. "So, I kind of try to keep my feet in all kinds of things, just to keep myself from being all metal. But, I sure love the genre. A great hard band is very exciting still."

Over the course of his career, Michael Rosen has worked in his share of different markets and he has a unique perspective on it. Everything, he says, changes when moving genres. "It's like being in a different culture. They speak differently, they dress differently. That genre does not like that genre," he says. "I'll give you a good example. When I did A.F.I. [Rosen produced the 1996 release *Very Proud of Ya*], it was like metal to me. I was mixing a song and I did something and they said, 'That sounds kind of metal.' I was like, 'What are you talking about? You guys are a metal band.' From that moment, I lost them. It was like the emperor had no clothes."

Minute differences within the genres are exaggerated more today, Rosen believes, than they were in the past. "Now it's like pop punk, hardcore, speed metal, death metal, grindcore…They're all separate kinds of things, and they all have their own dress code and their own lexicon of words that they use. I come home with a new vocabulary after every session. If I've been with a group for a couple of months, my wife will say, 'Oh, you got that one. What do those guys say?'"

Breaking out can be a challenge, as Mark Trombino has seen while he moves beyond the emo-punk scene that some say his band Drive Like Jehu started in the early Nineties. "That's so not true," he answers with a laugh, "but I never wanted to be in only one genre. Since the beginning, I've wanted to do other things. I have done some things here and there, but yeah the bulk of my work is all the same shit. I don't think it makes me a stronger producer. If anything, it makes me not as strong." Although he has had much success with such emo-punk bands as Jimmy Eat World and blink 182, Trombino believes he is still learning. "I think you can learn a lot from doing different things, but I have never felt like I mastered anything," he says. "I can keep doing pop punk till the day I die and never feel like I got it right."

Trombino had the opportunity to break outside the genre in 2002 when he worked with the hardcore band Finch. "That was new for me to do, a really heavy band. I was hoping it would attract more hardcore bands, but that didn't really happen. After getting canned from Jimmy Eat World [in 2004], my schedule freed up and I was able to work with Rilo Kiley, which was really cool because they're almost alt-country. It was awesome. I'd love to [produce] a singer/songwriter, like a female singer/songwriter sometime and put the whole record together. I was with a band, and the politics and everything that goes along with that…It would be nice just to work with one person and hire people for everything else."

THE EXCLUSIVE GIG

In the olden days of the music business, producers were exclusive to labels and studios, which gave them a consistent stable of artists to work with, as well as a steady income. These days, producers that are exclusive to labels are rare, if not non-existent. After all, it is just as much a gamble for a label to sign a producer to an exclusive contract as it is to sign an artist to a major-label deal. There is no difference; producers get an advance for work to be done with the hope that the bet will pay off.

Tony Brown has had that arrangement since he started at MCA Records under the tutelage of Jimmy Bowen. While he wanted to continue to work in the studio as a producer and sideman, Brown went to work at MCA for a specific reason. "The reason I wanted to become a producer and work at a record company is I wanted the security of working for a record company, plus, the ability to sit in the room when the marketing plan went down, when promotion plan went down, when they did the album cover, and just be involved in all aspects of the recording process. Plus, needless to say, one reason you want to be a label producer is because you get your salary as an executive. I have an independent producer kind of contract to the side, I actively participated in the records that I produced. There was definitely a financial benefit to being a producer-executive." After Brown left MCA to start Universal South, he continued his producer/executive dual role, while also getting back to performing with The Notorious Cherry Bombs.

When the phone rang at Walter Afanasieff's home, and it was Sony Records president Tommy Mottola, asking if the songwriter/producer was interested in writing a song with a new talent by the name of Mariah Carey, Afanasieff jumped. The collaboration was so successful—the song "Love Takes Time" was Number One on the *Billboard* Hot 100—that Mottola offered Afanasieff a deal to be exclusive to Sony. "What I was doing was an unusual thing at the time, which was playing and doing everything myself. [Tommy] noticed it being something that fit compatibly with Mariah at that time, and it worked so well that he didn't want me to ever not be available for that," Afanasieff says. "So, he took it upon himself to offer me a deal to sign with Sony Music so that when the time came for him to use me on a Mariah Carey record, or a Michael Bolton record, or a Celine Dion record, or whoever was at Sony Music at that time, he could guarantee that I'd be there working."

It was the early Nineties, and Afanasieff signed a two-year deal with an advance. "In that first two years, we had so much success with Mariah; I mean it was profound. One song after another was a hit," he recalls. "So, I paid back my advance probably within the first few months, and they renegotiated my contract and told me to keep going." Afanasieff's record speaks volumes, and the two made a good team. "It was a great experience, but it can only be a great experience with somebody that you trust and is there for you, and will move mountains for you as you move mountains for them," he says. "So, I was delivering what they wanted, and he was there for me doing what made me happy to be exclusive."

The contract had its down sides, as well. "I passed up opportunities after opportunities for thirteen years," he says. "I can't even tell you how many times I wanted to work with so many different people, and who wanted to work with me, and film scores and songs with this person and that person. It didn't happen, but other great things happened in their place. Everybody, everything runs its course, you know."

Afanasieff's tenure with Sony ended in 2003. "During the final renegotiation, things changed and [Tommy] left. My mentor, the guy who signed me, my father figure if you will, the guy who blessed me with such an incredible amount of stuff, was no longer there," he reports. "I didn't have that same chemistry with others, and I decided not to stay anymore, so my deal ran out."

6 LABEL POLITICS

There is a whole lot more to working as a record producer these days than sorting out songs and arrangements. Indeed, the business that happens before a note is recorded in the studio shapes the tenor of the sessions. How does the producer interact with the label's A&R rep? Or work with the label? Or play the buffer between the band and the label's representatives? These questions must be asked before the recording dates can start.

The producers interviewed for this book say that a good attitude rules when it comes to building relationships. Good attitudes almost tend to overrule positive results; a producer who can consistently combine the two will always be busy. However, staying positive can be a challenge, especially considering the tailspin the music industry has been in, and the reality that more is being asked of producers and engineers for less money. Not only that, with the continuing youth movement at the labels, A&R reps are finding themselves in the studio without the experience necessary to shepherd an album from start to finish.

The level and type of responsibility that A&R reps are given has changed gradually over the years, and many producers report that most A&R reps are now mostly invisible during the recording process. "There was traditionally always an A&R guy that was a music-lover, maybe he came out of being a musician and would be involved Artist and Repertoire," Ed Cherney explains. "They would bring songs to the table, would have good ideas, be here for the marketing, and just be the liaison to the record company, but they would be involved in the record the whole time. I make records now, I don't even see a label exec until the end. There would always be the execs that would come down and listen when you'd have a playback party; [now] I don't even see them. Now I work on stuff and send it off.

"A lot of the A&R guys are just cowering; they're desperate for their jobs and they're running scared," Cherney continues. "It's not their fault, and there are still music-lovers that come out of that place, but a lot of them don't have the experience. You know, my experience was that label execs and A&R guys knew how a studio worked. In most cases now, they don't. They are just absolutely clueless about the process of how music is made, and it's not their fault. I mean typically they are hired because they are a certain age and they can be the corporate face to the artists."

Chris Vrenna has worked with A&R reps as both an artist and a producer in the studio, so he has seen the positive and negative aspects of their involvement. "You've got the A&R guy who was in a failed rock band and that's why he's in there. He's a frustrated musician, but he still wishes he was the one actually making the record, so he tries to sit there and outsmart everybody with music-school jargon," he says. "Then there are a couple A&R guys that I just love and I respect them because they come and go, 'Look, I don't know what the hell I'm talking about but I'll tell you what I think.' They come in and they try and describe it in layman's terms, 'Something just doesn't hit me. I thought it was going to blow up a bit bigger there or something.' So, you take some of that to heart because, at the end of the day, people are just going to hear music and interpret it the way they're going to interpret it.

"There are a lot of variations that they want, because they're thinking about trying to get the sales department to get sales or for radio," Vrenna continues. "So, that's what they're thinking about, and sometimes I'm not thinking in those terms as much, but they're part of the process. I mean, they obviously believed in the band enough to want to bring them into the label, so you have to respect them a little bit, and I do."

Much like Vrenna, David Lowery has spent time with label representatives as an artist and producer. He's even more vocal with his opinions about working with A&R reps: "There are some that are amazingly helpful, and there are some that are totally fucking useless pieces of shit, and there are some that are useless pieces of shit on parts of a project you're working on because they shouldn't have signed that artist, but a different kind of artist they'd probably be great on."

To guard against the threat of a negative A&R experience on a practical level, Dave Jerden avoids talking to anyone other than the label's president. "The new kids that are A&R guys, I usually don't even talk to them anymore. I just deal with the head guys, and they're the ones that I actually talk to on the phone or talk to at the studio." The same is true of Jerden's interactions with a band's manager. "This is kind of unfortunate, but either I like the manager or I don't. If I like the manager and what he's saying to me makes sense [then I'll listen]. It depends on how long they've been with the band, it depends on how successful they are on their own, but because I work with new bands, a lot of time I'm working with new managers too, and a lot of these people just don't know what they're talking about."

Yet, there can also be issues with a label president who has oodles of experience and success. For example, Jerden points to the 2003 MxPx release *Before Everything and After* that was turned into the band's label president and A&R rep Ron Fair. "The problem I had with Ron with MxPx was that I just don't believe he understood what the [genre] was all about," he says. "Ron Fair is a person who knows nothing about punk music. I've known Ron Fair a long time. I knew Ron Fair when he was an engineer. He just knew nothing about the band, and his whole approach then with MxPx was more like pop singles. The whole thing was that we spent so much time in pre-production, rewriting two new punk songs and trying to turn them into [radio songs]. It was hard working with Ron—he only cared about one song on the whole record, "Everything Sucks (When You're Gone)." There were sixteen songs, and he didn't care about any of the rest of them; he only cared about one song and he drove me crazy on this one song."

Fair's hand was felt throughout the album's recording and into the mixing dates. "I've mixed every record that I've ever produced," Jerden points out. "I mixed the record, and he didn't even listen to it. He immediately went and hired [Tom and Chris Lord-Alge] to mix it. They paid them a lot of money, too. To this day, I don't think Ron listened to my mixes. He may say he did, but I don't think he did. I met with Chris after he mixed it, and Chris said, 'I just listened to your mixes.' When I listened to his mixes, the balances and everything were right, and there were a lot of harmonies and things like that. I've mixed stuff before and unless you listen to what the other guy's done, you're not going to know, you're going to mix it the way you want to mix it. When they started mixing it, [Chris] asked if there were any mixes and my engineer Annette sent over my mixes, and he just did what I did. So, I was really frustrated working with Ron on that."

Matt Wallace is saddened that he missed the heyday of A&R. "I'm too young to have really grown up in the era where A&R guys used to have pianos in their offices and they used to be the guys who would be, like, 'I found this song. How about your band covers it?' So I really missed that part of it," he says. "As a general rule, A&R people just drive me crazy. It's just the nature of the beast, but I should say as individuals, there are people who can really contribute in very, very positive ways. They know how to do it and really can help guide a record, you know. And I think that the smart ones or the ones with experience can give you just the right amount of information, not too much, in a way that the producer and the artist can understand it. Then you go forward from there, but if it's presented poorly, it's easy to get your back up and they run roughshod over you. You could be creating this beautiful thing, and they just walk in and go, 'It's crappy.' Then it's like, 'What?' So, when people can do it in a very graceful way with some experience behind it, it can be very beneficial.

"I think it's like any other business," he continues. "You'll find outstanding doctors who know their stuff, and you'll find doctors that you can't even imagine how the hell they passed the boards. There are a lot of A&R guys where I'm like, 'Dude! How'd you get that job?' Because there are no pre-qualifications for it, much like being an artist or a producer. You don't go to a school and get a certificate for it. And some people are really brilliant talent scouts but don't really know how to A&R a record. I'm sure the opposite is true—some people know how to A&R a record but can't really find the great stuff."

Frustration with A&R reps does not start or end with producers. Some acts, like System of a Down, keep them at arm's length while recording. "I don't listen to a word they say about my music," says the band's songwriter and guitarist Daron Malakian. "They are not even allowed to hear anything. If an A&R rep wanted to come to my studio right now and say, 'I want to hear the new System of a Down,' we wouldn't be there. I don't care what they have to say."

However, as Malakian points out, he will listen to label representatives regarding things other than his art. "I'll probably listen to them more if they're talking about how the marketing is going to be done," he says. "But I don't care for them to even hear any of it right now to be honest with you. We won't even let Don Ienner; he's like salivating, he just wants music. We tell him we're still working and he says, 'Okay.' Because they know that we've had our mind in one direction, we're not like one of the cheese-ball bands that they formed and produced and made into this one-hit wonder, and then they wonder why they didn't sell another album. Even when they've disagreed with us, we said we're going on this path. Let's just say that "Boom!" video [from the *Steal This Album!* release in 2002] we put out was not Columbia's first choice. Right now I'm sure Columbia would love another "Chop Suey!" but they're not going to get one. Another "Toxicity," "Aerials"— they're not going to get one. [Each song was on the band's multi-Platinum release *Toxicity*.] There is gonna be stuff that comes from that family, but it's gonna be different."

There have been positives and negatives in J.D. Foster's experience with A&R reps, as well. He knows that there has to be some interaction. "I guess that smart people do that," Foster says with a laugh. "But I'm not so sure I'm on that side of the fence, so I try to stay away from that as much as possible. The only people that I've ever found to be helpful in labels were the ones who had their ideas after they already loved what the record was about and they were ready to go out to promote and sell that. Every time I've ever had any experience with label guys wanting to be involved in the process itself, it's been a big annoyance for everybody. It creates this vibe of the authority figure in the room. I've heard some boneheaded things. I've heard A&R guys say to drummers, 'Hey, could you stop playing eighth notes and start playing quarter notes?' It's, like, 'Dude! That's exactly what he's been doing for half an hour.'"

Foster recalls a session he was working on with Richard Buckner when the A&R rep walked in the door. "He saw a board of completed songs and said, 'Oh, I really love this song. I want to hear it.' Then he wholly mispronounced the name. I mean, he had no idea what he was talking about. That's generally the vibe there. I've had bad experiences with record-company guys stopping the flow of things. Some people are cool [when] they show up and really don't say much about the music, but they have an American Express card and take everybody out to dinner. That'll work.

"I hate to be an old jaded guy, but I've heard it said so many ways from labels that they have the checkbooks, and they sort of feel like the artists are going to be around for a short period of time, and there's always a hundred people waiting in line to do that job," he continues. "So, being in the camp of the record label is a really smart thing to do, but they are not the people I particularly want to hang out with. I'd rather hang out with musicians than A&R guys. I would say, though, that's not the smart approach."

So, what is the smart approach? After all, the hard truth is that some kind of truce must be called for when it comes to label representatives and producers working together. Sylvia Massy Shivy has part of the answer. "I think the more you keep them in the loop, the happier everyone will be ultimately," she says. "I'll send them rough mixes, MP3s, so they can hear progress throughout the project even if they're not here in the studio. That way they are kept informed and feel a part of it. I'll accept their comments, and some of them are good comments. So yeah, I'll try to keep them as involved as possible, and I think that's the easiest way to deal with them."

Richardson echoes the idea that communication is key. "I talk to them all the time," he says. "When I'm doing someone's record I'm always on the phone. I think I'm one of the only record producers that sends them the rushes, like the drum tracks, the bass tracks, the guitar tracks, because it's so important today that everybody is a team, and if there's something that is not going to work out right, you need to have your team there and you need a plan. You need to say, 'Hey, look, this is not right. I need to do this.' 'Okay, let's do it.' If somebody hasn't been kept in the loop then he'll say, 'Well, Garth, somebody should have told me sooner.' I tend to always call and always keep them in the loop and always tell them every day what's going on, because they are the people that have to go in and fight there. They have to make sure that the marketing department likes the band and that people actually take it to sales and to radio. He's kind of the point man."

Building the initial relationship with A&R reps starts with capturing their attention with interesting records. "That's really the long and short of it for me," Brad Wood says. "Make records that people who listen to music for a living—which is the A&R people—like. So, the Fire Theft record was a really advantageous record for me to make, because a lot of people like Sunny Day Real Estate and a lot of people like The Fire Theft. How do you develop them? I don't really worry about that. I mean, make good records—that's how you do it. That's how you get them to want to work with you."

Of course, Wood has had his share of frustrating A&R moments. "There have been times where there have been overzealous A&R, people who are really over-eager. At least at the time it seemed they were over-eager, especially if they're not in town when the record's being made. These people may want to be kept in the loop to a fault, where you and your assistant and people in the studio are spending more time doing rough mixes and making cassettes or CDs and sending them and shipping them and incurring freight charges for the band, than you might feel is necessary. I've had those situations where [I've had to say], 'Dude, either you come out here and visit us or you've got to chill. I'm not sending you a CD every single day of the stuff we're doing.'"

At the same time, Wood tries to encourage those that are excited about the band. "They might drive you crazy, but when the record is done this guy's going to fall on his sword for the band," Wood reports. "He's going to be, like, screaming naked, running up and down the halls of the company, saying, 'This is the most important band in the world!' So, I've learned, through trial and error that this nut case that doesn't have a life outside of this band—that's the dude you want. I've had to learn [to say], 'Okay, man, you're going for it, you're psyched about this, you're all gangbusters, ready to roll, and I'm with you. I'm not going to go drinking with you, and I'm not going to talk about the band on the phone for six hours with you every single day, but I appreciate your enthusiasm and I'm not going to try to dampen it.'"

BAND VS. LABEL: THE PRODUCER AS REFEREE

Signing a band, hiring a producer, and booking studio time all add up to a pricey gamble for labels, especially in the major-label world. So, it is no surprise that both bands and producers are under the microscope as soon as they hit the pre-production portion of the schedule. Problems arise, however, when label representatives put producers in the middle, making them part buffer, part filter between band and label—it is the ultimate in politics. And in the midst of all that, producers are trying to get musical and inspired performances from the same singers and players.

With luck, a band's manager will take most of the heat, explains Ryan Greene. "If the band has a really good manager, then the band will never know a lot of what's going on behind the scenes," he says. Yet, Greene has had calls from labels that are looking for a radio song from the band he is working with in the studio, and those can be dicey conversations. "I sat down with a person [whom he wouldn't name] and said, 'Look, this is the bottom line; you're able to do what you do because this record label is giving you this opportunity. They're only asking for you to do this one song. You have thirteen other songs on the record, so the best thing to do would be to do the one song. It's not going to do any damage to any of the other songs. You may not like it, but put your heart into it because they're giving you this great opportunity—you're able to go on tour, play in front of hundreds and thousands of kids, doing what you want to do, and all they're asking for is this one thing. So why not just do the one thing? It's a lot easier to do it than sit there and complain about it day after day after day.'"

Much like Greene, Mark Trombino has found himself translating record-company demands into band-friendly conversations. Bands look to him for guidance based on his band experience with Drive Like Jehu and previous production credits. "That's got to give them a little bit of comfort to know that I come from that," he says. "They've signed to some shitty major label, they're going to have to make tons of compromises, and they've got some lame A&R guy whose musical take they don't trust or opinions they don't trust. They can hire someone like me, who comes from the same world and has been in a band, and I will be on their side. I'm not one of them.

"I end up positioning myself somewhere in between both parties," he continues. "I'll have tons of meetings with the A&R guy and we'll talk about the songs. I'll take all of his ideas—there are always good ideas—and I'll be the filter. I like that. I like taking his ideas and incorporating them with my own ideas and bringing that to the band, as opposed to both of us hitting the band. I think it's better for both of us if there is sort of a proper channel."

Trombino has not encountered the situation where the band has defiantly bucked the label's requests, but he has had to filter A&R requests for the band. "When I was making *Clarity* with Jimmy Eat World, the A&R guy had tons of ideas and he was super creative, but he represented himself in a way that the band didn't respect," he recalls. "But there was good stuff, so he never talked to the band directly. He talked to me, and then I brought his ideas into the band disguised as my own and they went for them. There were a lot of them."

Likewise, Matt Wallace attempts to find the middle ground between artist and label. "I cannot count the times that the label says something to the band and the band gets really worked up and pissed off," he says. "I'm the guy that's gotta kind of talk them down. 'Hey, guys. It's cool. I know that maybe they didn't approach us the right way or didn't say it the right way, or maybe they're high on crack or they don't know what kind of record we're trying to make, but let's try to weed through what they said and see what they really meant. Because sometimes people say things and they don't know how to say them. For better or worse, I always tend to take the artists' side because I think they're the ones that really need the support. Labels always do just fine. So generally, if push comes to shove, or just my general leanings, I always kind of go with the band and try to make more of an artistic record and certainly try to defend them when we butt up against the label."

Wallace goes on to point out that there have been times when labels have been helpful to the bands he's worked with, such as during the making of the 2002 Maroon 5 release *Songs About Jane* that came out on Octone, which is a J Records subsidiary. "That was a really difficult record because there was a lot of hands in it from the label and at times, I believe to this day, some really inappropriate scrutiny over the record that was very, very difficult to get beyond. But, that was a new label and they were learning how to do their thing. Sometimes I had to kind of walk them through it and explain, like, 'Well, this is how we do this, this is how we do that.' It took a bit of education on my part to kind of hip them to what's going on. Not everyone, there were some people at the label that had been around the block. So what was frustrating was that I had to explain things. But the flip side was their enthusiasm. I mean, even though it may have rubbed us the wrong way at times, at least we knew that their hearts were in the right place, that they were very enthusiastic and just wanted what we wanted, which was a great record."

Brad Wood, on the other hand, encourages bands to work with everyone at the label, from the A&R rep to the promotions department to the radio department. "If I'm doing my job right, then I don't think of myself as a buffer between A&R and the band as much as I used to, because the band should be hugging their A&R [rep]. There should be no layer in between. They can't afford not to be tight with their A&R guy," he says. "You have to be and you have to know your product manager, who is the head of marketing; you should be on a first-name basis with your radio promo guy. You should be on a first-name basis with those people, whether it's a major or an independent. You've got to be tight with these people, and the time to get to know them is when things are going smoothly and you're making the records and you're getting signed and everybody's all smiles and stuff. When you need them to work most for you, especially with a big company, you want to make sure that they can put a name with a face.

"I tell the bands I work with all the time, 'Dudes, what are you doing? Don't wait for your manager to tell you what to do. Get on the blower and call everybody at the record label that might have anything to do with your record. Once recording stops, that's when you actually have to start working hard.' The hard work is doing the stuff that you're not good at, right? I mean, nobody likes to do a nine-to-five job that they're no good at," he says. "Being in a band is pretty easy. I mean, it's still hard work, but, like, when they finish and the record is mastered, then they've got to sort through the artwork. They've got to make sure that the moron graphic designer has done the color separation correctly and hasn't come up with really bad clip art. They've got to make sure the credits are done right and that the spelling is done right.

"If you're on a major, you've got to make sure that the people in the system and your A&R people don't lose interest," Wood continues. "There's a hard road ahead, and it's harder than making the record, I think, because it doesn't come naturally, necessarily. Somebody in the band has to step up. Don't wait for your manager to tell you what to do, because your manager is probably paying attention to another band that's in the studio."

Even though he encourages his bands to stay involved at that level, Wood does not necessarily dive into the business aspect of promoting a record. "It's too much of a distraction," he says. "I focus on making the record. I don't buy that I'm a buffer between A&R and the band. I might have said that or thought that in the past, but I think the adversarial role is a myth. I mean, maybe it is a reality, but then those people are just in a bad situation. That's an unfortunate situation, and then I would act as a buffer. But, by and large, with most of the records I've made, you've got an A&R person that was really into the band, that wants to stay into the band, and wants the best for the band. If it's not a good fit between what the band wants and what he or she wants, there's a problem, and then you can help them massage that situation. Sometimes you can't. Sometimes you've got to be the bad guy. But that doesn't happen very often. Usually, people are so careful about who they sign, and for how much, and for what reasons that I'm usually surprised when there's that problem. It doesn't happen very often. I think it's mostly a myth."

J.D. Foster begs to differ. "You're definitely a liaison between [label] guys and what needs to get done," he reports. "It's certainly not my favorite part of the gig. You're also right in the middle of the budgetary control in a lot of ways, and I think smart money [would be spent] in hiring a production coordinator, so that wouldn't even be a worry."

Sylvia Massy Shivy has had tough times in the studio when she has had to replace a band's drummer, at the label's encouragement, during recording. That situation arose while she was producing Acroma's 2003 Universal Records debut *Orbitals,* and the label wanted to replace the band's drummer, Joshua Zirbel, with session drummer Josh Freese. "I wanted to have the Josh sessions be exciting and fun, but it was just the darkest day in the life of that band," he recalls. "I couldn't save them. There was nothing I could do, because I became part of the machine at that point instead of making it happen. But, ultimately, I think Josh was great and the record came out great, but they'll have this horrible, dark feeling about the record for the rest of their lives. But, you know what? It's about making great records. You have to put some personalities aside."

Some producers have found a way to capitalize on the chafing that goes on between labels and artists. When Walter Afanasieff was working with Savage Garden in 1999, the band members (singer Darren Hayes and keyboardist Daniel Jones) and producer believed they had turned in a collection of eleven great songs. The label thought otherwise. "We brought it to the record company, and they said, 'There's not a hit here.' Those are the times when you really don't understand the music business. We all worked so hard," he says, shaking his head. "You can do it for a year, say that this is the greatest thing in the world, and take it to the record company, and they [say] there are no hits here. So, like fools, we went back home with our tails between our legs, and I just looked at Darren and Daniel and I said, 'You gotta be kidding me. What are you going to do about this? Are you going to take that?'"

Hayes and Jones left Afanasieff's studio for ten minutes to think and then walked back in. "They said, 'We've got an idea,'" Afanasieff continues. "Daniel played it on guitar, and Darren sang, 'I knew I loved you before I met you.' I said, 'Okay.' Then we were all sort of challenged and dared by this record company, who critiqued our album that didn't have a hit. We were all on fire. I went into the studio and started a drum groove and some sounds, and changed a couple of chords that they had, and we all started doing it. Literally, about a day went by and we had this enormously cool poppy little number. They finished their lyrics, we started running into the studio that night, started laying down the tracks and the vocals, and about a day-and-a-half went by and we had this song, "I Knew I Loved You." Then we played that for the record company, and they freaked out. They said, 'This is what we wanted.' Now all the other eleven songs were genius, so we had a whole genius album. That was one fun experience."

THE COMPANY LINE

Suffice it to say, not all A&R reps are created equal. Some types may aggravate producers, yet there are others who are supportive and helpful during the recording dates. Of course, none of the producers interviewed for this book have suggested that all A&R reps are bad. Many realize that the record-company's representative is only doing his or her job, expressing opinions based on a host of criteria laid out by the label brass.

To shed some light on the labels' position, A&R reps Rory Felton (The Militia Group) and Kim Buie (Lost Highway) describe their experiences working with producers: How they pair artists with producers, and what they feel their role is once work begins in the studio.

The Militia Group has been in existence since 2000. Since then, the label has released thirty-plus albums and sold close to 500,000 records in four years. A&R responsibilities are shared among a number of people in a ten-person operation. Rory Felton, one of the label's co-owners and president, has had the opportunity to put a number of producer/artist teams together. When the label started to talk about putting the band Anadivine in the studio to record their debut, *Zoo*, the first thing that was discussed was their limited budget. It is not a surprise that indie-label recording budgets are low, and Felton reports that on average, the label spends between $5,000 and $30,000 to make a record. Once a budget had been decided upon with Anadivine, the two sides started to talk about a producer. "They decided upon a local producer that had worked with their friends' band from their same small town called Coheed and Cambria. The local producers were Michael Birnbaum and Chris Bittner, and they wanted to go with them because they agreed to do the record cheaply and whatnot."

However, the band was not entirely happy with the guitar tones once the record was mastered. "So we delayed the release and went to find someone to remix the record," Felton reports. "They went in the studio with Ed Rose for about three days to remix and fill [the sound] out more." While the label did not have a hand in picking Birnbaum and Bittner, Rose was a label suggestion. "We do a lot of records with Ed. We trust him. We know what he does. We know what we are getting into when we work with Ed and how he works," he explains. "He actually went out of his way to mix one song for free to show the band what he could do. That really showed a lot to the band, and they were really happy with the way Ed's mix sounded."

Felton observes that the label's smaller budgets have not pushed many producers off their radar. "We've seen that when producers work with us they have been able to get a lot more business out of it, because kids want to go to use them now because they made so-and-so's record," he says. "Some of the producers we work with have done so many indie projects that they are used to indie budgets and they're happy to do it because they love the music. Some producers will take a definite pay cut to do an indie record, because they understand we don't have the money like the majors do, and they want to do it because it's good for them to have the credibility."

That said, The Militia Group has not gone out of their way to attract big-name producers, although Felton has found a way to work with some of them. "Sometimes you can't pay them to produce tracks, but you can get them involved on a mixing level," he says. "For instance, the new Copland record is going to be mixed by Ken Andrews who's got a really good name up in L.A.; he does a lot of cool, credible stuff. Then Michael Rosen—who has done Rancid, and Santana, and AFI—did the Beautiful Mistake record for way less budget than he usually makes records for."

Once band and producer are in the studio, Felton will stop by to see how things are going. "We'll go down and visit the band in the studio and see how it's coming along, but as far as working in the studio [and having] kind of constant eyes on the producer, we don't like to do that. Usually, before the producer and the band are in the studio, we've heard demos and we know what the songs are going to be like, so we are pretty confident in what our band and the producer can do together," he says. "I go in the studio as a representative of the label that's paying for the recording. I want the band to know that the label feels a part of this recording and feel in tune to this recording and definitely wants to be involved with the record as a whole from start to finish. They are fine with that, because they understand the importance of having the label feel like they're a part of the record, as well as trusting our judgment on certain things."

Before Kim Buie came to Lost Highway as the vice president of A&R, she worked at Palm Pictures, a record label headed by Chris Blackwell and known for its diverse roster. While there, she worked with an eclectic group of artists and producers, which she has continued to do at Lost Highway. So, when she is looking to pair artist and producer, matching sensibilities is the first priority, no matter if those producers started on the technical or artistic side of the glass. "We always approach everything from the point of song first. There are a lot of different types of producers out there. There are the old-school producers, there are the new-school producers, there are the electronic producers, and there are the beat guys," she explains. "So, you've got to essentially look at the artist that you have and figure out what their strengths are, figure out what their weaknesses are, and then somewhere in the two it will help guide you to the kind of producer that you are looking for."

Buie learned the art of matching producer and artist from such Nashville legends as Tony Brown, Jimmy Bowen, and Emory Gordy, Jr. So, often she'll go for the right match over the hot-name producer name *du jour.* "I know that there are A&R people who [feel that] is meaningless [and] it's all about the name. 'I want the hot producer who's got the biggest hits on the charts right now for my act,' because they want a piece of that magic and they want to apply that to their artist. That's not wrong either; it's just a different attitude, it's a different mindset and a different mentality. It might actually be very appropriate for that artist, but for all I know it might be a pop act, and therefore matching sensibility is important because you do need somebody who's creative now. Then there are people who just, quite crassly, want the hot producer and whether sensibilities match or not is irrelevant. I'm not going to sit here and pretend that doesn't exist; it does."

While Buie was working with the band Butthole Surfers, the band's guitarist, Paul Leary, declared that he wanted to produce the band's next album (*Electriclarryland,* 1996). It wasn't a difficult decision to let Leary handle the sessions, since he had just come off producing Sublime's self-titled release. "That's when he stepped out into his own," Buie explains. "I think people saw that he wasn't just a member of a band, that he actually did something outside of that band that was successful and also sounded really good. He was appropriate for the band, and he brought out all the best highlights. He made a very smart record. It was absolutely right for that band and it worked. Whether it had been successful or not, a good record was made. The fact that it was successful just makes it all the sweeter," she says with a laugh. "So, in that case, nobody really questioned Paul Leary getting involved, but it is the rare artist that can actually produce."

There have been other times, though, when an artist has asked to produce and it does not come together. "It's like they write the songs and they create the music, so why do they also have to take that control? My philosophy is if they're a baby band, unless they've done something that already sort of proves that they are capable of creating something really amazing, you don't want them to produce themselves. I would rather have them learn from somebody else and then take that knowledge and go do it themselves than try to do it for themselves from the beginning. But, it's tough, they don't always want to hear it that way," she explains.

Once an act gets in the studio, Buie might find herself being very involved or not at all. She recalls an album done with artist Etta James and producer Barry Beckett where she was very involved. "Barry and I searched out the songs together and worked hand in hand," she says. "He pulled the band together; I take no credit for that, but in terms of pulling the songs together, and being there in the studio, and being a sounding board—sometimes my job as an A&R person is to walk in with the freshest ears in the room. I am not there every day, getting so closely married to the tracks that I can't hear them with clean ears." But that does not mean that Buie will offer unwanted opinions. "I want to be involved as I need to be," she explains. "It is always a shock to me when I walk in and have nothing to say. I feel like I am not doing my job because I have nothing to say, but literally I just sit there, and if it's really that good I go, 'Shit, I have nothing to contribute here. I am sorry, I wish I did. I wish I could say something, but it sounds so good, you just made my job really, really easy.' I get to walk away and go home with a smile on my face, and that doesn't happen that often, but when it does, it's just a surprise. Sometimes I have to temper my own ego: 'Surely there must be something that I have an opinion about here,'" she says with a laugh. "But you just have to give it up sometimes. When it's working, don't fuck with it."

Given her time in the studio, Buie has seen how best to work with producers, and how best producers can work with labels. "One of the reasons why T-Bone Burnett is so great as a producer is that he makes everybody feel like their opinion matters," she says. "Whether he uses your opinion or not is not the point, you feel like he listened, he understood what you had to say, and that your opinion was an important contribution." At the same time, Buie realizes that A&R reps need to know their place in the studio. "You have to respect the vision that is happening and the relationship that is happening between an artist and a producer. Unless it is taking an artist in a direction that is creatively sui-cidal, you've got to let the process go," she says.

According to Buie, there are two crucial times during the making of a record: The demo and the mixing process. "If before they go into the studio, when you hear the demos and like the shape of the songs and you feel like a great match has been made between producer and artist, then let them get in there. Stay out of the studio, stay out of their way, and let them get their work going. Give them at least two weeks to get something going and then step in for a couple days, check it out, be a fly on the wall, form some opinions, express them, and go away again," she explains. "Then right before the mixing happens, that's when you get a chance to evaluate everything that's happened. Get in any opinions that you have before they go to mix—if you feel like a few things need to be strengthened, or if you can convince the artist he can deliver a better perform-ance. That's your moment to get your last opinion in. Then the mix is where everything falls together, and that is where you step back in and you get a little more involved, and you listen to the mix. You make sure it's going down the way you think it's going to work, that there is consistency, that there is a flow and that the pieces are coming together.

"Ideally, it is nice to have a little bit of time between when the tracking ends and the mixing begins so you have room for that," she continues. "I can only speak for myself. To me, that's the right way to do it. It's the only way I know, and it doesn't always go in that way, but if it can be done that way, in my expe-rience, that is the best way to proceed and to let the process flow."

Although she has a reliable list of producers, Buie is always on the hunt for new names. There are a number of ways she finds them: Producer and band demos will come across her desk, or she picks up indie or major label records, receives notes from producer managers, or gets suggestions from other A&R reps or the RPM Web site or print directory of producers, engineers, and mix-ers used by music executives across the globe. Once she has the name, Buie likes to meet with a new producer for an interview of sorts. "I ask them a bunch of questions from a set list that I have," she explains. "I generally get really inter-esting answers, and it tells me a lot about who they are, how they are, what they are, what they haven't done yet, what they'd like to do, how they work and where their sensibility lies. It gives me a sense of their personality, so when I am trying to match sensibilities and personalities with a band and producer, having met them helps with the puzzle pieces."

THE DIFFERENCE BETWEEN MAJORS AND INDIES

Music is music is music, but the music *business* has changed dramatically over the years, as more and more independent labels have been born. Where inde-pendent labels were once a haven for off-kilter acts that could not find a home in the major-label-dominant world, these labels now sign some of the most popular bands on the scene. Today's indies are much more than mere products of vanity or minor-league labels for artists that are not quite ready for prime time. Even for well-established artists, indie labels can offer a level of creative control that can be hard to get with the majors.

For almost any independent, however, money is still an issue. Recording budgets can run up to $500,000 in the major-label world, but it is not unheard of for an indie budget to come in at $30,000 or less. On average, though, most producers still want to work with indie labels. Many will put their fees on a sliding scale in order to work with bands that inspire them, and because they enjoy the process.

When Shivy works with major-label bands in the studio, she finds that an entire team comes with them, from A&R reps to managers. She's seen a big difference in the type of people coming to recording dates since she opened Radio Star Studios in Weed, California. "I've been contacted by some really great, completely independent bands, unsigned bands," she says, "and I've been able to work with them directly, without interference from labels or managers. I think I'm having the most fun I've ever had making music. It is not having labels involved and not having managers involved. It's complete freedom, and I think the results are really great. So, in a perfect world, I'd rather not work for a label at all, but I know it's a necessity."

The curse of major-label bureaucracy has haunted Craig Street on a number of occasions. "I think more problems happen with major labels, because I think [with] major labels you're dealing with a lot of different things. Major labels, at this point in time, for all intents and purposes, are these corporate entities that are multinational," he says. "Even the most creative people who have a major-label job don't really have a big say. They do, but they don't. They'd like to think they do, but in the end there's some blank person at a corporation who's saying, 'No, here's what sells. We just want ten more of this. We don't care about the rest of it.'"

On the flip side of that, Ryan Greene points out that indie labels are more apt to be concerned with the band. "I think independents are more into making sure that the band is happy. 'You guys want to do a record? Go do your record, turn it in, and we'll put it out.' Majors are not that way," he says. "You'll have your A&R guy come out making sure the project's going well. You're pleasing everybody from top to bottom when you're working with the majors—A&R person, his boss, the marketing, promotion…Independents are really about making sure that the band is happy."

J.D. Foster has also seen that approach from indies, and he adds that the people who work in those labels are a little more fanatic. "I think there's a big difference, at least in my experience, because the major-label method, by and large, seems to me to be to grab a bunch of schlock and throw it against the wall. Anything that sticks gets used, and the rest doesn't. Whereas indies don't have that luxury financially, so they get behind everything. I have a theory and that, for some indies—of course, some indies want to get big and they're looking for the next Nirvana or whatever—the people there are obsessed. If there's any obsession at major labels, it's about shareholder prices. Of course, nobody would do this at all if they weren't looking to get something out of it, but there's a different philosophy. So, I find it much easier to deal with the small labels than the big ones. The whole [label] is like three or four people and that's it. They are all the people that are going to make the creative decisions. I recently took a demo to a label, and the guy—typical A&R thing—first of all asked me how old the woman singing was and she was too old for him. He basically said, 'Well, if you told me she was eighteen years old, I'd have three other guys in this office listening to it right now.' Which only meant that it was halfway there," he explains laughing, "to whether they could do something or not. Whereas on an indie, if one person likes it, then that's it."

It is not as if indie labels are the music-business panacea, however, as Brad Wood reports. "I don't see the evilness [in major labels]. I've been ripped off, but I think that my biggest disappointments—and the most painful of not getting paid for the work I've done, you know, the most flagrant rip-offs—were all indie labels," he says. "Major labels? You do the work, you get paid. Well, with indies you do the work and you don't always get paid, because their bottom line is much more sketchy, and their checking account might just be bare or they might just be lying to you. You can't raise them on the phone, you can't find them. Then they pop up again two years later with another band that they've managed to sign to a seven-album deal. You know, indie doesn't equal angel. Just like major label doesn't equal devil. That doesn't equate. That's a naïve assumption."

7 THE COURTING PROCESS

"**M**usicians don't cause ulcers, but they are carriers," reports one producer who asked to remain anonymous. He was laughing, but he wasn't joking. And many artists could probably counter with a similar comment. This is why performers and producers swap demos back and forth, talk at length on the phone or in person about the potential of the songs, and check out each other's reputations before the two parties decide to work together. The music industry is rife with stories about producer and artist clashes—guns being drawn, chairs being thrown, or out-right fistfights—happening over "artistic differences." The time in the studio for both is highly emotional; dreams and careers can be made or shattered. Finding the right combination of artistic temperament and producer sensibility can be just as combustible as it can be magical.

Both parties in this creative relationship are definitely looking for certain characteristics before they commit to entering the studio together. The "courting process" has resulted in pairings that have lasted through multiple album cycles, where artist and producer feel they are contributing to a noteworthy catalogue. At the same time, there are one-off relationships that create strong career albums. The keys to both are building trust and intimacy for the time that the team is working under the pressure of the red light.

One step that has changed during the dance between producer and artist is the way producers now find themselves chasing artists before they are signed to a recording contract. Not only does that give the producer a heightened level of responsibility for the band (not to mention the costs associated with recording an album), it makes the communal feeling of the studio dates more crucial. The producer is taking on some of the business challenges that were once tackled by an A&R rep, and so he or she is now more aware of what it takes to get an artist from start-up to full-fledged recording and touring band. This may also result in more than the standard three points and producer's fee that they would collect for polishing and recording songs.

How Producers Pick Artists

There are a number of factors involved when a producer starts to look for an artist to work with in the studio: A collection of songs, an amenable personality, and a combination of attitude and perseverance. Most producers say that the commerce of the music industry does not crowd into the decision making. Rather, the belief seems to be that good art will command strong commerce. The key at the outset, for the producers interviewed here, seems to be a collection of songs that can stand on their own.

"I pick artists by songs and by guts," Garth Richardson says. "I get sent a lot of demos and I basically go by what I feel. I get it, I listen to it, and I can tell by the first song. I put it in and go, 'I don't like it.' Then I go on and I say, 'You know, there's something there.' I do have a knack of listening to someone's demo and knowing how it's going to sound finished."

However, having finished songs is not critical to catch a producer's ear. If that were true, many artists would be better off going into the studio with an engineer, who could simply ensure good tones, rather than seeking a producer to encourage good performances. Brad Wood gets demos sent to him from his management company or will often get referrals from bands he's worked with in the past. He is pretty specific when it comes to accepting new assignments. "It has to sound like something that's interesting and have good songs," he says. "There's no methodology to it at all, other than seeing a band or an artist play and being into it. It could be about anything."

Likewise for Joe Henry. "I'd work with anybody who I thought was exciting," he says. He also says he has no purist reservations that require him to eschew pop music. Obscure does not necessarily equal quality: "A lot of music that I revere more than anything else was just wildly popular, successful music. I don't think the things are mutually exclusive, I just think that people have developed a really false and narrow point of view about what can work and how it can work. There's all kinds of ways it can work, we see examples of it all the time and yet, people still always look at a very small demographic and say, 'This is what would interest them, and nothing else will, except more of this.'"

Henry is just one producer who consistently follows his instincts rather than betting on a "sure thing." In 2000, Dave Jerden had to choose between two acts: Sum 41 and Big Wreck. So, he traveled to Toronto, Canada, to decide. "Sum 41 was more of an obvious thing to do, because they were young, they were cute, and all this other kind of stuff," he says. "They had all the combinations, but that's not the reason I do this stuff. The reason I do it is to have fun. There's so much depth and weight to what Ian [Thornley, Big Wreck's singer/guitarist and songwriter] was doing. He took me by his studio in Toronto and he played what he was doing on his own. It just blew me away. My first reaction was, 'Why do you want me? Why do you need me?' But he wanted to work with me, so I said, 'Great.' I called my manager, and he asked me which one I wanted to work with, Sum 41 or Big Wreck, and I said, 'I want to work with Big Wreck. I think there's just a lot more there. I'll have more fun doing it.' I probably could have knocked a record out in a couple of weeks with Sum 41, and it would have been a lot easier, but working with a high-pressure record is a lot of work and there's just so much to deal with." While Big Wreck's *The Pleasure and the Greed* was satisfying to Jerden, the Jerry Finn-produced *All Killer No Filler* gave Sum 41 a multi-Platinum career calling card.

Over the years that David Lowery has been producing records, he's gotten calls from bands, managers, and labels with the message that he'd be able to help massage magic out of some raw songs. "I've tried all those things, but ultimately I won't record anything that I don't actually personally like," he says. "Although, sometimes you do really well if you're not emotionally involved in the music. You can make all the hard decisions, but I'm not doing that now."

J.D. Foster admits that he hasn't turned many artists down, but at the same time the gig needs to make sense for him to take it. "I feel personally that the best musician in the world can't pull a rabbit out of the hat if there's not already one in there. That's what I look for: Is there any kind of rabbit there? Do these people have anything to say? Because no matter how easy a gig it's meant to be, or however low the stakes, it's gonna be time out of my life that I'm not spending with my family or doing my own thing where I'm going to have to take on the emotional issues of others," he says with a laugh. "Is it worth something artistically? That's the long and short of it."

Certainly, songs are crucial to successful recording dates, but so are personalities. That is why Matt Wallace begins the vetting process with a long view in mind. "I'm looking for a band that is hopefully together enough to be able to withstand the signing process, live through the recording process, and also be able to go out there and tour and have the record heard," he explains. "If you get people who are fragile, they're never going to get past at least one of those difficult points. The artist will just flip out, and we'll stop making the record." Wallace speaks from experience; he has seen sessions go south when a band he has signed on with has trouble with substance abuse or personality issues. "It's happened so many times now where I've had to deal with people doing all kinds of stuff, and if it's anyone but the singer/songwriter you can limp through it and hire other people. But if it's the main person, you're in trouble. You meet 'em, you really like 'em, you have dinner, and then all of a sudden they're drunk, and you're, like, 'Uh-oh.' Then the first day recording, they end up going out and getting crack. It's a big drag. I've got to put trust in them as well, and I've got to make a leap of faith that they're going to want to make a great record."

"Don't work with assholes," Ed Cherney simply states. "Don't work with people who are deliberately mean and hurtful." Beyond that, he says, there has to be some sort of creative resonance between artist and producer. "You have to hear something," he explains. "If you feel an affinity towards it, you work on it. It's real simple."

There are also the producers who pick artists to work with based on who will round out their discography. "Sometimes I look over the past year and see what I've done in my career and say, 'Okay, I've done this band and this band, maybe I don't need to do anymore of those types of bands.' I took on My Chemical Romance [the 2004 *Three Cheers for Sweet Revenge*], who is a very different type of artist. For me it's sort of a darker [sound], like if Iron Maiden met The Cure," Howard Benson says. "It was very weird-type stuff, and I wanted to do it, first because I thought the band was great and the lead singer has his own thing—he lives in his own world—and I love bands like that. They want to try draw you into their world, instead of trying to be in your world. That's always what makes great music, when you have people that are very set in their world. So, I met [singer Gerard Way] and thought, 'This guy is kind of weird, he's got great songs and I haven't done a band like this, so let's go.'

"There was another band that came along at the same time, and I won't name who they are, but they were just the same thing that I had just been doing over and over again, and I was just bored," he continues. "I won't lie, a lot of times if a band comes to me with a huge sales base they'll get a big look, and that band had a big sales base, but I said no to them because I didn't want to be involved in their career and I didn't like what they were doing. They may succeed, but they're certainly not going to do anything for me."

John Porter went out of his way to work with a number of blues artists in the late 1990s for a simple reason. "I love the blues and I made a conscious effort to work with a couple of them while they were still around," he says. "That's what I loved as a kid." To that end, Porter produced albums for B.B. King, Buddy Guy, Taj Mahal, John Lee Hooker, and John Mayall & the Bluesbreakers. He believes his being a fan ultimately helped the sessions, and that is true of almost any artist he works with in the studio. "Oh yeah, absolutely. If I'm lucky then I'm a fan anyway, even if it's a bunch of fifteen-year-old kids. If I'm really into what they're doing then I'm a fan anyway. But that's one of the perks of working with somebody like B.B., who I love, but it doesn't change what you're there to do, what you have to do, or how you would do it. I'm not overawed by musicians. I love what they do, but they're just musicians."

HOW ARTISTS PICK PRODUCERS

As the old saying goes, it takes two to tango, and while producers might be the ones being asked to dance, it is the artists who do the inviting. When artists are looking through a list of producers who may guide their recording sessions, they look for some very specific characteristics; they want a producer who is honest, supportive, creative, and, yes, has something of a track record in their genre. Occasionally it is a small thing that a producer says or does not say that clinches the deal. It might even be how they act or carry themselves that gets them in the studio with a band. When The Ataris were shopping for producers for their major-label debut, *So Long, Astoria,* a number of names came up, says bassist Mike Davenport. "Lou [Giordano] was always my choice. Ric Ocasek said, 'I don't get it.' Mark Trombino told us to keep writing. So, I kept pushing Lou, and the minute [songwriter Kris Roe and Giordano] spoke, it worked."

The same situation played itself out when the Counting Crows were looking for someone to produce their sophomore effort, *Recovering the Satellites.* As guitarist Dave Bryson discussed earlier, Gil Norton ultimately got the gig because he clicked with singer/songwriter Adam Duritz. "Gil's first phone conversation with Adam was completely talking about this image he had for this song and this lyric and how we were missing the point," Bryson recalls. "Adam was like, 'He's right. He totally got it.' That was a huge part of Gil and he was that way the whole time. He was always working toward the song."

For Rufus Wainwright, it can just be just the type of person he is looking for, and that person may not be the one with the most suitable musical background. "I've had some pretty harrowing experiences with certain producers and Marius [deVries] has been a complete dream. I like him a lot, because he's a nice person and he's very British in his sensibilities in the studio. He's extremely efficient and diplomatic." Wainwright felt so comfortable with deVries that the two wrote much of the 2003 *Want One* and the 2004 release *Want Two* together. "Basically, I would come in with a song, we would put down a click track, and then I'd put down a scratch vocal with a guitar or piano," Wainwright reports. "Then we would hang out together and play keyboards and figure out what kind of bass line we wanted, or what kind of horn line, or find some weird synth sounds."

As a producer, David Lowery has been in that situation where an artist is looking for some musical direction and he has freely given it. As an artist, he has looked for that in varying degrees from producers Dennis Herring, who produced Camper Van Beethoven's *Our Beloved Revolutionary Sweetheart* and *Key Lime Pie;* and Don Smith, who produced Cracker's self-titled debut and the 1993 follow-up *Kerosene Hat.* "Dennis is not really the songwriting guy who will tell you when [a song] is screwed up. Sometimes he'll suggest a part—he knows when it's not working and it's screwed up and you need to do this or that," he recalls. "We interviewed a few producers [for Cracker's debut], and we went out to see Don Smith out in an industrial park in Chatsworth. He was mixing some record, and there was incense burning everywhere, candles were lit, there was a big knife on the mixing console and a bong in the corner. There was just some totally crazy vibe around him, and we liked that vibe. Don is very much about hanging out with the bands, going to the bar with the bands...It's like he's your partner in crime, but he also comes from an engineering background. So, he sets the mood so you get a great take. You never really feel his stamp; he definitely works in the background. He pushed us more in a sort of rootsier classic rock direction from where we were."

For the band's third release, *The Golden Age* in 1996, it made sense to Lowery to change producers and go back to Herring. "The songs that were written for *The Golden Age* seemed like they needed a real in-studio arrangement kind of production," Lowery reports. "Don Smith is the kind of guy who would say, 'Here's the band,' and maybe he would add some kind of organic thing. Whereas Dennis was pretty flexible with working from anything. 'Let's just start with an acoustic guitar and cut a track. Just sing the song for a while, let's put some keyboards to it, let's try out different things.' If it's not working, Dennis will go in a completely different direction, where I think Don would just go on to the next song. I wanted to have strings on certain songs, so it really became an arrangement issue, and I needed somebody who had some chops as far as arranging. We mapped out a lot of the string arrangements before we turned it over to David Campbell [a noted session string arranger in Los Angeles], and Dennis would say, 'Make sure that the strings play the third in this part of the song.' He could really talk to you specifically about the music."

Artists will also turn to producers who share a similar background, as is the case of the Dave Grohl and Rye Coalition pairing. The former Nirvana drummer and Foo Fighter frontman was selected by the New Jersey-based rock band for a number of reasons. "The span of his work [was important], and he just seemed like the right choice," explains the band's drummer Dave Leto. "We had the ideas, but he had more experience than we did and he understood where we came from because he did the same thing. It just seemed like a good match. We're all kind of funny, and he's a funny guy. We got along."

The other producers that the band were looking at included Josh Homme from Queens of the Stone Age, Led Zeppelin's John Paul Jones, Garth Richardson, and Phil Spector. "We wanted Phil to do it from jail," Leto says with a laugh. "We thought it would be very newsworthy. We met a bunch of people, like Garth Richardson and he was really great, but we just figured Dave would be a good one to go to."

When Grohl got in with the band, he brought a wealth of songwriting experience, and that helped the band shape their songs. "We rehearsed for [about] ten days before we recorded, and we had all these songs written. He understands how to write a song effectively and he helped us trim the fat off," Leto says. "Instead of having a song be twelve minutes long, which is what I wanted, he said, 'Make them make sense.' He pushed each one of us to give the best performance we could." It was a change from the experience the band had working with recordist Steve Albini, who recorded the *On Top* album and a handful of singles. "Steve won't interfere with bands writing songs. He gives input like, 'That was a shitty take' or 'You guys could do better,' but he would never say that we should have moved the chorus or something," Leto says. "He's just there to capture your band. He made it sound like you were standing in the middle of all of us, which is amazing. He's a great engineer, but we produced all that stuff."

System of a Down looked around for different producers, but it was hard to get any better for the band than the man who signed them, Rick Rubin. "How do you not pick him? If he's willing to record your albums and work with you, it's just a cool thing to be a part of," Daron Malakian says. "Some people have had a bad experience with him, because some people want a knob twirler. That's not what I am looking for. He's like a guru. Rick comes to band meetings if it has nothing to do with music. He's a part of our band just like George Martin was a part of The Beatles."

THE KEY TO THE ONGOING RELATIONSHIP

In the early days of the music business, it was nothing new for an artist and producer to work together over a career span of releases. At that time, it was not so much choice as contractual obligations on both sides. With the era of independent record producers came the opportunity to work with any number of artists in the course of a career. However, a handful of producers found a base of bands with whom they worked repeatedly throughout the 1970s and 1980s. The Don Was and Ed Cherney team, for instance, did a handful of albums with Bonnie Raitt, The B-52s, and Iggy Pop.

There are a number of producers of this era who built a reputation with a band that enabled them to continuing working together. Garth Richardson is just one of them. Tony Brown and Walter Afanasieff, while under production contracts with record companies, continued working with the same artists from release to release. John Porter likes working with an artist over and over. "I do like working with the same artists, because if you've got a good relationship, you can get better," he says. "Half the thing is knowing how far people can go, how far you can push them, what they're capable of, and under what conditions to get the best out of them. That all comes with familiarity, to a certain extent."

There are others, though, that do not believe artists and producers should work together more than twice. "My track record is always do two albums and that's it," reports Dave Jerden. "It's like we've explored everything that needs to be explored. I did two Alice in Chains records, I did two Jane's Addiction records. It's like, what else is there to say? All of a sudden you're just repeating yourself, and it's not that much fun anymore. The reason I do it is to have fun. I don't make enormous amounts of money or anything, but I have fun doing what I do. When you're doing it for money, you become a hack."

Michael Rosen views his repeat work as a quiet pat on the back. "I'm really proud of that. I like the fact that most bands I've done have asked me back to do it again," he says. "To me, that's a sign that you did your job and they liked what you did. You get a comfort level. I did three with Vicious Rumors, three with Rancid. It's like being a part of the band. If you really connect with them, then you are a part of the band. You make decisions; you help them out, and you kind of become part of their trip. So, they keep coming back to you to help with that particular side of it."

Rosen allows that a part of a producer's job is to bring an objective pair of ears to a project, but feels certain that's still possible with artists who come back to work with him. "The flip side of it would be that whatever we did together is a part of their sound now, and they need that part of our sound to continue. I can be pretty objective about what their songs need. I mean a great song is still a great song. [But] if they're going to go for a makeover, then they'll probably go to somebody else. If they were going to go from being a pop band to a polka band, then I might not be the guy for that," he adds with a laugh. "That's one of the things that you talk about when you meet with a band. What's their vision? What do they want to do with the album? And you have to give them yours, because just like a band the best thing that works for a producer is to have a vision. So, when I say to the band, 'Okay, I think it should be a little Americana with a little power-pop. That's what I would go with.' They can say, 'Okay, well, we're not really feeling that.' Then I'm not the guy to do it, but you know it."

Sure, meshing personalities and similar songwriting ideas is helpful to continuing a relationship, but there is no better cement than success. "Nine times out of ten longevity gets built around, not just friendship, but success," says Tony Brown. He should know, after multiple albums with artists such as Vince Gill, Reba McEntire, and George Strait. "When you're successful and you're also best friends, it's hard to find a better working relationship, especially in this business where, even if you do something that you think is really good and it fails, you both are proud of the product. That's happened to me, and I still continued to work with the artist. That says a lot about where you are both coming from—some of my favorite things that I've ever produced have been some of my biggest failures—and some of the things that I thought were just okay have been very successful.

"I think it's success and a good working relationship," Brown continues. "You get in the studio and spill your guts to the world. I think that's what an artist and a producer do with each other in front of great musicians and an engineer, and once that commitment and belief in each other is there, you don't want to screw with that unless you have to. I've seen A&R people just screw with it and I think, 'Why would you do that?'"

With Mariah Carey, Walter Afanasieff built the first artist/producer relationship where both parties felt like it was worth continuing. The roster of Afanasieff's recurring clientele grew to include Michael Bolton, Kenny G., and Celine Dion. "What happens is that these artists understand you; they know what you're about, and you know what they're about, and they trust you can deliver and guide them and produce them into what they feel is a place that no one else can do," he explains. "When another person would say, 'That's it, that's the keeper vocal,' I would say, 'No, it's not there yet.' No one else would have done that, but I do, and then finally they'll do something that's so perfect. I think that when you have that relationship, you reach these heights in those moments so that the artist and the producer feel enormous satisfaction."

While Afanasieff has had a long career with some of those artists, he has also seen what has happened when they moved on to other producers. "They'll say, 'I didn't sing as good as if Walter had been producing.' The other producer won't comp the vocal the same way as I do. I'll get an emotion out of the song. The height, the depth, and the 'grandioseness' of something is a little bit more important to me than to someone else, and these folks all know that about me," he says. "That's the style under which I work. I'm a perfectionist, so they keep coming back, and I'm glad for it. I think that's wonderful. I'm honored that these folks want to come back and work with me. Sometimes you don't see that happen and [the artist] goes off and gets busy with somebody else. I wonder why that person doesn't continue to come back, and then in some cases, that person just withers away and you never hear from them again. I think, 'Well, I would have taken a different course. I would have come back to me, because I would have gotten them to sing better or I would have chosen a different song or written a different song. Somehow fate would have been different for them.'"

Obviously, a series of albums with a consistent team is helpful to both artist and producer, but Dave Fridmann does not go out of his way to convince artists to come back to him over and over. "Oddly, I don't and at least on many occasions I have had to tell people clearly, 'We shouldn't do this one. You should go do this with this guy.' Or else I'll tell them, 'Your record label is freaking out, so don't do it with me. Go do it with somebody else.' When it's right, it works," he says. "If we did a good job in the studio or if the rapport between us is all good, then we're going to work together again. You spend six to eight weeks over a few months' period with some people and you talk to them once or twice until it's time to go do their next record. You're in this intimate relationship again and then you're out of it. Most of the people I work with are friends of mine, and any time any of us can hang out, we do because we enjoy each other's company. In general, though, the bottom line is if they're doing well then they're gone and there's no way to keep in touch. I don't know, it's not like I'm going to send them a fruit basket or something. If they want to come back, they'll come back."

BUILDING TRUST AND INTIMACY

It's one thing to set up a session for success technically; it's another to establish the type of environment where an artist feels safe enough to take a risk that will push a song or an album from interesting to exhilarating. Artists need to feel that anything they try—from a guitar solo that can soar or falter, to a drum fill that may carry an emotion beyond believable or dissolve into a rumbling mess, to a vocal track that bends and pushes the boundaries—will be welcomed in a spirit of acceptance and experimentation.

Just how intense can it get between producer and artist? "I don't mean this in any sexual or romantic sense, but you come to fall in love with certain people as a friend," says Walter Afanasieff. "You respect what they do, and if you hang out long enough you bond with them and they with you."

While that tight-knit feeling is part of the reward of a good pairing, the level of honesty and intimacy required for the successful consummation of a session can also be emotionally exhausting. At least that is Chris Vrenna's experience. He starts the process with long discussions about song concepts, where he gets the opportunity to see how their personalities will mesh and to make sure he is the right producer for the band. "I don't want people wasting their time or their money. Be honest with people when you first go in there and just lay it out on the table. I've always tried to have no ego, no pretense—at the end of the day, we are all just making music. All of us want to make a really fun cool record."

"I always try to be as brutally honest as I can," Vrenna continues. "'This song I don't think is very good, and here's why. This, I think, is fantastic and here's why. My favorite thing about you guys is...' I'm trying to form a bond with them, and I let them know that I don't have all the answers, but I'll tell them what I think and I'll stand by it. At least for me, in my experience, people seem to respond to it, they appreciate it. That's why you're there. They don't want you to say, 'It's great guys,' because some producers that I know just want to turn a production over every six weeks, and they won't back up and take time to work on things. They just want to run it through the assembly line, so it sounds like everything else on KROQ [a Los Angeles radio station] and then move on to the next one. I don't know, I don't do that many productions, because when I take them on I get pretty emotionally attached."

In the long run, though, Vrenna believes that the emotional attachment is helpful. "I care a hell of a lot more about it, and I don't just see it as just a way to make rent," he says. "I always say to the band, 'Look, when I'm producing,

I'm a band member. I'm your fourth band member right now, I'm your fifth band member right now.' I get that involved, as if I was the one who created it originally. Maybe some people would think that's a bad way to go, but music is an emotional art form, and people are laying out feelings through lyrics. So, I take on projects that I can feel that way about myself. Not that I'm a fan, but I'm almost taking that approach, not just simply to please the record company. Where's the radio single and how fast can I get these guys through this thing under budget? I take the completely opposite approach to that sometimes."

The process of building trust from the outset is one mirrored by many producers, including Brad Wood. "First of all, you listen to their music, so that you know what you're talking about," he says. "I usually take pretty copious notes. When I put a CD in, I rarely listen to it while I'm driving or doing anything else; I pay attention and write stuff down. If it's something that I really like and I want to do, then I go back and listen to it a bunch more times and write more notes. I find out the tempo, the key signature, a major point that I like about [the song], and then write down any arrangement suggestions. Then, if you get to the point where you talk to [the band] on the phone or meet with them, you lay out what you think works and what doesn't. I think anybody is flattered when anybody, even a stranger, takes the time to pay attention to their labor of love and thinks highly of it, even if we've just started out. That's what I did when I started, and that's what I do now."

When he is working with an artist for the first time, Rick Rubin will spend extra time in rehearsals. "It usually takes a couple of days to see if we're in sync with each other," he says, "and if your ideas make the artist feel like something good is happening with their music that inspires them. That makes them feel better about the relationship."

Matt Wallace agrees. "Generally, [building trust] starts when you meet the band for the first time. You get a vibe for people. They ask you how you make records and what you do. That's when you start building the trust, the band starts getting a feel for you and if they like you that's the beginning of, 'Okay, I think we're gonna trust that this guy is not gonna screw us over and not let us put out a cheesy record.' But there's certainly a leap of faith on both sides where we say, 'Okay, we're going to commit and we are going to start making a record.' Even then, there's a building of deeper trust as time goes on where the band hopefully will start trusting and realizing that when they see me in action that I make choices—there's the cheese choice, and there's the other choice—that don't involve being cheesy. Then they're like, 'Oh, if we're going to let our guard down then he's gonna just all of a sudden make it cheese.' So, they see the way I do things and they can trust me. It takes awhile. Some artists, you get a week into it and you're ready to roll. Other artists, it takes a long time, and by the end of the record you're finally getting that trust and you want to kind of go back and redo things because they finally realize that you're not there to screw them. You're there to help them make the best record they possibly can."

There will come a point in nearly every session, Mark Howard says, where that trust will click after the artist has heard something you've done. "Then they will believe it or will say, 'Wow, I never expected this,' or 'This arrangement is something I would have never thought of.' From that point on, as soon as you get that, then you have their trust and they'll come to you and ask your advice," he says. "Until then they are always trying to drill in their two cents, or they're trying to tell you what they want. I always kind of go for what they want and ask them, but when they see that what you are doing is what they believe in, then you're home-free and things are a lot easier."

It is a tricky relationship to establish, Wallace adds, because some artists are reticent to turn over their music to someone who is not in the band. "Anyone who is not the singer/songwriter or in the actual band is an outsider," he explains. "Whether it's someone's Mom or it's the label, the producer, or the postman, they're all outsiders with opinions, and everyone has reasons for their opinions. Mine happen to be, hopefully, more professional, because I want them to make a great record—hopefully a record that might sell something, as well. I always ask the band, 'What do you want to do here? What's your plan? Do you want an artistic statement, or do you want to make a record that's going to try to sell at all costs? Do you want to find something that can encompass the two?' I'm very straightforward. I don't play any mind games and pit people against each other, which I've heard other producers do. I don't do any of that stuff. I don't have the patience or intellect to pull it off. I tell the band, 'I'll give you my opinion, and after you've heard it enough times and if you still want to go in another direction, I will join forces with you and we will go do it your way. It's your record. Your name's on the cover bigger than mine or the label's.'"

Listening to the artist, and realizing the producer's role is sometimes complementary rather than dominant, turns out to be a very big factor. Ed Cherney calls it "the ability to get along with the other kids" in the studio. Although the producer is the one at the helm of the recording sessions and is the hired sounding board, it is still the artist's album. That artist is going to have to spend the next eighteen months out on the road playing those songs. More than that, the album may or may not give that artist the opportunity to return to the studio to record a follow-up. "It's not a place you want to be acting out," Cherney adds. "They might let you get away with it once or twice, but a lot of times you have to supplant your ego. Most of the time you do. You are there to really be the conduit between the artist and their ideas, and for the technology, then you make their ideas and performances peak.

"My mantra was to be honest, open, and giving," he says. "It was always about the music and the artists, and rarely about me. I just tried to leave myself at home.

I could bring my unique perspective, which gets me in trouble more times than not," he admits with a laugh, "but it was just always about the artist and I was willing to do anything, jump through any hoop, to make the artist's performance better and to move their artistry forward. I think most of the time they got that."

It is during the building trust and intimacy stage that producers become counselors, parents, siblings, cheerleaders, or the like. There is more, though, explains Garth Richardson. "It's like I'm basically giving birth to their first or second or third child, and I have to be very sensitive to that," he says. "Every band is different—sometimes you have to be a father figure, sometimes you have to be a bro, and sometimes you just have to be the guy who is there. I tend to give everybody rope, because the last thing that I'd want is someone telling me what to do. So, I give everybody space, but I also know that whatever they do has to be right and it has to be the best."

When and where the initial meetings between producer and artist takes place varies. It could be at a studio. It could be over a cup of coffee. It could be at a home. Tony Brown prefers to have the initial meetings in the office for a specific reason. "I like sitting across from an artist that is not so social where it's easier to realize that we're talking about business," he says. "We're not going to be stiff, but this is business and this is their career and what we have to achieve here is as important to me as it is to you and I'm going to prove it to you. If you're talking about certain kinds of music or a certain writer you're turned on to, it's easy to turn around and play something [for them]. You can actually be more productive in an office setting than out in a restaurant. I like having a place where I can put my hand on something and say, 'I know a song that you should consider recording.' They say, 'Well, play it for me and I'll tell you if you're full of it or not.'"

Being that up-front can be a bit of a double-edged sword for a producer. Brown explains, "You may play it for them and they say, 'I totally understood where you were coming from on that, but I could never do that kind of song and here's why.' Jimmy Bowen used to tell me that the artist is right nine times out of ten. It's their music. Always have an open ear to the artist, and if you agree with them, then in your mind you can say, 'I just learned something about this artist that I didn't know five minutes ago.' They may have also picked up, 'I just learned something about this producer who didn't know his butt from a hole in the ground,'" he says with a laugh. "I think you learn something sitting across from each other in a situation in an office where you have access to music and they can play you something."

WORKING AS THE NEXT PRODUCER

Even with the boom of self-produced releases, the odds are high that any artist or band a producer hooks up with has already worked with another producer.

Clearly, this presents positive and negative implications. On the one hand, the band will already be familiar with the way a session runs and how the technology works. On the other hand, the band may have preconceived ideas about the sessions and be resistant to new methods.

The ante is upped when a producer steps into the studio with a band that is returning to follow up a successful release. Don Was has been in that situation a number of times and the one that stands out in his mind is the recording of the Barenaked Ladies 2000 album *Maroon,* which followed the band's commercial break-out, *Stunt,* (including the chart-topping song "One Week"). "You knew that Warner Bros. [the band's label] was going for it, and you could feel a certain marketing that carried over across the record," he says. "You can see [the marketing] gearing up while you're still making the record—you have MTV coming down to the studio, you've got the president of Warner Bros. coming to hear the record, and people are calling you at home about the record. Then you go to the Grammy Awards and the people from *Billboard* say, 'So, tell me about this record. What's it like?' I have never seen such a rush."

Was saw the other side of that situation when he worked with Hootie & the Blowfish, who had released a pair of multi-Platinum records earlier in their career. By the time the band and producer paired up, it seemed as if the band had dropped off their label's radar. "It was like Atlantic Records had cut the umbilical cord on Hootie & the Blowfish, and these guys were free-falling from space. There was no external heat on the record, and I just knew that it was doing badly. An infant child could have spearheaded the marketing better than Atlantic Records did. You almost have to go out of your way to do that bad of a job." While Was felt it then, he didn't bring it up to the band. "It was something that went unspoken because it would be too depressing; you don't want to start bringing that up when you're trying to make music. The benefit of it was that there was no one telling these guys what to do, and they were pretty free to make the record they wanted to make," he says. "I think they made a great record. I just think it wasn't their time."

Even more so than by label and industry pressure to follow-up successful releases, artists can be paralyzed by the stress of coming up with another hit song or set of songs. Three years after the Jimmy Eat World released *Bleed American,* (which was eponymously re-titled after the 9/11 tragedy), the quartet started to work with Mark Trombino on their next release. "That's an example of a band who had a big record, toured their asses off, and then it was time to make the next record," Trombino reports. "With the combination of the pressure of having to follow that up with the fact that all their lives have changed— they're all married, kids, big houses in Arizona—they haven't found the inspiration they need to write the next record. We went ahead and started making it anyway, and it just became obvious that they weren't ready to go."

Trombino was fired. "Granted this is my perspective, but they needed a fall guy. It obviously wasn't their fault, so they blamed me for them not having their shit together," he says. "So, they hired somebody else, and they're going to finish the record with somebody else. [Gil Norton was hired after the band took a break from the studio. That album, *Futures*, came out in 2004.] They blew $300,000 making a record. We were like eighty percent done, and they needed to write two more good songs to put on there. Maybe more, but that was the deal from the beginning. We knew that they didn't have a record, but we said, 'Let's get started and see what happens. Maybe you'll be inspired once we get in the studio and you'll write "The Middle" part two. It never happened. It was a struggle just to get lyrics. Jim [Adkins] just had nothing to say. He's a weird dude, and he's in a really weird place. I think it's the case of him waking up one day and realizing, 'Oh my God, what's happening?' He's married, he's got a kid, he's got this pressure to follow up *Bleed American,* and he just doesn't take pressure well."

That is part of the reason Dave Jerden prefers working with new bands who aren't under that kind of pressure. The one time, he says, that he broke that rule was when he produced *Ixnay on the Hombre* for The Offspring, who were coming off the multi-Platinum success of *Smash*. "The Offspring was the only big band that I've ever produced that were big already," he reports. "Breaking new stuff is like winning the lottery, but to me it's much more satisfying because it could be anything. With The Offspring, I had to make the transitional album with them from *Smash*. The first album that I did with them, *Ixnay on the Hombre,* still had one foot in *Smash* and the other foot in something that they were trying to do. When we did *Americana*, it was like we could do anything."

Howard Benson has been the producer for two bands who had major success with a previous release: P.O.D. and Hoobastank. "I'm pretty good with sophomore records. I've kind of learned to put myself in a position of having them stick to the sound that they've got, yet make it sound forward-moving and push it more," Benson explains. "Second albums, I think, have to be a little bit more focused; they have to be more directed. Now that this band has established who they are, you want to maximize that. I always say to the band that it's like the Nike swoosh. You spend your whole career trying to get that brand, and once you have it you have to maximize it, so when people say the names [of musical styles] they immediately think of certain bands." That became especially true and important as Benson went into work with Hoobastank, who had worked previously with Jim Wirt on their 2001 self-titled debut. "When people say Hoobastank, you want them to think of a particular sound, and that's what we were really trying to get on the record [*The Reason* 2003]. We wanted to stick with what they did really well, which is their incredible songwriting," he says. "They're incredible writers, and the singer [Doug Robb] is phenomenal."

As for P.O.D., Benson worked on the band's 1999 major-label introduction *The Fundamental Elements of Southtown*—which had a pair of charting songs in "Rock the Party (Off the Hook)" and "Southtown"—before he started in on the 2001 release, *Satellite*. "P.O.D. had a huge jump from the first record to the second record, but we knew walking in with *Satellite* that we were going to make a great record. We were doing rehearsals in San Diego in some dusty rehearsal room with no air conditioning, and you could just tell. We would walk to 7-11 and Sonny would sing parts to me on the way over there, like the opening line to "Youth of the Nation." I called my manager and told her that the song was going to be huge." Not only was "Youth of the Nation" a Number One hit, the band charted with the singles "Alive," "Boom," and "Satellite."

Hoobastank and P.O.D. are two strong examples of Benson's sophomore magic, yet not every second release has gone so well. He is quick to point to Crazy Town's 2002 *Darkhorse*, which he says was "a disaster. It was a combination of things. First of all, I don't think they were ever taken seriously by the fans. They were pop artists, really. We went in to do a modern-rock record and probably tried to make them into something they weren't by trying to make them more credible," he says. "When you really think about it, Crazy Town was never really going to be credible. Then with the artists themselves, there were two singers who couldn't decide who wanted to be the star. It was like constantly going back and forth between singers about who wanted to sing less. It was a tough project for me, it was very, very tough."

What helped an otherwise tough set of sessions, Benson adds, was a supportive Atlantic Records A&R rep. In the final analysis, he believes a good record was released. "We still had some great songs," he reports. "We had a great A&R staff, the label cared, and the management was great. It didn't sell. That's just how it happens sometimes. Maybe there really wasn't anything wrong with that album, maybe it just didn't happen. I feel that a lot of times those are the things that you just sort of chalk up to experience. I had the same thing with the Adema record [the 2003 *Unstable*]. Everything was fine with that project; it's just that when it came out, honestly, nobody cared. It didn't matter what we did.

"I always feel like you have to get through these layers of stuff first before the kids even hear it," Benson continues. "You've got to get past your marketing department, your promo department, the CEO of the company, and then you gotta get past the program directors at all the radio stations. There are a lot of people that have to feel good about a project for it to be successful; sometimes all it takes is one or two people not feeling it and you're in trouble. You can really take a band like a Hoobastank or P.O.D. to the next level, and some projects you just can't. It's just not going to happen no matter what you do."

FINDING ACTS TO GET THEM SIGNED

These days, more and more record producers are turning the tables on major labels by going out and finding artists before they can get snatched up. For some it is a matter of rejuvenating what they view as a stale art form; for others it is a way to recoup expenses and enjoy more of the profit from a band. "There's a whole new way of doing thing now where a lot of people like me are finding bands, finishing records, and selling them to people," Garth Richardson says. "I think that's going to be the way."

"There was a time you would get a call from an executive at a label, if you had history there or that you were friends with or you had some camaraderie with, and they would have an artist," Ed Cherney says. "They would say, 'Would you like to work with this artist?' Well, it happens the other way around now. "You find the artist, you develop the whole thing, you record and mix the music, and then you take it to the label. It's just entirely different. I don't think it's bad, but it's definitely a world of entrepreneurs, and we have to do that."

So, Cherney is out in clubs looking for bands again. "I've been lucky enough to have the kind of career that my phone would ring and it was people seeking me out," he says. "But it's a different world. You have to make your own success now. I go and talk to kids at schools and I really try to get that message across, that that's just the way it works. You're responsible for yourself, and you're responsible for finding the artists you want to work with."

According to David Lowery, this is not necessarily a new phenomenon in the music industry. "This is sort of what people did back in the Sixties," he says. "We find stuff, then we get the money for it, and then we sell it to the record labels. I think it's better for music in a way, because more records are being made with more of an artistic vision than a commercial one. But, I'm not sure that these are the records that are getting on the radio."

Richardson began taking more control in this way after a sour experience working on a Kittie album for Artemis Records. "It's getting harder and harder [to work with labels]," he says. "You do the math. The [Kittie] record cost them $40,000 to make. My record-company advance was, I think, $5,000. The record sold 800,000 copies, and they paid me $60,000 in royalties. I am owed another $320,000, which they know, and it's too bad. The record labels are basically hurting, because they never dealt with the whole downloading situation. They basically have to keep paying their big fat salaries and the people that make the records end up screwed."

Benson actually made the shift to dealing with bands directly years ago when he felt like he was being pigeonholed as a hair-metal producer and that genre was falling out of favor. "I was screwed, because I didn't have any projects and I remember thinking that I had just had my first kid and I had no work. I was sitting at home and I was like, 'Oh, my God, I'm extinct.' It was my first real crisis moment, and I went to South by Southwest with the intent of finding a band. I was going down there to find one band, get it signed, and produce it. That's exactly what I did. The first rehearsal hall I walked into, I found a band called Seed and thought they were amazing. I got Giant Records interested in them, and I got them signed and then got to produce them." The experience got him a job at Giant as an A&R rep. "It was amazing, because I remember thinking that you always had to find new talent," he says. "That was the only way to survive, and that was my first real dramatic lesson on survival. Seed didn't sell that many records, but it got me a gig at Giant, and I was able to get in there and I learned an amazing amount."

The first time Lou Giordano made the move to find a band was when he was still working at Fort Apache Studios in Boston. The engineers at the studio had struck a deal with MCA Records to deliver finished albums. As Giordano explains it, the other engineers—Paul Q. Kolderie, Sean Slade, and Tim O'Heir—had found bands early on, but it took him awhile to find his act, Mercy Rules. Putting the deal together was smart for MCA; after all, they had four great engineers looking for unsigned talent in what was then an independent music hotbed. It was an eye-opening experience for Giordano. "We never realized until we had that label together how different our musical tastes were, and that was when I found I really didn't fit in with those guys," he recalls. "That label was the beginning of the end of Fort Apache for me, because I was not seeing eye-to-eye with those guys about the music they liked."

However, years later, the idea behind that label inspired him to start looking for bands again. "I've just started, with Todd Parker, who is an engineer I work with, a little production company, and we're going to basically be our own A&R staff. We're going to go out, find bands, and sign them to the production company. Then, we'll record songs and try to get them deals, because we're constantly finding bands. Why give them to somebody else? You can sit around waiting for people to call, you can target bands that are ready to make records, and the next step is to go out and find bands yourself. There's a lot of ways to do it. I'm not going to give away every secret, but everybody knows it's just being in the right place at the right time, and hopefully you want to avoid people who are looking for two- or three-million-dollar deals because you can't necessarily give them that directly, obviously. Perhaps if we happen to come across a band that is striking the exact resonance with what's going on at the time, then maybe they'll get that kind of deal."

The first signing for Giordano's new company in 2004 was an Orange County, Calif., band by the name of The Tanks. Giordano has found bands to be receptive to the idea. "The thing that you can do for them, that they won't get with a big deal, is get their product into the market a lot quicker," he says. "We're not recording demos, we're recording masters."

FIGHTING THE GOOD FIGHT

Whether implied or stated, a producer walks into a session as the leader. An artist or label hires a producer to take charge, to guide the sessions, to assist with song arrangements, as well as vocal and musical performances. But producers know that there's a delicate balance between taking charge and taking over. Craig Street has said that collaboration is the key to a successful relationship, which includes opinions from artist, engineer, and producer. That type of communication fosters feelings of unity and accountability.

There are times when that communication comes easy and times where it creates conflict. Michael Rosen isn't so sure that conflict is bad in the confines in the studio, however, because it has the potential to bring band and producer together and may even push them to try things that might have stayed as ideas, to push beyond their comfort level. "I've always told my bands, 'Inside this arena, inside these doors, we can fight like bastards. If you think you're right, fight me. Prove it. Speakers don't lie; they are right there, make it happen. Play it. I'll be as honest as the day is long. If it sounds good coming out of those speakers then you're right. If the speakers say no, then you have to admit it.' I don't mind fighting with them. I don't mind going toe-to-toe. I've fought with a lot of bands about what I think is right—maybe to my detriment in certain cases, to where I've kind of lost people. But I'm going to keep fighting for it."

Even with that approach, Rosen allows that the band must buy in to whatever he is pushing. "When I'm done with this record, I'm going on to the next project, but that guy is going onstage to sell it. So, I don't try and push it," he says. "They have to feel good about it. It's their advertisement. If they get up onstage and think, 'Nah, that's just not us. I can't do that,' then it doesn't do them any good."

8 PUTTING THE TEAM TOGETHER

Except in the rarest of situations, making a record is not something that happens alone. In most cases, the collection of people in a studio during the recording process includes the artist or band, an engineer or two, assistant engineers, studio staff, and, of course, a producer. Along the way, additional musicians may join the fray for that special touch, or a Pro Tools specialist might be brought in. A different engineer might come on to mix the project, and then there are those A&R visits. Except for those intense sessions when a producer and singer hole up to capture vocal performances, most studio dates include a team that work toward the ultimate goal, a successful album.

For artist/producers, finding just the right people to join that team is crucial, whether they be fellow musicians or engineers. When Ben Harper put together the team for the *Diamonds on the Inside* sessions, he looked for one thing. "I insist that there be people that are like-minded and will listen to direction," he says. "If I feel that their heart's in the right place, that's where I start. To me, that's a part of production, as well, because working in those close quarters, I'm not trying to surround myself with people who make it harder."

Harper has long worked with bassist Juan Nelson, percussionist Leon Mobley, and drummer Oliver Charles, who made up Harper's original Innocent Criminals back-up band (and returned after drummer Dean Butterworth and percussionist David Leach departed). He brought in guitarist Marc Ford and keyboardist Greg Kurstin to play on the *Diamonds* release. Ford and Kurstin were much more than session players on the album. "They are friends of mine who I have known for over a decade," he says. "So, all these guys I know and they know me, they know my music and I theirs." What about bringing in session players? "That would be easier, but then you get a session-player-sounding album," he explains. "If there is one thing I can say, none of my albums are that."

Harper's approach is consistent, not just in terms of the musicians he hires, but also with technical personnel, such as engineer, Todd Burke. Burke worked on Harper's *Fight For Your Mind* and *Will to Live*. Their history was important as Harper stepped up to produce his own album. "It is sonically crucial and personally crucial, no question," he says. "There is gonna be friction, but it's gotta be the kind of friction where you say, 'I know and respect this individual, and I respect where he's coming from, and he respects where I'm coming from, and there will be friction until we rub it through.' There are challenges, but they are not ego challenges, and they're challenges that can and will get worked out for the better of the album," he says. "It's not that somebody is trying to get their point across so they can have a stamp on the record; it's because they want you to be the best at what you are doing."

Joe Henry has that exact relationship with engineer S. "Husky" Hoskulds and musicians Jay Bellerose, Chris Bruce, David Palmer, and Jennifer Condos. Finding musicians that fit, personality-wise, is crucial to Henry. "The world is full of really talented people who are creeps, and I don't have anything to do with them anymore. For years I did that thing where you work with somebody and you go, 'Well, he's an asshole but he's an amazing guitar player.' You know, life's too short," he says. "There are unbelievably wonderfully talented people who are responsible, fantastic people to be around. I do think making records is a really exciting and really fun process, and when people are enjoying themselves they're a lot more creative; it's just a fact. I look at people who are going to embrace the process in the same way. People that I'm really going to enjoy having a meal and a bottle of wine with at eight o'clock when we order food, because that's a big part of the dynamics. You can have one person there who is the pebble in the shoe, and it's like someone just put a hole in one side of the balloon and lets the air out of the whole thing. So, I really think about people whom I know are going to approach the process really open-heartedly, and who really enjoy the process, because they're going to be creative. They're going to listen, you know? You know, they're not going to be offended if you say, 'Hey, that's beautiful but this needs to go somewhere else altogether.'"

The Henry-Hoskulds team is crucial to the artist/producer: "He's as important as any musician in the room," Henry says. "Husky is not for everybody, not for every occasion. Aimee Mann doesn't want her shit fucked up that way, but I've always encouraged him to bring that to the table because it influences how people hear and think."

As an example, Henry points to the song "Richard Pryor Addresses a Tearful Nation" on his 2001 *Scar* release, where the entire team worked together to get the right feel for the song. "I was really kind of afraid of [that song], because I knew that it was going to be kind of like my statement of purpose in a way, because it's how I came to understand what the record was supposed to be," he recalls. "I wanted it to be orchestrated. I knew that Ornette Coleman was going to play on it. But, I didn't know how we were going to get there, because it's written kind of like a classic blues, but it can't be played like a blues number. There's nothing worse than hearing a rock band try to play the blues. Fortunately, I had an amazing group of people in the room. I had two of the greatest drummers alive right now, I think, Brian Blade and Abe Laboriel, Jr., and Marc Ribot, who is one of only two guitar players that I really care about. I mean, I could live my whole life without hearing a guitar solo, but Mark is somebody who is just endlessly interesting as a musician. So, we ran through it maybe once, and came and had a listen. As soon as Brian Blade heard the way that Husky was treating the kick drum, the kind of prominence it had, he was like, 'Oh, I hear what you're doing with that,' and he started playing differently. It was an event, it was a moment, and everybody responded to it."

When Craig Street went in to work with Chris Whitley on the 2000 release *Perfect Day*, both had a firm idea of what they wanted from the recording and from engineer Danny Koppelson. "Chris and I decided we were going to do a disc of covers, [but] we had no budget, so we're going to do the thing in two days and were doing straight to two-track, so it's basically live. So, what I wanted to see was basically how far could we push a room with three guys in it and the microphones and the tape. So I told the engineer, 'No reverb, can't use any reverb at all. No plates, no mechanical reverb or delay, no digital reverb or delay. Nothing. You can't use it. Everything that you do, you have to do it [with a] microphone.' So, we got so that there were mics all over the room. On one song, the mics for the drums might be these mics that were like thirty feet away, and so the drums sound like you just did a ton of processing to them. It sounded like we totally destroyed them. Then there was another mic that was right up against the drum. The same thing with Chris; sometimes we'd use a vocal bleed from something way back in the room. Sonically, I just think it's an amazing record, because it sounds like all this stuff was done and nothing was done, it's three guys in a room with some microphones going straight to two tracks."

From the beginning, Street, Whitley, and Koppelson knew what had to happen for this record, partly because of the budget. "Me and Chris knew it was going to be straight to two-track, because we didn't have the budget to afford mixing," Street recalls. "So, we spent our extra budget on analog tape. We said, 'Okay, instead of buying a two-dollar DAT or a one-dollar CD-R, we'll spend like fifty dollars on a reel of tape, and that's going to be our extra expenditure and I'll talk with the engineer and tell him specifically what I want. Then it was playing around with certain things, like an artist will say, 'This is what I'd like it to sound like,' and then I'll translate that through myself to an engineer.

"That's why all of those things are critical. It's critical that I understand in the work process what an artist means when they say something. If they say warm, I want to know what they mean by warm and I have a really short time to learn that. By warm, do you mean warm like sitting out in the desert at Palm Springs, or do you mean warm like sitting next to a fire in the middle of winter in upstate New York, or do you mean warm like being next to somebody in bed? What do you mean by warm? Because they are all different; they are all warm, but they're all completely different things. So, a producer needs to understand that really rapidly if they're working the way I am.

"In the best of all cases in the world that I inhabit, it's completely collaborative," Street continues. "It's important that the artists have an opinion. It's important the producer has an opinion. It's important that the engineer and the musicians have opinions. I don't hire musicians that come in and are like session guys. They don't come in and look for the sheet of paper. I mean, string players do because they're playing an arrangement, but even string players that I hire have opinions. I hire string players that I work with all the time; they know what I like, and they are not afraid jump and say, 'You know Craig, if I bowed my viola this way, I think it would sound much better with the track,' and they're right. I don't play viola, they do, and so as a producer, I trust that.

"When I go to the engineer and say, 'This is what I want it to sound like,' the engineers that I work with know me. So, they know, 'Oh, okay, he's probably talking about this.' I'll say, 'I want the sound of this thing,' and they'll say, 'Well, we can't really use that here, but we could do this.' So, it's always collaborative like that," he continues. "The artist is the same thing and it has to be. I think it has to be a free environment. It has to be an environment where everybody feels like they can say something. The bottom of it all is that the artist is the client, so I think it's completely okay that you go through a process and at the end of it all the client says, 'You know what? I was wrong, this isn't what I want to do.' So, sometimes you go back in and you work on it another way, and sometimes you pass it off to somebody else and they do it and it's fine like that, because creativity is about exploration. Fun is about exploration."

That exploration is possible without a level of comfort, but it is definitely helpful to have an engineer or two who can use technology to translate ideas into reality. Dave Jerden regularly works with two engineers, Elan Trujillo and Annette Cisneros. "The three of us make records together," Jerden says. "I've been with Annette since [Jane's Addiction's] *Nothing's Shocking*, and she's really quiet, really thorough, and has great attention to detail. We've been working together for so long that we don't even need to talk a lot of times. How it works is she sets up the mics and stuff, and I do the fine-tuning on the sound always. I'm still the engineer in the sense that I work with her, but on her own she's a great engineer and she's a whiz at Pro Tools."

There are a few producers who like to twist a knob now and then, but having a dedicated engineer can be more ideal. "If I'm tracking with a band, I prefer to have an engineer that I really dig for a number of reasons," says John Porter. "One is that I don't have to worry about watching levels. Two, it's good to have somebody you've got a rapport with, a pal to work with because it makes things go better. I do enjoy doing it, but when I'm there with musicians I'm more into the music than I am into technology."

During his early career, his mentor, producer Jimmy Bowen, was pushing Tony Brown into the engineer's chair. "That's the one area where we had a parting of the ways," Brown recalls. "I said, 'I don't like twisting knobs.' I prefer surrounding myself with engineers who are on the cutting edge, and I've always done that. I've always tracked down engineers in town who were on the cutting edge like Justin Niebank, Chuck Ainlay, and Steve Martin. They're always the ones that say, 'Hey, [George] Massenburg has just created this new compressor, and I want to try it out.' I always say, 'Absolutely. If you can work it, I want to hear it.' I just love being around an engineer who loves trying new things. I really want to spend my time concentrating on the performance."

Brown will go so far as to let the engineers pick the formats—digital or analog—as long as they can make it work. "We just did this album with The Notorious Cherry Bombs, Rodney Crowell, Vince Gill, and myself. We got the whole band together, and Rodney wanted to cut it on analog and not Pro Tools. I didn't have a problem with that. There have been a couple of times when we were doing one more take and the second engineer didn't pay enough attention, and before we finished the track, the analog tape ran out. I said, 'Well, that's the down side to analog.'"

That doesn't stop him from letting engineers pick the gear, though. "I let my engineers deal with technology. Jimmy Bowen used to drive me crazy, and I found that most engineers hated when he walked in the studio, because he would start twisting the knobs," Brown says with a laugh. "They would say, 'He likes the delay set on a certain setting, and when he sees where I've got it set he won't even listen.' They said to me, 'That's why we love you, because you at least listen.' I don't know how to tell them technically what I want; I can just refer to a record and go, 'You know, I really want to delay the sound like this particular record.' I just play something for them, and I find a lot of producers do that. They always have a stash of CDs where they refer to a Bonnie Raitt, Wilson Pickett, or Beatles record. I find that works just fine for me."

When Ben Harper went in to work on the Blind Boys of Alabama sessions, he and engineer Jimmy Hoyson had a conversation about the sound the producer was hoping to find. "I let engineers do their job," he says. "When I came in, I said to Jimmy, 'Think Muscle Shoals and Stax' before any sounds were down. I was looking for open-aired drums with the option for close miking."

John Porter adds he will be more or less specific and direct with his suggestions based on what type of rapport he has already developed with an engineer. "If it's somebody that we've had a working relationship for quite a long time, then it goes without saying almost," Porter says. "I don't like to cramp people's style. So, if somebody says that this guy's good, then it doesn't matter whether it's a musician or whether it's an engineer or tape-op or whatever it is, I like them to be able to do what they can do. I don't want to impose on them too much. Same with me. If somebody has me, trust me that I'll do my best, but don't try and trip me up before I'm done."

That said, there are certain technical things that Porter likes to have during a recording session. "If we're in a nice room and we're tracking a band, I like to put the drums on a riser if there is one," he says. "I like to know how the drums sound with basically a mic on the kick [drum] and an overhead. I like a pair of old AKG C-12s. I like to put a [Neumann] FET 47 about three feet in front of the kick drum. Very simple. Beyond that, there's not a lot." Beyond microphone choices, Porter likes things to move quickly. "I don't like to see people sitting around. I like to get recording pretty quick. I think it's rotten for a band [to wait]. You don't want them to get bored; they want to be playing. That's what they're there for," he says. "So, let them play."

BRINGING IN SESSION PLAYERS

Session musicians can make a tremendous impact on the mood of the recording dates, almost as much as the producer and engineer team who are capturing the performances. There are three main reasons for bringing session players in: A producer is building a band around a singer/songwriter, a band wants other/additional instrumentation on one or more cuts on their album, or a record company has asked to replace a band member during the recording of an album.

There are legions of stories where a drummer has been replaced on one song or an entire album, including Sylvia Massy Shivy's story of replacing the Acroma drummer with session player Josh Freese. There's also the case of the Counting Crows' drummer Steve Bowman being replaced by session drummer Denny Fongheiser during recording of the hit song "Mr. Jones." In these types of situations, opinions may be divided. Don Gehman points out, "I find that if you're gonna make a band sound like a band, you have to let the people in the band play. I generally don't pick bands that are terrible musicians; I usually pick acts that can pull off at least the songs they've written. Past that, you're looking for some kind of character that makes them unique, and that doesn't mean bringing in session guys to fix things. Usually, there's a way to figure it out."

Dave Jerden has seen the difference between band and session drummers. "I'd much rather work with a band drummer that can't play as well as a session player, because session players tend to want to just keep good time, whereas band drummers have parts," he says. "They don't think in terms of the overall thing, they think in terms of that part in a song. So I'd rather work with a band drummer because they've spent a lot of time working those parts out, and ultimately my goal is when somebody hears a band that I've done on the radio, they can say, 'Ah, that's MxPx' or 'That's Alice in Chains.' How you build in those identifiers is by those parts that the band worked out for themselves that are germane for that band and song and that band and song only. When I was working on the first Alice in Chains record, the drummer Sean [Kinney] broke his arm before I went up there to start pre-production. We tried using the drummer from Pearl Jam, and he had a totally different feeling. He's a good drummer, but it just didn't sound like Alice in Chains to me, and the only person that could play Alice in Chains correctly was Sean. Now I've worked with a lot better drummers than Sean, but Sean is the best at Alice in Chains."

On the flip side of that, Tony Brown reports, "Jimmy Bowen always told me that if I was cutting a record and I thought I needed Dean Parks to be the guitar player on that record—in my mind, as a producer, that he would be key to achieving the end result [to get him]. Like MasterCard says, "It's priceless. Don't even think twice about it." In Brown's experience, it is crucial for producers to expand their possibilities while working towards what is best for the artist. "The worst thing that you can do is keep in a tiny bubble," he says. "If you never get an opportunity to meet some great musician because you never had the nerve to hire them, because you thought that the record label or the artist would think that you were trying just to be cool for cool's sake, then that's your fault. If you thought that bringing David Lindley in to play slide on this song would have been the ticket and you didn't do it? Your fault. You learn so much being around great talent, and if you expand your relationships with people that know more than you know, then you will draw from them."

What is important for producers like Brown and Jerden is to create something memorable. Brown does it by bringing in unique musicians who will add just the right amount of spice to a track. Jerden, on the other hand, tries to keep bands intact so that they will retain their unique flavor. Both would probably agree, however, that bringing in the same session player over and over again breeds consistency, in a bad way. "It just makes everything sound the same," Jerden says. "I like the Strokes because the Strokes are doing exactly what they do, as opposed to a lot of bands that are out there that I can't tell apart."

Often, a band's unique sound and how they got there can't be heard on demos. Don Was says he found that out when he was called by Hootie & the Blowfish to work on their 2003 eponymous release. "I think they are a great band. I didn't necessarily know it from their records," he says. "Their records were obviously well made and very popular, but they labored methodically over those records and they were a little too correct for me personally. I thought of them as being precise. They asked me to come in and listen to some new songs.

Thank God, they didn't play any demos, but they played the songs live for me. I had never been to see them live, and I didn't understand that even though none of them would end up playing in the youth orchestra, the whole is greater than the sum of the parts, as it is in all great bands. Somehow, you get these disparate characters that meld into this one thing. That is what the band is, and that's why they have an incredible feeling, interaction and [there is a] great conversation going on among all the players. You could have gotten some guys who might have played more precisely, but at the expense of destroying the feel, which you know is what made the band. So, I would rather have the guitar player in any band sit there and figure out the mandolin part than call a session guy who might be a virtuoso but who just becomes a whole different story than the person in the band. You'd want to keep that balance and personality intact, or if you don't like it, don't work with the band."

Brad Wood concurs, saying that most of the time it is a band's chemistry that gets him interested in working with them in the first place. "The chemistry and the pieces of a puzzle that fit, no matter how misshapen the pieces are—it's still the puzzle that works," he says. "I have the tendency to be a preservationist of what the chemistry is, so I never hire session players ever to replace someone who's in the band. I will hire a pedal steel player or a string section, but I won't bring in a hired gun. I never have, not once, and I'm really proud of that. It's helped me to get work, because drummers, who are usually the guys on the hottest seat of all when it comes to that kind of stuff, if they're paying any attention to the credits on the record that I worked on, they'll notice that there's no Hollywood drummer there. I don't hire drummers. I just flat-out refuse, because if you're good enough to be on a good independent or a good major, there's something there. It's the engineer's responsibility to use his or her skills to make the band sound as good as possible, not to cheat necessarily, but to take the time it might take to make sure that those drums sound as good as they need to be. Also, as a producer, to not get so hung up on the perfection aspect of it."

Wood takes out some insurance on avoiding the perfection trap by going back and listening to records that have been influential to him, such as the Clash, The Beatles, and the Rolling Stones. "I like to be reminded that Topper [Headon of the Clash] had his drums all over the place and he was sloppy, but he's one of the best drummers who's ever picked up the sticks. Keith Moon? All over the map. Did it make a difference to the millions and millions of people who love those records? No. So, let's not assume that because the drummer drops a beat every now and again that you can't use Pro Tools to fix it or, back before then, tape. I've done tens of thousands of edits, and even then I've left sloppy stuff in because it felt right," he admits. "I don't care if some guy doesn't get it, some *Modern Drummer* dude says, 'Hey, that guy's no good, because there's a dropped beat.' Well, Charlie Watts drops beats all the time, and I'm on his side, Ringo's side. As a producer, you've got to remind yourself of that, if that's the kind of music you like. I have a tendency to forget and get perfectionist, because you can do that with Pro Tools. It's really easy to, but I don't want to make a Boston record. I love those records, but I don't want to make those records, because that's no fun."

Yet there are the times when a player must be brought in, and experienced producers have built-in resources to find those people—it might be through other bands they've worked with; a suggestion from an A&R rep; a careful look at credits from other releases; or it might even be a player's manager who will call and make the musician available for a session. These players will often be brought in for recording dates where a singer/songwriter is making an album, and producers view their responsibility as "casting" a session.

"The thing I learned from Don [Was] and Quincy [Jones] is really how to cast some musicians around an artist," Ed Cherney says. "It's like casting a movie, and that was my favorite part. If we wanted these kinds of textures and this kind of feel, then I knew all these great musicians and I would put different bands together to place around the artist. Then we'd get into the studio and create these sound montages and the arrangements around a great song."

Mark Howard worked that way when the Vic Chesnutt *Silver Lake* sessions began. Chesnutt's touring band couldn't make it into the studio for a variety of reasons, and the producer had to find players to fill in. That, in itself, was a challenge—one that actually changed the dynamics of the sessions for the better. "At the last minute, I had to find all hired help and he wasn't into that, so that was a struggle right from the beginning," Howard recalls. "But I got a bunch of guys that he really loved, so he fell into it and had an amazing time. It was a fun record for him to make, and we surrounded him with a lot of really great players. We had Doug Pettibone playing guitar, and it pushed Vic to play these amazing solos. He said, 'I just had to take the solo, it was right there.' It was amazing and Doug could have taken it and it would have been good, but Vic played it great. Then on the song "Sultan, So Mighty," we had these three black singers that were amazing, and they pushed Vic to sing like this bird and the soul came out of him. He said, 'I didn't know I could do that.' By surrounding yourself with great people, it pushes you to the next level and you can bring things out of you that maybe you just didn't think that you had."

That is exactly how Joe Henry approaches building bands for his sessions, whether it is for his own releases or when he is producing one for another artist, such as Solomon Burke. "Sometimes it's just a matter of putting the right people in the room and they start hearing each other, and it's amazing how quickly it becomes something musical," Henry says. "Things happen as you're discovering." Where that came crystal-clear for Henry was while the band was recording the song "Flesh and Blood" for Burke's *Don't Give Up on Me*. The demo the band and

Burke had to work from was a piano and vocal recording and, according to Henry, the only discussion that went on before they hit the 'record' button was Burke asking bassist David Piltch to switch to an electric bass from an upright. On the first take, the song came together. "We just started it digging in, and it happened exactly as you hear it," Henry reports. "There's this, to me, unbelievably beautiful moment of decay at the end of the bridge that nobody knew was going to happen. Solomon went up like an octave and just stayed there, and everybody just kind of stopped playing. Nobody had talked about that happening or how to climb back in once that happened. But I heard it and it's like something just kind of climbed back up out of the ashes. On the kick drum, Jay [Bellerose, the drummer] just brought it back up. It was heart-stopping, and everybody responded to it. You don't get that by talking about it, and you don't get it by playing it again. We played it again, and everybody was ready for the breakdown and to come back, but it was nowhere nearly as exciting or as musical."

The Henry anecdote goes directly to the point: A producer's highest goal when hiring a band is finding the right players who will bring in even more than musical talent. Matt Wallace says it is about knowing the player's temperament and abilities. "Sometimes you just go with your instincts," he says. "I think you make educated guesses. The record where I really had to utilize that was a Khaleel record I did [*People Watching*, 1998]. I had multiple drummers, bass players, and different people on that record. That was just knowing that the different flavors for each song had to have a specific kind of guy."

THE ENGINEER'S PERSPECTIVE

Many of today's producers started their careers as engineers. That experience has given those producers a unique perspective on how to work with an engineer to get the best results during a session. The key to a successful relationship seems to be trusting the engineer, allowing him or her to take some risks, and communicating clearly about the requirements of the session.

As an engineer, Ross Hogarth has worked with a number of producers who have unique approaches to recording, and each taught him valuable lessons that he carries into his production work. He makes particular mention of Don Gehman and Pat Leonard. "I'm not downsizing my participation as a producer, but I think it made me a better producer because I have worked with other producers and I see what works and what doesn't work. Don was an engineer himself, and I learned quite a bit of engineering from him about things that I thought he was good at," Hogarth says. "On the things that we did, we would do a lot of the work together. Don I think appreciated my "whatever works" attitude, because I would push him to do stuff that he maybe wouldn't have done and tried stuff that he wouldn't have tried.

"It was the same thing with Pat, but different. Pat's a musician, Pat's a songwriter, and Pat is a great technical talent as far as wanting to hear stuff and be willing to experiment, but he would totally give me my space. He would tell me what he kind of wanted in a sense of like a big drum sound or a really small drum sound. Or he'd want the kick drum to be fat, and there are different ways you can make a sound. If you're always going to make something sound the same way, it's going to be a pretty stale, plain production, I think. So, he was really good at communicating to me, and I was good at deciphering what he was going to want and how to get it, and making his life really easy in that respect and really supporting him as a musician and a keyboard player."

During Ed Cherney's engineering career, he worked alongside such producers as Quincy Jones and Russ Titelman. For a fifteen-year stretch, Cherney was Don Was' first-call engineer. So, Cherney knows what makes producers different. "I think the level of how neurotic they are," he says with a laugh. "Some really know what they want and really know what it takes. Many times when you're doing this you are stumbling around in the dark, and hopefully you trip on something that's good and you recognize it's good. Sometimes that's fine."

Then there is a producer like Jones who comes in with very specific ideas. "Quincy comes in with charts; he has the thing written out and how it should be played. Other times you're improvising, so you don't know. You have an idea with a producer if they want it dry or wet, but you have to think and feel on your feet," Cherney says. "You try to make it so you can communicate. Hopefully, they can communicate with you with the fewest number of words, you're in sync, and you get the performances that you need."

Cherney also acknowledges that things have changed over the past decade or so when it comes to the number of producers and engineers working on a project. "If you look at an album, there are five or six different production teams," he says. "If you look at the engineering credits, there are a minimum of four, five, six engineers, and there are Pro Tools engineers. It's rare that you're seeing one engineer mixing the whole album, or recording and mixing an album. I was lucky enough to come up in a time with Bonnie Raitt or Eric Clapton, when you basically did the whole thing. You recorded every note of music, you did every edit, you did everything, and then you mixed it. Well, it doesn't happen like that anymore. So, the way you communicate, that dynamic, is a lot different from what it traditionally was."

One thing that has not changed over the years is the fact that artists and engineers—like grandchildren and grandparents—have a common enemy, the producer. When Mark Howard was working on the Grammy Award-winning Bob Dylan release *Time Out of Mind* with producer Daniel Lanois, this type of united front developed, although it came on gradually. "When you make a record with somebody, there's always the first period of not being sure about the trust and whether you trust this person, and as an artist they have to trust your opinion on things. Once you establish that trust, man, you can go all the way, but if you don't establish that trust, it's a very difficult road making the record because you are up against a lot of wall along the way," Howard says. "On Bob Dylan's *Time Out of Mind*, we'd do like three takes of [a song] and Bob would come in the control room and say, 'What take do you think it is?' I'd say, 'I think it's take two.' He'd listen to all three and go, 'How'd you know? You were right.' I just went by what I felt, really, because they were all great takes. That happened like six times and he established the trust in me, so I became his guy. He would trust me more than he would trust Dan, and it became where he would come to me first, he wouldn't go to Dan. He'd only trust me with his vocals."

The relationship peaked when the team started to record the song "Not Dark Yet" and Dylan decided he wanted to change a couple of lines. "They were my favorite lines and I said, 'Hey, Bob, this is my favorite line in the song. I'll put [your new vocal] on another track, but for me to lose that, that breaks the chain.' He said, 'Oh, yeah? Okay, let's leave it.' He trusted me, but if Dan said he liked that line, he would have gotten rid of it right away. Dan would come over and poke his head over the console and say, 'I really love that.' The first thing Bob would say was, 'Get rid of it.' Bob and Dan have a funny working relationship," Howard says. "Not that it's a competition, but something happened during the recording where Dan was going for something and Bob really thought we'd already gotten it. Dan was striving to go the extra mile, and it pissed Bob off or he just started acting like he didn't care. He cared, but he just didn't want to go through it all again."

Finding himself in the middle of the Dylan-Lanois struggle was a tight-rope walk for Howard. "It was exciting and uncomfortable at the same time," he says. "I had Dan on the one hand telling me what to tell Bob and I got Bob talking to me directly, and it's like having to make decisions without pissing off either party. The respect from Bob was enough to keep me going and give me the energy to make my stance. I think it helped me a lot, but I think Dan was frustrated because of it."

PRODUCERS WHO ENGINEER THEIR OWN SESSIONS

Although there is a plethora of engineering talent available these days, a number of producers prefer to handle all of the technical duties when they are recording a band. Their reasons may run the gamut from saving money (or earning more money themselves), to simplifying the process by removing a layer of communication, to ensuring that the sound will represent exactly what they want. The down side to this practice, much like when artists produce their own albums, is that the producer may lose perspective. What these self-contained set-ups typically have going for them is an artist who is not afraid to say something if the session is not gelling.

Over the course of his career, Ross Hogarth has bounced between engineering, producing, and mixing. In 2004 he produced albums for Melissa Etheridge and Coal Chamber, engineered and mixed John Fogerty's *Déjà vu (All Over Again)*, and mixed a solo album from Rob Dickenson, formerly of Catherine Wheel. "If you ask me what I am, I am an engineer," Hogarth says. "I'm a musician, and I produce because producing is a natural progression in the evolution of someone who's creative. But as a profession I chose engineering over being a musician at the time when there was a fork in the road where I had to focus on something that might make me more of a living without the hassles of being a musician."

Trading in his budding musical career (he still plays guitar and keyboards) was not a sacrifice of creative opportunities, though. "I believe as an engineer the creative sense is the communication between someone who wants to get their ideas across musically," he says. "As an engineer I have to translate that into the sonic picture and I have to translate that into a technical place. Someone will say, 'I want this to have a certain mood or I want to have this song feel a certain a way.' Well, what makes it feel that way is how it sounds. Choices of sounds, choices of balances, is it dry, is it wet, is it dense, is it sparse? I think a lot of times engineers like myself who are creative, don't get credit for a lot of stuff we do." With that in mind, Hogarth moved into the production chair for a simple reason. "Why would I want to explain that to someone when I already know what it should sound like? So, now I'm producing. Now I'm the guy that is not only in charge of the sound, but is in charge of the whole overall vision. So, why should I even bother having to explain that to someone else when I'm the guy that can do it best for myself?"

This dual experience has enabled Hogarth to avoid some fairly typical shortfalls that producers encounter: Lack of technical experience or musical vocabulary, or the inability to communicate what's needed technically. For Dave Fridmann an engineering background gives him the freedom to move quickly with a band like The Flaming Lips, especially when the band will try just about anything to work out of a position where they're stuck. "Sometimes you just have to throw an oblique strategy at it and move forward. We do that often," he says. "We'll say, 'Here's the worst idea I can think of,' and we'll just start throwing them out there and keep recording. 'You've got a bad idea? I don't care, let's record it. Let's not sit here and think about it; let's actually make music and see what happens.' If you think about it, you can eliminate every possibility, and in the meantime, nothing gets on tape. If you try some stuff it may inspire you to do something else at least that you will keep."

That mentality helped while the band was recording the song, "The Spark That Bled" on the 1999 release *The Soft Bulletin*. "We were standing around scratching our heads for an hour or two, and then Wayne [Coyne, the band's singer] got mad and said, 'This is bullshit.' Nobody had a drum idea for the song, so he just went in there and said, 'Fuck you guys, I'm playin' drums.' He just started playing and the drums are retarded. He actually just played kick drum. The whole beginning of the song is nothing but kick drum and then there are stick clicks. That's just Wayne playing the drums and I was laughing my head off, but those are the drums we kept and we moved forward. You can always get stuck, you can always get arty, you can always get sent back into the studio by an A&R person or something like that. But, you know, it's just really important from a production standpoint to just always put the best face on it and move forward. Don't let anything stop you from going forward. Even if you hate the idea, even if you think it's stupid. At least half the time that I thought, 'This is the stupidest idea I've ever heard,' it ends up being what we do and liking it and being glad we did it. You have to have faith in the people you're working with that somebody's going to come up with something."

The band, likewise, has to have faith that the engineer/producer has the studio set up and ready for recording anything that happens. That is precisely why Fridmann believes it is important to have those skills. "It's vital, and that's why it's nice that I do both parts," he reports. "It makes it a lot easier. You have to make sure that everybody on your team is doing the same thing. You have to be willing to take the best idea, even if it wasn't yours, even if it's the opposite, even if you just spent the past two hours arguing against it. If it turns out good, you gotta take it and go with it, and admit that it's good. You [also] have to have an engineer or be an engineer that if someone says, 'Oh, you know that song on the Elton John record? You know the one? Let's throw that sound in there…' You have got to be able to have those tools. So, yeah, the engineering part of it is vital."

At the same time, Fridmann knows that Pro Tools skills are helpful. "There are things you can do in Pro Tools that no amount of analog goofing around is going to do, but from an engineering standpoint it's more about knowing that if you need that snare sound what kind of snare you need, what kind of microphone, what kind of room, and what kind of compressor. You need to have those engineering skills at your disposal instantly," he says.

When Mark Trombino is working with a band in the studio, he handles everything himself, from engineering to editing to mixing. "It's cheaper," he explains with a shrug. "I'm pretty particular about some things, especially when it comes to computer stuff. I'm very particular with the way files are named and the way that the tracks are laid out. I come from a computer background, and there's a way that I like to work. I fantasize about hooking up with some kid that is going to share a similar taste in music and sound and stuff like that and then kind of like grow a relationship together. I found this assistant over at Ocean Way that I've been working with that I think is that guy. Eventually, I'm hoping that he can engineer and I can kind of sit back, but it's harder to afford that extra person."

By engineering sessions, Brett Gurewitz feels like he brings something to a session other than his music talents. "I wouldn't know how to produce without engineering. It's one of those things that I do," he says. "It's one of those things that I bring to the table. I don't mean to diminish producers who do not engineer, because many of them have a profound impact on records, and groups find them instrumental."

THE BALANCING ACT

Many engineer/producers may find themselves in difficulty if their role in the project is not well defined from the outset. One such individual lost a long-standing relationship with a band because he asked to share production credit on an album even though he performed more than just engineering duties. The band balked, taking the production credit, and then didn't work with him again. Another engineer/producer interviewed for this book walked a fine line during a session because of the artist's temperament and lack of willingness to listen to another viewpoint.

It takes clear communication before a session even begins to avoid those problems. When Mark Howard first talked to Tom Waits about working on the *Real Gone* release, the guidelines were clear. "Tom has produced all of his own records, so he called and asked if I'd be interested in helping with his record," Howard recalls. "He knows I'm a producer, and he asked if there was any way if I could just help him on the engineering side. I said,' Yeah, it would be my pleasure.' As it went along, because I'm a producer and I did have comments early on, I made them. [But] we didn't have a relationship established yet. I didn't think it was a problem, but he called me up one day and said, 'I'm feeling like you're a pharmacist and I'm a patient and you're trying to make me take Xanax and you know I maybe I should be on Percodan. Maybe you're right, I should be on that but maybe I need to take the Percodan to find out that I need the Xanax, so I really need to kind of do the Percodan.' I took that as an okay, shut up and sit down." (By the way, Howard does a spot-on Waits impression while he tells that story.)

Once that was set down, Howard understood a little better how to work with Waits. That doesn't mean it was easy, though. "He's got all of these terms," he says. "He's not a technical person, so he would say things like, 'The drums are a little beige. Can you put a little hair on them?' I was like, 'Okay, that means I've got to brighten them up or bring them out in the mix more.' So, he's full of these great terms and he knows how to get things out of you. Tom's kind of an eccentric person and when he's searching for something he doesn't know he's looking for, he just keeps looking and looking." That way of working was exhilarating for Howard, who prides himself as an extreme person who likes to find new, undiscovered sounds. "I was quite mild compared to where he was going," he says. "It was a challenge and it was exciting, too, because he was pushing me to do things, where I thought I'd already pushed them and he pushed me over the edge."

There did come a point during the *Real Gone* sessions when Howard had to take the reins. "I had to take charge a couple of times, because after four or five takes of a song, Tom didn't know, and every day we went in and operated on these things," Howard recalls. "I said to him, 'Look, you need to take time and listen. We've been working for a month-and-a-half and you haven't sat down to listen to these. You need to do your homework. You need to figure out what you want to do. That's a production thing, where there are decisions that you need to make. You're the artist, and it has to come from you.' As the producer he should have made his arrangements the way he wanted them, but as you get fried in the studio you start to lose your vision. At the end of the sessions I stepped out of the engineering chair into the production chair, helping him with ideas although he asked me earlier not do it." The key, Howard adds, was that there was a relationship established early on and the trust grew throughout the sessions.

Dave Jerden has called the balancing act between engineering and producing a left-brain/right-brain issue. He says it boils down to the difference between being creative and being technical. "It is really hard, because when you're an engineer you're just trying to please yourself or the producer, but when you're a producer you're trying to make something that's going to sell, which is a whole other thing," he says. "Plus when you're an engineer you're working for a producer, but when you're a producer you're working for a record company and a band and everything else. It's just different. When you're an engineer you care about what the snare sounds like, and when you're a producer you don't care that much. I do care about the sounds I get, but the sounds I care about I'll hammer square pegs in round holes to get the sounds that will work for a song and the album."

When Jerden started in the studio, he didn't have to climb the ladder from assistant to second engineer; he came straight in as an engineer. "I felt I got lucky right off the bat and fell right into it," he says. "I have the ability. Steve Lillywhite caught me off guard when I was working with the [Rolling] Stones and he was producing. You'd get people like Jimmy Page coming by, and Paul Schafer would be leading the band. I switched from recording the Stones to recording a live-to-two-track jam. Steve said to me, 'You know something? You're really good at getting the sounds really fast.' It kind of threw me, because I thought that's what an engineer did. I mean you get sound really fast, right, and an engineer's supposed to be good at that. But then I realized that I had a talent for that, and I really can't do anything else. I'm not a good carpenter, I'm not a mechanic, I can't really do anything but make records and I'm really natural at it."

Jerden admits, though, that didn't make him a natural producer in the beginning. "I listen to some stuff that I produced early on, and it sounds terrible," he admits. "Sonically it sounds good, but overall it just doesn't work, and I understand why. For me, it didn't work because I didn't know how to think as a producer. Even when you work as a producer, you don't how to think as a producer until you become a producer."

LONG TERM ENGINEER-PRODUCER RELATIONSHIPS

The relationship between producer and engineer is obviously a crucial one, and over the past couple of decades, certain partnerships have equaled top-selling, award-wining releases. More than that, though, because of an established team's relative comfort in the studio, artists seem to be more willing to come back and work on their next release. The heyday of these partnerships came in the 1980s with the producer-engineer teams of Don Was and Ed Cherney, and Steve Thompson and Michael Barbiero, and stretched into the '90s with Daniel Lanois and Mark Howard, and Mitchell Froom and Tchad Blake. It is no coincidence that the engineers in these teams became outstanding producers in their own right.

The Don Was and Ed Cherney pairing lasted fifteen years and resulted in some of the biggest hits of the 1980s. From Cherney's perspective, the relationship worked so well for a number of reasons: "We were about the same age, we came from the same area of the country, culturally we were brought up the same way, and we just got along," he says. "I think we complemented each other. For a long time my work was better because he was there, and I would like to think that his work was better because I was there."

Was says, "I think it's really imperative to have people that you can trust. It's funny to think about worrying about whether something is even getting to tape, let alone whether it sounds good on tape. That's a full-time occupation, and now with Pro Tools you have the further thing of having to keep track of where everything is—you don't want those little things. You don't know what song it comes from or what instrument it is, so there is a tremendous amount of record keeping involved, and that may really distract you from being able to tell if the vocalist is sincere or not. That should really always be what you're interested in. On the other hand, if it's not going well, that can be more distracting. If you don't like what's going on tape, if someone's taking too long to do everything you just want to push him aside and say, 'Put a mic there, let's go, let's go, just play it, come on.' So, it is really good to not ever have to think about it, and that's how I always felt about Ed.

"I don't ever go in and tell a guy what to do or what to use," Was continues. "I don't care what console he uses, I don't care what equipment he rents, as long as he doesn't spend a lot of money. Mainly you want people who know how to give off a positive vibe and also be invisible; you don't want them to darken the room at all, you want upbeat people."

When Steve Thompson was looking for an engineer in 1979, he had some specific ideas in mind. "I was looking around for engineers that could be very adaptable to different forms of music, and Michael [Barbiero], to me, was the best at adapting to any musical style you could throw at him," he says.

The recipe for Thompson-Barbiero's success was simple enough to explain, according to Michael Barbiero. "I'm a recording engineer, and Steve is not," he says. "Steve was the one that managed to keep the overview while I was focused on the minutiae, and that worked out well. I have produced some records myself and I know how difficult it is, when you are involved in worrying about the real-time work of engineering, to maintain the overall view of the overall production. You have to be willing to let go of the details at some point and go for the feel, which is by far more important than perfection. I learned that from Steve. He is a very good motivator, and at the same time he has some creative ideas to bring to the party. He understands a song structure and what makes it work. Since I have more schooling in music theory, I could interpret what he was saying to the band in terms of what he's saying."

Thompson believes this partnership is akin to a marriage, where the two know each other's strengths and weaknesses. "You know what each can bring to the plate," he explains. "The good part about working with Michael was that we could tag-team things, so somebody could be fresh at all times. We split up the duties, and I couldn't say that one person did this and one person did that. It was whatever it took, and it worked out great."

Mitchell Froom's intuition told him to find one engineer to work with as he was launching his production career in the mid-'80s. It was not a snap to find that person, but when he ran into Tchad Blake at a Los Angeles recording studio, there was some good chemistry right away. "He gave me a tape of the *Barbarella* soundtrack and he said he liked a solo record that I had done [which was actually the soundtrack to *Café Flesh*, an adult film]. I had this opportunity to score a play, but I only had two days to do it. There was just no money, and I said, 'Why don't we try this?' We had fun doing it," Froom recalls. "My instinct, living in L.A. at the time, was not to be all over the map and not use twenty different engineers and session cats and all that. I just felt that that's the way it should be in order to do something more distinctive. Tchad was an interesting guy with a lot of cool ideas. He was also a guitar player. It just seemed like if we started working together that we could get to the point where the work that we did together would be far superior than the work that we could do separately."

It took five years, Froom recalls, for it to click. "It wasn't until the *Kiko* album [Los Lobos, 1992] that we hit on it. I could tell the difference, because right after that record I was getting calls as a producer and people would say,

'Oh, by the way, Tchad is doing it right?' So, I saw more and more that the combination became something that people liked."

Each of these partnerships lasted a solid number of years until the engineers evolved into producers and started to get jobs on their own. There is a part of Mark Howard, though, that believes his tenure with Daniel Lanois may have lasted too long. "I was twenty-two years old when I met Dan, and I worked with him for fifteen years. Not that he didn't pay me a lot of money, but I was saying, 'Can I get a raise? Can we up my thing?' He'd say, 'Well, you're not making a lot of money now, but in the future you're going to make a lot of money off of these relationships. It will happen later in life for you, don't try to take it all right now.' I still feel that things have moved quite slowly, because maybe I stayed in his camp a little too long. Although I worked with U2 and Bob Dylan and all these great opportunities came my way because I hung in there for so long with him, as a producer and establishing my own thing I felt like maybe I stayed too long and I should have branched out earlier on."

THE BOSS

Garth Richardson, who has also spent his share of time bouncing between engineering and producing responsibilities, learned from his father that he had to be careful not to be to friendly with bands when they started recording. "My father said, 'Garth, never sleep with the band. Never become one of the boys, because as soon as you become one of the boys the band loses your respect.' Once you have to be the bad guy, they go, 'Ah, it's just fuckin' Garth.' But when you're the boss and you have to say, 'Do this now,' they'll do it. Somebody has to be the boss, and the record label hired you to make sure the job gets done. We do have times where we go out and get drunk, because you do need to let off steam, but you also have to make sure that you're not one of the boys. A lot of times, I'm the bad cop and my engineer is the good cop. The engineer is always buddy-buddy with the band and because the band can get away with shit with him, they will usually use that engineer on their next disk. And then when he becomes the boss, they go, 'Well, how come you aren't what you used to be?'"

9 SELECTING A STUDIO AND TECHNOLOGY

Even after a producer has found an artist and lined up a team of engineers, there is still some research that needs to be completed before a note is recorded. Namely, a producer needs to find a place to record the album (whether at a home or commercial studio) and pick the kind of technology that will be used to capture the performances. Picking the right studio contributes to the vibe of the session, and the technology often determines how producer, engineer, and artist will work.

Finding the right studio has become especially important as recording budgets continue to tighten and label expectations grow. Gone are the days when a band would fly to an exotic locale and spend months on end working on a concept album. Even if a band decides to stay close to home, the odds are that they still can't afford to book a studio exclusively, unless they are in the upper echelon of artists that can practically guarantee Platinum sales. What's happening more and more is that bands book a week of time in the studio's main room to record portions of an album, such as drum tracks, and then retire to a less expensive set of rooms for bass, guitar, vocals, and overdubs. Or else they will record the drum tracks at a proper studio and then move camp to a home studio to finish off the balance of the tracks.

Of course, these new economics have made a dramatic impact on the studio business. Seemingly, there will always be a call for top-tier studios in recording hot spots such as Los Angeles, New York, Nashville, and even Miami. Yet, in a city like San Francisco, which used to be a destination for many artists looking to record an album out of town, the business has slowed down considerably. Nina Bombardier manages Fantasy Studios (Berkeley, Calif.), where acts such as Santana, Creedence Clearwater Revival, and Journey recorded in their heyday.

She points out that there is a trickle-down affect in the music business. "I don't care who you are owned by, where you get your money, what your focus is, or what your future plans are, all studios are victims of what goes on in the industry. We're kind of at the bottom of the food chain in a lot of ways, because if the record companies aren't strong and aren't signing acts that they give money to, to come into a professional recording studio to record, then we have no customers," she says.

For Fantasy, the business model has changed since 2000. "Most of our customers these days are people off the street, making demos and CDs of their own, because CDs have become like business cards," Bombardier explains. "Many years ago, making a record was an earned privilege and it took teams of people working together to make a band what it was. We're still in the position to serve whoever it is out there that wants to record, no matter what their budget, no matter what kind of music, no matter what their needs. Our role as a studio has changed in many ways; we're doing a lot more for the client in many ways than we ever had to before. Where ninety-nine percent of my clients' projects used to be billed to record companies, ninety-nine percent of my clients now are not."

The good news for producers and musicians looking for studios, though, is that prices have come down at many spots. For a place like Fantasy, where the management takes pride in having a destination-type studio, that's a hard reality to face. "Even if a band in L.A. wanted to come up here," Bombardier reports, "there are a thousand studios in L.A. choking each other to death with the rates."

Also contributing to the slow death of recording studios is the continuing boom of the digital audio workstation market, which includes offerings from manufacturers such as Fairlight, Digidesign, Steinberg, and AMS Neve. Any of the products offered from these companies enable artists, without even the help of a producer or an engineer, to record their own tracks. Each of these technologies gives artists the ultimate freedom to avoid the expenses of a recording studio and, for that matter, the trouble of getting a record-company contract.

However, it is fair to say that even with the accessibility of DAWs the majority of albums are still recorded, at least partially, in a studio that is stocked with the most up-to-date technology and a staff to help.

How to Select a Studio

For the most part, producers and artists consider a few main issues when picking a studio: Gear, room acoustics, and vibe. "The right vibe is crucial, because you can bring in the right gear," says Ben Harper. "The best places are set up for the right vibe and the right gear. You can bring in the right gear and you can actually bring in the right vibe. We lined the inside of the studio for *Diamonds*. There were tapestries everywhere; you'd have thought we were never leaving." Harper produced the Blind Boys of Alabama sessions at the legendary Capitol

Studios, famed for hosting artists such as Frank Sinatra, Nat King Cole, Dean Martin, and others. "We didn't do anything like that at Capitol," he says. "It's so full of the ghosts of music past, and you never lose site of the fact that you're in that building, in that studio where they stood. That's always there. It would almost be sacrilegious to hang stuff up, in a weird way."

When Daron Malakian started to look for a place where System of a Down could record the tracks for the multi-Platinum album *Toxicity,* he went to his record collection. The album he pulled out that he wanted to mimic was *Date with Elvis,* a 1986 offering from The Cramps. "I was looking for a thicker sound for the band, and I thought if a room can make The Cramps sound thick then that was the room for us," he explains. The Cramps album was recorded at the part of Ocean Way Studios that is now Cello Studios in Los Angeles. "We were already ready to record a thick-sounding record, so I thought, 'Imagine what it would do for us.'"

The key for Los Angeles-based producer Mark Trombino is to find a studio that feels like a home base. "It's taken me awhile, but I'm starting to find places where I really like to work," says Trombino. "I've done that where I've kind of latched onto a certain studio and I'll do a few records there, and then when I want to book it and it's booked I have to go somewhere else and I love that place and I go there all the time." During the early part of this decade, he found that spot at Ocean Studios in Burbank, California. It has the combination of gear, acoustics, and vibe that works for him. "The people are awesome, the gear is awesome, and the studio is great," he reports. "The thing I like about Ocean is the vibe. I like that it's one room and you're not sharing a lobby with five other studios. I like that I can walk out the door and it's not gross out. I like that I can walk down the street into a restaurant or something. That's a lot of vibe stuff. On top of that, Ocean has amazing gear, and it has one of the larger vintage Neve consoles in L.A. and a big drum room."

Lou Giordano, who started his career at Fort Apache Studios in Boston before moving to New York, found a studio he could call home in Hoboken, New Jersey. "There is a studio there called Water Music that I work out of quite a bit," he says. "It's really great whenever you start a recording project, because there's a lot of initializing that has to happen, and with your own studio you're already familiar with the acoustics and everything is wired up the way you want it to be, so it's just less time wasted getting everything working." In addition to working out of Water Music, Giordano is looking to put together a home studio.

Wood echoes the idea of finding a home base, adding that picking a studio based on popularity is not a smart move. "The hot spot means it's going to be expensive," Wood says, "and expensive is bad. I've never booked a studio based on that, ever. I book a studio based on how good the rooms sound, including the control room, what the aesthetics are, and then the equipment. I really couldn't care less about the equipment. I have all my own equipment, and if I have to, I'll bring my own equipment. Often I'll use my own equipment and bypass every single thing in the room. There have literally been times where I've said, 'I need an outlet and I need you to leave me alone,'" he adds with a laugh. "I'm just not going to let anything hang me up and I prefer as little interference as possible. So, if I'm in a tracking studio, I almost never use their gear, because I like my gear. I've got a lot of it, and if they have a great mic collection, that's gravy. But I like my mic collection. I've got a lot of great mics."

Wood says he looks for windows that look out on something pleasant, as well as things like a nearby restaurant for late-night dining and something for the band to do. "Is there a ping-pong table? Is there satellite TV? Is it an individual lounge, or is it a multiroom facility? Is somebody going to be smoking crack in my bathroom? That's been a problem," he admits with a laugh. "Is Fred Durst going to be on a cell-phone rant, pacing up and down like a raving lunatic? Or is Rick Rubin going to park his Bentley in the loading zone every single day so that we can't get in and out without him having to have his shit moved? That's a problem. I am a paying client, and I insist on being treated as well as Rick Rubin. Rick Rubin is infinitely more talented and more successful, but I insist, if I'm going to work in a multi-room studio, that I be treated with some modicum of respect. And that comes from being a studio owner. I'm an old-school business guy. I mean, if you laid out the cash, you're the man.

"People want to be taken care of, so the aesthetics are super-important," he continues. "I can't work in a cave. I don't like dark studios. I like natural light. I work during the day, into the evening. I like to see the change of day. I like to know what time it is. I'm not afraid of clocks, you know what I mean? I'm not one of those freaks that needs to be in a tomb. I like to be interactive with my world outside."

Harper, Malakian, Trombino, and Wood are in good position because they live in Los Angeles, where studios are plentiful. "It's awesome, because bands get to know each other and, actually, Fred Durst doesn't really go on tirades. He's actually really nice," Wood says. "I was yakking it up with him and his band and it was really cool. I got to know [producer] Jerry Finn when he was working next door, and we could sit around and have a beer late at night. We were having a good time and that's the whole point of it, to try to maximize the bonding. That's my job as the producer, to pick the perfect place to bond."

THE PROS AND CONS OF BUILDING YOUR OWN STUDIO

Many producers have taken control of the studio environment by building their own facilities. Some have dedicated parts of their home—garage, bedroom, guesthouse, dining room—while others have gone out and found space in another building where they could set up shop.

There are a few intrepid modern-day musicians, such as the Counting Crows and Incubus, who have set up temporary studios in homes to record albums. Mark Howard spent the beginning of his career moving from rented house to rented house with Daniel Lanois and a bevy of gear. "I've been doing these kind of installations in houses and warehouses with Dan," he says. A house's interesting environments, he says, become part of the production. "You are put in a space that you've never worked in before, and you're going to have discoveries that you wouldn't actually get in a conventional studio," Howard explains.

The experience of building those studios changed the way that Howard sets up when he records. "The control room is in the studio, so [the band] is recording right next to the console," Howard explains. "Communication is a huge asset and I can say [to the players], 'Hey, maybe not so hard?' I can relay that without going to the glass where they may not hear me or it's hard to get their attention. It's so fast [this way], and I find it difficult to work in that environment now where you have to go through the glass or the door and running back and forth."

Howard built this type of setup at The Paramour studio, up in the hills of Los Angeles, and showed it to Tom Waits when they started recording *Real Gone*. "Tom had never worked that way before and he was freaked out about it," Howard recalls. "I invited him to Paramour, and he played me his tapes and I got him to do a couple of vocals on top of them, just as a test. He got to see how it worked and he really liked it. He said, 'Hey, can you come on up to my place and we'll do this same thing up there?' So, we rented this little schoolhouse, set up shop in there, and we've been going great. Now he says, 'Man, now I can't work any other way. This is the best way.' The music can be playing and you can run around the room, playing any instrument. Before he had to go out on the floor, couldn't hear the music, and it was a bit of a struggle."

The catch is that Howard is now addicted to building studios. "I've been doing it with Daniel for fifteen years, and he always says, 'Hey you don't need to do this anymore, you can just go work in normal studios and forget about the gear.' But it's just become a part of me. I get hungry for it, to go somewhere else and have like a nomad studio. I've been to Mexico, New Orleans, San Francisco, and the desert; it's just like I've got all these locations under my belt and I just can't stop."

It is clear that Howard thrives on the constant challenge of building new studios and getting good tracks in strange environments. In addition, because he is always pushing himself technically, he does not become stagnant in his approach.

That nomadic method doesn't resonate for Walter Afanasieff, however. He built a studio in his Marin County home while working with Mariah Carey, Celine Dion, and Savage Garden before moving to Los Angeles and purchasing a share in Chalice Recording Studio. "It's kind of like I don't like sleeping in strange beds, like when you're in a hotel room," he says. "Those have been the worst nights of sleep in my life, just because it's somebody else's bed. My thing is I'm so comfortable with my own place, my own way, my own stuff. It was very hard for a lot of years having to take all of my equipment, put it all in racks and cases and ship it every week to another studio in New York somewhere, because Sony Music wanted me to work in New York. It was very frustrating, and during that early part of my contract with them, I decided to build my own studio. As a result, I've had my own studio and now I'm spoiled. I hate going to other studios; I can't stand it. I'll do it, but I just never know what I'm going to get unless I've been there and I love it.

"I love a few rooms in [Los Angeles]. I don't mind working there, but it's always this temporary feel," Afanasieff continues. "It's not your place that you come to every day. It can be like anything—the bathroom, the coffee cups. I remember having to work at Sony Studios when they first built it in New York, and it was amazing to me that someone had built this huge multibazillion-dollar facility and I would sit at the SSL, which was great, and have to turn my head sideways to look out into the studio at the singer. I thought that that was a poorly designed thing, at least for me. I know that a lot of studios are built this way, and I know there's a very famous studio designer who does this, but if I'm listening out of my right and left ears I want to be able to see exactly what I'm hearing."

Another issue that bothered him while he was at Sony Studios was the lack of privacy. "Their bathrooms were outside in the hallway, and there was a huge video-production facility down the hall where they were taping some MTV show. I'd go for a pee run and have to get in line behind thirty guys," he recalls. "Things like that drive me crazy. So, having my own place has just been a dream." On the other hand, Afanasieff won't build a studio at his house again because he feels like there needs to be a separation between home and work.

Howard Benson has split the difference by dividing his time between Bay 7 in Los Angeles, where he tracks most of a band's sessions, and his home Pro Tools rig. "I don't own Bay 7, but I work there a lot. I don't want to own a studio; that's a bigger problem. I have enough to deal with," he says with a laugh. But having that home base is important. "We can set up drums in like two seconds, so that's a very good thing for us. We're very efficient. We can have all the tracks cut in three days or so." Those tracks then head home with him where he tinkers with them in Pro Tools. "I like to sit around late at night and fix the arrangements," he explains. "A lot of that happens at my home studio when I'm away from everybody and it's quiet and I can focus. During the day it's usually recording, recording, recording."

While budget concerns have pushed some artists and other producers to move from studio main rooms to smaller rooms, Sylvia Massy Shivy's Radio Star Studios in Weed, California, enables her to work close to home and save bands money. Massy points out that the typical budget she will see to record a band is close to $100,000, which is less than what she would need to record in Los Angeles. "If I was still in L.A., doing sessions at L.A. studios, the budgets would have to be $150,000 to $200,000, because I'd have to put the band up in a hotel, as well as hire a studio, rent gear, and get transportation for the band. Those are things that I don't have to charge the client now. I think it makes for better records because there's more time to be creative. You don't have to move from a great tracking room to an overdub room in order to save money; we just keep working right here. There's an apartment in the complex for bands to stay in, so there's no cost involved in putting them up in a hotel. It's all right here."

The 2004 *Andiamo* release from Authority Zero may have sounded a whole lot different had Ryan Greene not had the ability to return to remix the record in Motor Studios in San Francisco, which he co-owns with NOFX singer/bassist Fat Mike (né Mike Burkett). "I remixed two songs on that album for free, because we were locked into a deal with the studio where we recorded this record. The studio gave the band a great deal, and it was an all-in deal and that was all the money that they had," he says. Although it was a good deal for the band's budget, Greene did not know the room's acoustics for mixing. "I was going to mix that record blind, and you can't fix a ghost," he says. "If you don't hear it, you can't fix it. I have time, so I'm going to do these mixes and I'll send them to mastering. These will be the mixes that go on the record and I'll be happy. What do you do? I'm fortunate enough that I have a studio that I can do that in."

Even so, Greene is not so sure that opening a studio was the smartest thing to do. "I think that opening up your own studio is the craziest thing you could ever do in the music industry, especially nowadays," he says. Nevertheless, he is quick to point out that if he moved out of the San Francisco Bay Area, he would put a studio in his house. "Absolutely, I'd do it in a heartbeat. Why not? I'd set up an overdub room and go somewhere else to mix, somewhere else to track drums. Why not? Because the records aren't about how great they sound, it's the vibe. Pretty much everything that you do is going to sound good enough to listen to," he explains with a laugh.

SELECTING TECHNOLOGY

The analog vs. digital debate has been played out so much since the mid-1980s that it is no longer worth discussing. Most producers now recognize the positives of digital (editing flexibility, increased capacity, and speed) as well as the advantages of analog—a warmer sound. Only purists and audiophiles will argue that digital has yet to get beyond the crisp and sterile sound that it was known for at its introduction into the audio world. In fact, most of today's hardcore fans would be hard-pressed to hear the difference between a recent analog recording and one recorded to a digital format.

What is true today, more than ever, is that producers are splitting the difference, utilizing analog outboard gear and consoles in combination with digital audio workstations. "I've got every format," Dave Fridmann reports. "They're just different-flavored tools. I have a lot of compressors, and they all sound a little bit different. That's really the essence of it. What I love about digital: You never lose a take. You never have to go, 'Oh, God! We didn't improve on that one. I wish I had the old one back.' But what I love about the analog is, when you've got it, it's really there and you've got it and no power outage or missed keystroke is going to get rid of it. There's finality to the analog, which has its place as well that I really appreciate.

"I think a lot of the bands I work with appreciate it as well," Fridmann continues, "knowing that it's done. When you go through a Pro Tools session and you punch in fifty times, you've just begun to work. You haven't actually finished. You think you might have enough raw material to finish. You go through an analog track and you get to the end of the song and you've punched in fifty times—the track is done. It's done, and there's something to that that's relieving, I think, to musicians. They know when I say, 'We've got it,' we've actually got it. There are just different tools."

Producers are also using both analog tape and hard-disk recorders with digital audio workstations on some sessions. "I like analog for tracking," explains Sylvia Massy Shivy. "We have a Studer A820 [24-track analog machine] that we use to record all the basic tracks, and then we dump it directly into digital. We'll edit the drums where they need it, and then we continue overdubbing on digital from that point. There have been a few projects where we've done it all analog and going back after you've worked on Pro Tools for eight years was really challenging and fun. And it sounds great, but I don't know how I ever lived without the digital editing capabilities—the ease of moving one chorus performance of vocals to the other choruses and creating parts that the guitar player will never play correctly. It makes for better records, I think. It makes the artist sound better."

A number of producers have turned the analog vs. digital decision back to the bands they are recording. For a fair amount of time, Lou Giordano would start each session recording drums to two-track analog tape and right into Pro Tools. "Then I set up a blind test with the band and asked them which one they thought sounded better," he explains. "They always picked the Pro Tools. So, after doing that test a half-dozen times, I didn't think there was much point in using tape anymore. People don't really like the sound of it."

The point, Giordano adds, is that bands want their recorded tracks to sound like what they are playing in the studio. He bases that opinion on the experience of the bands that he has worked with over the years, which was also articulated well in an article he read about the Strokes' studio philosophy. "They got so used to the thing sounding exactly like what they are hearing from the monitor and not a two-inch representation of it," he explains. "At least in their case, they preferred the direct digital sound. It sounds more like what you hear when you're setting up the sounds and working on the drum sounds for half a day to get everything sounding right, and that's what you want to hear back off of your playback machine. You don't want to hear something that's different. Unless it's something different and way better, but I think people are getting much more used to the sound of digital and it doesn't have such a bad name anymore, because people are using it correctly rather than pretending that it's analog tape and continuing to do all the things that we used to do to get the tape to sound good. You just don't have to do those things anymore. You do other things. There are times when I've used both formats within a project and it's really just what sounds the best."

Sound is certainly at the top of the list when it comes to picking through technology but so is ease of use, and that is why Mark Howard has moved away from Pro Tools. "I get frustrated with the whole mousing-around routine," he starts. "Then you've got this guy in front of the screen and you're like, 'Okay, can you do this and blah, blah.' I'm not sure if it's a loss of control thing, or you're waiting on somebody, or it's like, 'Okay, here we go, we're gonna record, and sorry we gotta reboot.' It takes the wind out of you and I've been put in that spot." Howard uses the Otari Radar system instead. "It's damn reliable, and I can do everything Pro Tools can do if not faster, and I think it sounds better."

DAW setups also offer the ability for producers and engineers to expand the amount of tracks recorded much more easily than they can by synching up analog machines. That helped Ben Harper when he was working with the Blind Boys of Alabama on *There Will Be a Light*. Harper and engineer Jimmy Hoyson started with analog and then moved to Pro Tools after discovering that the amount of vocals that needed to get to tape was growing with each song.

Perhaps it is Mark Trombino, the former computer science major, who sums up the benefits of working in digital best. "I've always fantasized about being able to do in the box what you can do in the box now," he says. "It's such an easy way to work. It's fun, it's spontaneous. Plus, I'm a control freak, so having that much control over something is pretty nice. I like the speed at which things happen, the stress-reduction that happens, and the cost savings." That does not mean, however, that he jumped on the digital bandwagon from day one. At first, he would record to tape, dump the tracks into the digital domain for editing, and then dump it all back to tape. "Gradually, it kind of became more and more digital, until finally I started thinking about just breaking away from tape entirely, but then I would have to convince myself that it was okay," he explains. "So, for like five records in a row, I would set everything up so that I could record to tape and Pro Tools at the same time. Then I would A/B it and the band and I would listen to it. Finally, I figured it was okay to go all-digital, and sonically I'm good with it, too. I don't think I'm taking any sort of sonic hit."

Nick Launay, on the other hand, finds that staying in the analog domain helps him keep musicians closer to their music. "I have a very different way of working, apparently, than most producers," he says. "I still do everything in analog, and I don't use Pro Tools. The way I go about getting performances out of people is, I set the band up in the same room, all looking at each other, sometimes without headphones if it will work that way, and I record everybody at the same time. I don't do overdubs on backing tracks. I don't record the drums first then overdub the bass and overdub the guitars; never have I ever done that on any album—ever. I always record whatever the band is live. If it's two guitars, bass, and drums, that's what I'll record."

Plus, Launay will go for complete takes of a song rather than piecing it together digitally. "I will do it until they hit their peak of recording that song and that arrangement. When they start dropping it and it's not happening anymore, that's when I'll stop. Basically, I will do as many takes as it takes, and then I will listen to all the takes and I'll make notes and they go down and I will chop between the takes a complete band. In other words, I take performances of songs," he explains, "and I'll chop it up by doing two-inch editing."

"If I was working with a band that couldn't play, I would use Pro Tools, but I don't choose to work with those bands," Launay continues. "The only time I use Pro Tools is for the plug-ins. There have been times when I've worked with a band who does very vibey takes of things, and maybe some of the timing needs fixing within that, so I'll use Pro Tools for that. But when I am working with a normal kind of rock band, I won't do it that way. I definitely don't get into moving kick drums or snares around. That, to me, is a big no-no. Even the worst drummer who can't keep time will play really well if you make the circumstances right, for example—stoned enough, drunk enough, awake enough, the right lighting, happiness, you know—whatever it takes."

After all, Launay comes from England's ramshackle punk heyday, "Where bands had just learned how to play their instruments, jumped onstage, and made a racket that was a beautiful racket," he says with a smile. "That's what it's about to me. You just never know what's going to make the take work, and it can be anything. It isn't always about musicianship. I much prefer to work with a band that's got a vibe and a mood and a whole feeling than listen to a band that's really, really proficient at playing their instruments. To me, that's like so what? I would never work with Yes or Rush. I hate that stuff. It's not musical, it doesn't have any mood, it doesn't do anything for me at all. I love Iggy Pop, I love the Stooges, I love all of the mistakes on their records. I love the fact that they are out of tune, playing the wrong chords, and the bass player is playing the chorus two bars before the chorus hits and they left it in and its amazing.

It's wrong but it's great. I love all that."

Clearly, the importance of technology is to make the artist feel comfortable enough with what is going on in the studio to take enough risks to create a memorable performance. However, as Walter Afanasieff knows, sometimes building that comfort level has nothing to do with big expensive technology. "You can have the best console, the best engineer, the best circumstances, the best everything, and you can be sitting there as a record producer and the littlest tiniest thing will fail and everyone starts going down with the ship immediately," he says. "It can be as little as the wrong pair of headphones or the wrong headphone mix, and the artist doesn't know to even say what's going on; they just know that they can't hear something or they don't like what they're hearing. That causes them to inwardly collapse. Their vibe goes out the window, and they become complete, utter monsters. So you're sitting there with the power of SSL and the power of anything and everything, but that artist out there in the control room doesn't know how to communicate what's going on.

"I had this exact experience with Barbra Streisand," he continues. "It came down to the fact that she had been using a microphone her whole career, an M49. I didn't know really anything about microphones; I just knew what sounded good. So, we're in the studio and all of her people are in the room, and I'm just sitting there—it was my first time working with her—and I'm sweating bullets and nervous as hell, and she just was not singing well, and she wasn't hearing well, and she was getting in a foul mood, and she was just blaming me for it. I didn't know what to do, so I finally realized that I was just going to go on my instincts here. I'm just going to say what I think is true: 'Why are we using this microphone?' [She said] 'This is my microphone; I've used this microphone for fifty albums.' I said, 'Well have you ever tried using a different microphone? There is really a beautiful new microphone out called the Sony whatever.' I can't really remember exactly what it was, but we put that up. Then I said, 'Let's try the headphones that I have.' So, we changed the mic, changed headphones, and she came back after a little lunch and went in the studio. Her first words were, 'Oh my God, this sounds amazing.' We rolled the track and she was like, 'Oh my God, I've never sounded this good.'

"There are guys that know all the answers," Afanasieff says. "They can have all the best gear. I never was into that. I just rely on sounds, you know, what my ears think."

Using Technology to Find Perfection
More and more, it seems, technology is coming to the rescue in the studio. Thanks to the ease of digital editing, performances that are out of tune, out of time, or just plain poor are being fixed up so that fans will never know the difference. One producer interviewed for this book, while watching a video on

Country Music Television, quiets down, points to the screen, and says, 'Listen. That vocal is so pitch-perfect that there's no way she could do it.' A plug-in called Auto-Tune, which is utilized in Pro Tools, enables an off-key vocal to be moved into the right pitch for the track. A product called Beat Detective cleans up drum tracks that are out of time. There are plug-ins to fix practically any problem that would have required a re-take in the analog era.

There is also no shortage of opinions when producers are asked whether they think it is okay to fix a performance with technology. "Oh hell yeah," exclaims Dave Fridmann. "Why not? Wouldn't you? Seriously, I can't think of a single reason why not, and I can think of a million reasons why it's unnecessary on occasion, but if you've got the time and you've got the will and you notice that it's wrong and it's bugging you, why not change it? I'm just as happy to continue to try and perform it and get it right, but there's instances where something is the right thing but it's off for some reason and you can take something else, copy and paste it, and do whatever you want, and it's great."

"It's kind of like watching a Sly Stallone movie," Garth Richardson says with a laugh. "He didn't jump off that cliff. That's all done by a computer, and nobody would say, 'Well, man, that scene fuckin' sucks, he didn't really jump.' People want to be entertained, and that's what film does now. Tell me any person that you have ever known that has gone up against seventy-five guys with machine guns and not got shot once! The bottom line is, if it's a great song, it's fine."

For the most part, bands want to be able to play live what they record, says Sylvia Massy Shivy. "But I think it's a completely different animal. I think live shows should be completely different, not necessarily a mirror of the record. I like to do things that you could never perform live in the studio. Jeez, I think it really ties the producer's hands to make a record that only represents what the band can do live."

Both Shivy and Walter Afanasieff carry the film metaphor into the recording studio. "Actors get make-up," Shivy says. "Auto-Tune can be used as an effect, like the Cher kind of treatment, or just to fix a few of those high notes, or you can take a mediocre singer and make him sound great and natural. It depends on the degree and the music that it's fitting into. It depends on how far you want to go with it, but, yeah, I think it's absolutely fair."

Afanasieff adds: "I think it's okay, because at the end of the day, a CD is different than a live performance. When you are doing a recording, it needs to be done so that everyone appreciates it—it's the best that it could be, it's the absolute finest that we can achieve in the studio given the money spent, the people hired, the technology afforded, and I argue with some of those guys that say it's just transferred to the stage like that," he says. "A lot of people don't have the ability, but they are great artists, great performers, great talented people, and not everything they do in one take in the studio is what should be on their record. There have to be multiple takes, everyone does it. I don't care if you're Tony Bennett or Mariah Carey or Celine Dion, Whitney Houston, Aretha Franklin—everybody has multiple takes. Frank Sinatra used to do three takes.

"So, with the exception of a live performance that goes down as being an astounding performance, and yeah, there are those performances…" Afanasieff continues. "But I guarantee, if you took that astounding live performance and you put it into a studio setting and heard it dry without an audience and really looked at it as being what it was, you would find so many flaws. You would find that extraordinary live performance out of tune, out of time, flawed, and you would have to do another take until you found the best of the best and put it together. Then you'd find yourself saying, 'That word that he or she sang was so great, but it was just a little out of tune.' So, I don't see anything wrong with Auto-Tuning it or pitching it. I think that just enhances what we know is needed for that final CD."

As an artist, Ben Harper will not rely on a tool like Auto-Tune to get his vocals right, but he will not shy away from moving performances from take to take. "I'll re-sing, but I ain't tuning," he says. "It's not on my radar. I'm not beyond sliding something from somewhere else, as long as it works musically to have something identical all the way through [a song]. But I'm overly sensitized to the sterilization process. I'm not letting it creep in. When I start listening to older records, to the pure—and I'm sorry to use this word—*magic* of the old Van Morrison records and the Bob Dylan records and the Al Green records, you realize we've removed ourselves from that rawness. I strive toward imperfection as a producer, I really do—the beauty of imperfection—because that's something that's been lost. You've got to be brave; you've got to be ready to hear yourself raw or to hear other people raw and imperfect. To commit to imperfection is the biggest step an artist can make, and I haven't gotten all the way there, but I've gotten further to it than I've ever been."

According to Lou Giordano, the amount of technical wizardry done in the studio depends on the artist's comfort level. "Some people really just want to sound good and they don't want to have obvious mistakes, but they don't mind if there is some human imperfection to it," he explains. "Other people are insane and just obsessive about fixing to the point where everything is squeaky-clean perfect. I don't really back that method very much. If an artist really, really wants to do it, I'll do it up to a certain point but I think that it adds way too much time to a project and it does strip the life out of it." He points to a recent project where the singer had quite a bit of character and emotion in his vocals, but couldn't find the right pitch. "I found that it was more honest to present his voice with some of the imperfections rather than Auto-Tune it all out and fix every little thing," he reports. "For people who are not a part of the music industry, it's those moments where the singer really shows his imperfection and shows his true emotions, that people really react to and they say, 'Wow, that's my favorite part of the song, where his voice cracks.' I've heard that many times, and when you explain that was a mistake they say, 'But it just sounds great. It sounds like he's real, like he's not a robot.'

"Sometimes it takes a lot of convincing to get the artists to agree to use those moments, but it's really what people react to when they hear a band. If they like the singer and they like what he's singing about, then everything else is getting a free pass," Giordano continues. "It's hard for people who work on the music from day to day and have their heads so far deep into it to step back and realize that's what it is all about. It's not about how tight you played the track to the click; it's not about how in-tune your guitar is. Listen to any Lou Reed or Velvet Underground song. His guitar was out of tune, and people loved it. So, it's not about how perfect you are, it's about what you're saying and how you are saying it."

This is coming from a producer who is known for acoustically perfect releases, including the 1995 album, *A Boy Named Goo* from the Goo Goo Dolls. "There was some cleaning up that had to be done, and I want to present the music to people in a way that they will get it, and sometimes that does involve being a tuning Nazi and really picking things apart for pitch and everything," Giordano says. "Sometimes that's what the artist wants, sometimes they want to be out of tune." For example, Giordano recalls working with the band's singer Johnny Rzeznik on the song, "Long Way Down." "On that song, Johnny sang the chorus over because he thought it was too in-tune and made him sound like Michael Bolton," the producer recalls with a laugh.

When Ross Hogarth was working with Ziggy Marley on his 2003 release, *Dragonfly,* the artist had his own ideas about what technology to use and when to use it. "Ziggy's attitude was that when it came to drum grooves, he wanted a couple of songs to have a certain hip-hop feel," Hogarth says. That feel had to be found by building a loop with software, "because a real drummer could never play a loop like that—they breath. There was an element where Ziggy wanted it to feel really relentless, so there was no question that we were going to have to chop up and grid some of the drums or at least make them feel that way a bit, and not stiff, but just sort of more loopy."

The approach changed, though when it came to Marley's vocals. "If you did get into comping things too tightly, like picking too many words apart, you would take the soul away from it. The soul being something you can't put your finger on, being something like God-related, and that has to be in the music because that's the thing in his world and I am a total believer. I think that Ziggy has a message of peace and love that he needs to get out there to the world, and if he himself feels like his soul has been taken a little bit away from the music, I think that would detract from that message," Hogarth explains. "So, there are some notes that are a little bit out of tune here and there that I could have easily Auto-Tuned, but I didn't. I agreed that this is what the world needs to hear because it's about the heart and soul."

Although tools can be used to clean tracks up, "you can't fix feel," says Dave Jerden. "You can put things on a grid and chop them up so they're precise and right, but you cannot make a groove. You cannot do it, and anybody who says you can for rock 'n' roll [is wrong]. I still think a good performance is a good performance. Occasionally, I'll use pitch-correction stuff, but I still get a good vocal performance that's sung right. Even if the guy can't sing, I'll still spend the time trying to get him to sing it right and on pitch, because I can hear all that, and to me it sounds phony. I hear so many records that are spot-on precision-wise, but something's been lost. I'm old-school: I'm used to working with tape and getting a good performance. It's fun for me as a producer now, since I know how things are done, to go back and listen to records from like the Fifties and Sixties that I grew up on. For instance, that song "Wooly Bully" [Sam the Sham & the Pharaohs' surprise hit song from 1965], everybody's heard that song. They had the slap on the hi-hat, and the [drummer] isn't playing with clicks, so the time is going in and out on "Wooly Bully" with tape delay. It pushes and pulls and creates tension at the right spots."

David Lowery echoes Jerden's stance, recalling work done by his friend Dennis Herring. "I know Dennis did that Buddy Guy record [*Blues Singer*, 2003], and he said that he edited a lot of that together, but I can't imagine him fixing notes. Why would you put Buddy Guy's guitar back in tune? If you had this really passionate solo, why would you put in perfect pitch? I'll give you an example of how one artist's imperfections were their character," he says. "The [2003 self-titled] Liz Phair record. It's awful. I mean, it's not a Liz Phair record because the Liz Phair character was built around her imperfect sort of singing and not that good of guitar playing. That's part of the persona. Lou Reed doesn't really sing in tune, either. If you put him in time, what would that be like?"

Yet, Lowery does see where technology can help further a band's creative abilities. "With Camper Van Beethoven, we recorded a lot of shit in Pro Tools, but we weren't correcting time or pitch. We were using it so we could flip a whole section around backwards and take a section from someplace else," he says. "So, if you preserve the character of the artist, then it's okay with whatever you do."

"It's appropriate to do whatever it takes," Ed Cherney says. "The technology is there, I say use it. I would love to see great artists where you don't have to tune every word. I've got friends that sit in the studio and pull their hair out trying to make a compelling performance out of a piece-of-shit performance. Look, there's certainly an over reliance on the technology. I think Nashville is an example. It would really bug me when I would hear great singers with great songs in Nashville and their vocals were tuned up the wazoo. I don't know if they were making music better by doing that, and I resent hearing some great singers tuned so hard, but it's like anything else—it's the nut behind the wheel. You have these tools, and some people can use them and some people can abuse them. You can use this stuff to make great art, and you can use it to ruin it, too." Cherney's work on the Rolling Stones' 2003 DVD *Four Flicks* wouldn't have been possible, he says, without the use of some polishing software. "We recorded that all over the world at four different venues, and if I didn't have the technology I would still be sitting there trying to fix it. Ten years ago I wouldn't have been able to make that DVD because there were some great performances, but in every song there was a place where it was less than stellar and I was able to pick up guitar licks from other nights and I was able to do stuff that I think made it really great."

Part of what producers are facing these days is the competition between bands and the race for radio airplay and record sales, so one album needs to sound like another, one single needs to sound like the one at the top of the charts. "It's the result of a billion record labels signing a billion bands," Mark Trombino says. "They're not all going to be good. Out of all the bands that are signed right now, how many are actually any good? Ten? Five? The rest of them need some help, and their record needs to sound as good as the next guy's on the radio. So, [tuning and pitch-correcting software] is a necessary evil in the business. Also, people are growing accustomed to hearing things that way. I can imagine that back in the Eighties, when people started using drum machines, it felt stiff and now it doesn't feel so bad. We've all grown pretty used to it, and I think when people started Auto-Tuning it was probably the same thing and it sounded artificial. But now we expect people to sing that way."

Ross Hogarth has also felt that pain. "Record labels expect to hear things a certain way, and they want things to be a certain way," he says. "If you don't deliver it that way to them, they're probably not going to like it. You can't cut off your nose to spite your face, because if you're doing a heavy-metal band and what's been set in stone before now is that everything is kind of [syncopated], the only way to do that is to chop it up and grid it and make it feel that way. It's sort of project-dependent. Am I tormented by it? Quite often, I am tormented because it's gotten to the point that people do things in Pro Tools because they really need to. I mean, we made some pretty damn great records pre-Pro Tools with bands that could play great together. If bands can continue to play great together, then Pro Tools will only hopefully help them make better records because the creative process is deeper and more expansive.

"There's an element of Pro Tools that's really scary and I try, because of my years of pre-Pro Tools analog engineering and producing, to never lose sight of that," Hogarth continues. "Sometimes you have to stop, step back, and say, 'I'm looking at something down to the sample rate. This is crazy.' I have to listen to it from twenty seconds back and make sure what we're doing isn't absolutely nuts. Again, there is a history of music up until the point that machines came into play, and it's pretty damn fine stuff. You can't loose sight of that, and I think bands have to continue to look at their own performances; artists need to look at their own performances before they start to blame the box."

At times, Hogarth has heard bands say that they'll chop up the audio in Pro Tools, fix a few things with the plug-ins, and they'll be done. That kind of attitude rankles him. "It's like, wait a second. Play it again or sing it again, or come back tomorrow and do it again, but don't come back later and hear how I Auto-Tuned you all night long."

Whatever an individual producer feels, the reality is that these tools are now part of the musical landscape. Howard Benson does not think there's any need for discussion. "If you don't use Auto-Tune, you're nuts. I look at it like tuning a guitar," he says. "I mean, are you not going to tune a guitar? So, if the singer is just a little flat or sharp, you can fix them. It's minor, minor stuff now. I don't really even think about it, but we use it very minimally when we have to. You don't even hear that on our records at all, it's so invisible."

10 MANAGING THE BUDGET

While songwriters in gentler times professed that love made the world go around, when it comes time to work in a recording studio these days, there's one thing that makes things happen—money. Granted, funds are not being provided in barrels like it once was, but a certain amount of money is still needed to hire a producer, an engineer, and session players; and to purchase raw materials and rent gear that might be needed. Other things that come out of a recording budget include catering, lodging, travel expenses, and, of course, studio time.

Of all the line items in a recording budget, which can range anywhere from $10,000 to $500,000 and up, one of the few variables is how much a producer is paid. More and more, it seems, producers are being asked to compromise on their asking fee in order to stay busy and keep a high profile in a highly competitive business. Where certain creditials might have meant a higher fee in days past, one well-known producer admits to jumping at a $10,000, all-in budget because he needed the work and it was the largest budget he had seen for a number of months. Chris Vrenna found himself in that situation when he worked with the punk band Strung Out on their 2003 *Live in a Dive* release. "We did the whole thing at my house for $10,000. It took us twelve hours a day for three weeks. If you prorate my salary, I might as well go work at McDonald's," he says. "It's not about the money, but people need to live."

While no one would suggest that production work is being compromised because of the lower budgets and salaries—meaning they would sacrifice a level of quality—many producers are finding ways around spending money by concentrating on pre-production and choosing to edit tracks rather than having a band or singer continue to perform a particularly challenging song.

These tightened purse strings are also having a negative affect on engineers, but those who make their living as mixers seem, so far, to be immune. "I've had it happen with records where the label says, 'We've got this amount of money. You've got to spend this and make the record; we don't have any more,'" Matt Wallace reports. "You're like, 'Man, if I could get more bread, we could spend more time or rent these instruments.' You grind, you work really hard to turn it in nice and cheap, and then all of a sudden the label trips over a bag of a hundred-and-fifty grand, and they hire some guy to mix it. He's some big-shot guy with an expensive studio and a huge fee. It's like, 'One-hundred-fifty grand? We had less than a hundred to make the record, you took us to task for it, and now you found this big pile of cash?' That stuff pisses me off. That's not playing fair.

"If they are going to do that, then they have to at least give us a little more money to make the record right. I've had records where I'm grinding all my friends and the people that I work with," Wallace continues. "I say to them, 'Look, I'm working really cheap, I need you to work cheap. Can you contribute your Pro Tools for free?' You do that stuff, and then they find this money."

Nick Launay knows that pain. "I think my part of the Semisonic record [*Feeling Strangely Fine,* 1998] was around $300,000, and then they went off and remixed it. With all of those people, they probably blew another $300,000 on that," he says. However, the mixing end of it does not get his ire up as much as labels spending money on videos. "The American Hi-Fi album [*The Art of Losing,* 2003] was actually very efficient; it was probably right around $200,000," he says. "Then they got us to cut three more songs, so maybe it got up to $300,000. Then they were talking about the first video being a million. So, we spent two or three months in the studio, then they went and do like a three-day shoot for a video, and it costs a million. What are we doing? Is the video what it's all about, and we are just a soundtrack to the video?"

Another troubling trend that Wallace has observed is when labels don't honor the contracts he makes on-the-cheap with session players, beat-makers, or engineers. "Labels say they're not going to pay them, because they didn't make the deal with them," Wallace says. "That's completely erroneous, because all of the musicians went through me. Every single one of them. I didn't contract with the label for any of them. Most producers just make the decisions and get the musicians. I've never called and said, 'Hey, I'm using so-and-so. Is that okay?'"

"The big phrase now with everyone I know in this business is that we're all working twice as hard for half the money," Wallace continues. "Most of us are at the point now where we're saying it's really not a lot of fun anymore, because you want to make at least some kind of living. Most of us work ten, twelve hours a day, six days a week, and if you really figure out what you're making per hour, it's not that great. It's not so much fun anymore. It used to be fun. I was making a little bit of dough and got to make a great record. Now I'm always watching the clock and making sure the right protocol is established. If I decide to spend a little more money or you need to hire so-and-so, now I've got to call people or have my manager send in a fax saying what's happening, so that they can't come back and get you later. It's frustrating, and it's taken a lot of the fun out of it."

"I've had some good projects that I find fiercely enjoyable, like this Caleb [Kane] project. I think the music is exceptional. I love it, but it's just getting to say, 'Okay, I'm gonna go work long hours and have to really fight for every dime I get and make records really cheaply.' Plus the fact that I'm having to build a studio again and ultimately subsidize a record. It's not as creative and fun as it used to be, which is too bad. I think a lot of the labels have established this aesthetic where hits are most important, but you can't spend a lot of money and you gotta go for more of a common denominator."

The numbers on Brad Wood's productions have ranged from less than $20,000 to over $300,000. "My fee is in there somewhere, depending on how bad I want to make the record, what my time schedule is, and the budget that's available," he says. "I think that [budgets] are getting smaller. It reached a peak and there were times when I said, 'I can do this for half of what you guys are talking about.' Bands would come and say, 'Our advance is X number of dollars.' I would tell them that there was no way it would cost that much. I didn't know how I could spend that money. Then [the band] would either take the advice and go back to the label and take less advance, or other times they'd take the advance and be happy about it. Oftentimes the record label would say, 'No, that recording advance is for recording, so you better find a way to spend it.' That's weird. Those days are over, though, for the time being, maybe for good. I don't think that's a bad thing, because I think people have overspent for lots of stuff."

Sylvia Massy Shivy understands that her Radio Star Studios enables her to save bands and labels up to $100,000 on a set of recording dates. "I have an advantage with the studio. I have every piece of gear that I could ever possibly want, so I can pretty much name the price of the studio," she says. "But, where I thought that it might have been an advantage, it's somewhat of a disadvantage because labels think that I don't have to pay a staff and things like that. So, I think that it's harder to convince labels to pay separate for the studio." At the same time, having the space enables her to save money for the band in some areas, and allows them to spend more time in the studio.

"It's terrible to run out of time, and it always seems to affect the most fun parts of the record, which are the final overdubs," Shivy continues. "I found a way around that, though, because I look at the schedule and say, 'Okay, I'll just kick 'em in a few days on the tail end so I can get the record the way I want it.' So, I'll actually give the client some extra days, if that's what it takes to do it right."

The philosophy of doing what it takes to get it right might make a producer popular with bands, but labels tend to get a bit antsy when the studio clock keeps ticking and the bill keeps growing. "I never watched the clock," Ed Cherney says. "I always forgot about the money. It was never about the money, and that's probably why I had some of the problems and arguments with the labels that I did. Most of the time when I was producing, it ended up with bad feelings between the label and me because I did whatever it took. I felt that if I could get the music right, everything else would take care of itself. If you look at the artists I worked with, I did three, four, five, six albums with every one. Typically, if you look at most cases, you get one shot with an artist, and then they're off doing the next thing with somebody new.

"The budgets are absolutely out of this world," Cherney continues. "Labels actually get together and decide how much they are going to pay a studio. Typically, it's not enough to keep a studio in business. I see that a lot, and these studios are struggling. I also see producers working on projects for spec. The label will only pay them if they like what they did, and I see people jumping at those."

The decline in budgets—and some producers accepting jobs on spec—started in the late 1990s, coinciding with a decline in CD sales, as well as corporations overpaying for companies and catalogs "They are just as tight as they can be and they are sweating bullets," Ed Cherney says. "They're struggling to stay in business too, and it trickles down. That's why I'm putting a studio in my house. I can mix records for people that have little budgets and deal with people whose music I'd like to work on. I couldn't do that if I had to go into a studio and pay twenty-five hundred a day. Now I can work at my leisure and spend as much time as I want at home on this stuff."

A fellow studio owner, Mark Howard, observes that his own space has enabled him to work with bands that do not have major-label budgets. Howard shifts between bigger budgets of $150,000 and $200,000, and projects with a lower budget, like the $30,000 that was spent to record Vic Chesnutt's 2003 release, *Silver Lake*. Part of the fee, obviously, goes to pay for Howard's time. That also varies from project to project. For instance, he was paid $50,000 to work on the Lucinda Williams album *World Without Tears*, and he was paid $15,000 for Chesnutt's sessions. Howard suggests that the numbers even out in the end, since he spent almost two months on the Williams project and a week or so with Chesnutt.

WORKING WITH THE BUDGET

So, the glory days of recording budgets are over. That is not news. What that means is that producers are finding ways to work around lower budgets. Many, like Matt Wallace, have worked on albums that have exceeded band and label expectations, in terms of creative realization, sales numbers, and chart success.

After a year of low-budget and indie projects, Wallace was not thrilled to work on another album for little money. "But I'm the kind of producer that can make records for cheap, because I've got a great engineer I work with who's very flexible with what he needs to get on a project," he says. "I'm certainly flexible with my dough."

That philosophy was tested in 2001 when Wallace worked on Sugarcult's *Start Static* and Maroon 5's 2002 release *Songs about Jane*. Wallace worked around a $100,000 budget by handling the Pro Tools editing and some of the engineering himself. "I don't like to do that, but budgets are tight and you have to be creative," he says. Another way that he has found to avoid the money pinch is by opening his own overdub room. "That means the engineer and I can keep some money in our pocket in a really tight budget," he explains.

Even with all his experience, Wallace was not prepared for the budget presented to him in 2004 to record the Squad Five-0 2004 album, *Late News Breaking*. "My manager made a budget, sent it to me, and as I was looking through it, I noticed that under producer it said zero dollars," he recalls. "It was the first time in my twenty-year career I had seen that. Capitol had to buy this band from another label, and they didn't want to spend a lot of money. So, Wallace called the label's A&R rep. "She said, Okay, here's what you gotta do.' She explained it to me. 'First of all, we'll take the travel and lodging out of the budget. We'll put it in A&R. So, that will get you some money. Then just write up a budget to record, and once it's done, if Andy Slater [the company's president] likes it, then we'll get the money to mix it.' Fortunately, I had that advice, because going into it I very seriously talked to my manager about doing the record for no money. I wanted to keep working and keep my name out there, which of course, would be financially heinous."

When Daron Malakian records with System of a Down, budgets aren't a big concern, however when he has stepped outside of the band and produced other acts he has seen how things can get dicey. "I did the Bad Acid Trip drum tracks, bass tracks, and most of the guitar tracks [for *Lynch the Weirdo*] in one week at Sound City," he explains. "I was cut for time, so I just said, 'Fuckin' play it again, play it again.' I got probably two or three great performances, because we didn't have enough money to buy enough tape. So, you gotta be satisfied a little sooner. You don't have the time to say, 'We gotta play it twenty more times.' You get stuff done quicker.

"System's budget is huge," he continues. "I can ask for stupid shit and it's just there. It's just not an issue, but it does get a little frustrating sometimes when it comes down to working with a band who has a $30,000 budget. For some indie bands, that's a lot of money to record an album. I don't come from there and I would like to work with more of a budget, but if you can't, you can't. What do you do? You do what you can. You get all the best performances down."

For bands that cannot come up with a reasonable budget, explains David Lowery, he will be honest with them from the start. "I'll get in there and say, 'Look, this isn't realistic.' Eventually the band is like, 'Yeah, we need another five or ten grand to really do this right. We're going to go out and do some shows. We're going to wait for the next quarter when we get the sales of our last record in.' Or the other way that people do it these days is credit cards," he reports. "That's actually true. Something really interesting is happening in getting things financed these days."

The band Rye Coalition knows how to finance albums, as they have gone from recording their own music to signing with the independent-label Tiger Style to signing a major-label deal with DreamWorks Records. (When DreamWorks was sold in late 2003, the band was moved to Interscope Records in March of 2004.) During the band's Tiger Style days, the budgets were just enough "to get into the studio and bang it out in a week," Dave Leto explains. That changed when they signed the DreamWorks deal and got a budget in the neighborhood of $200,000. "It was the first time that we've ever had the luxury of taking our time recording-wise. That's not a luxury that's afforded from being on a small label. No small label could afford that."

That impressive budget also enabled the band to shop for producers. "I think you get what you pay for," says Leto. "Maybe there's a chance of people being open to [our record] if someone they respect had something to do with it. Whereas, if we just did it ourselves, there might not be that much excitement. We wanted that and we got it. It's like, whatever—we were going to owe money, regardless of what we do."

Perhaps one of the most unfortunate things about the tight budget climate is that producers and bands are finding themselves watching the clock. That is especially true for the smaller-budget bands for whom time and money run out awfully quick in the studio. While it might seem like working quickly and being conservative with studio time would be a smart way to work within a budget, it often leads to spending more money because more time is needed in the editing and mixing dates.

But when the pressure is on, there are ways to save money. Wallace did it by handling the engineering for the Squad Five-0 album; Malakian did it by pushing the band through the recording dates at a studio. Joe Henry did that with Solomon Burke's *Don't Give Up on Me,* and Craig Street worked some low-budget magic on The Holmes Brothers' 2003 offering, *Simple Truths.* Like Henry, Street recorded the album in three days and mixed it on the fourth. "You work like a demon. Extra musicians come in and cut deals. That's how you [work with a low budget]. You make sure you're taken care of in the pre-production department, so that you know what you're going in with, and that's how you do it," he says. "You leave yourself a day or two extra for things that might be surprises that pop up."

And, of course, producers and artists alike are building their own recording spaces as a way of avoiding that ticking clock. "That would be the joy of owning my own space," says Ben Harper. "To be able to turn off that clock once and for all, and to be able to have a space that was at arm's reach to where I could have the freedom at a moment's spark of an idea to take it to tape. I need to follow the music—the music inside is as perpetual as the wind, and I need to be able to follow that."

GOING OVER BUDGET

Mark Trombino's experience with The Living End's project—going over budget and then having the money taken out of his back-end deal discussed in Chapter One—is not a new issue for producers. There is a clause in every contract that covers potential overages, holding producers accountable. What is striking about Trombino's experience is that this clause was actually enforced. More often than not, records go over budget for myriad reasons that include the label requesting more songs, the band working inefficiently in the studio, a band member having an issue with drugs or alcohol, or heading into the studio before the band has an idea of what they want to do.

"I have gone over a couple of times, and the unfortunate thing is even with my best efforts of trying to make everything work out just right, it goes over," reports Matt Wallace. "If the label is cool, they won't take you to task, but in recent years the label can take some or all of your money if you've gone over a substantial amount of money. I think it's lame. In the old days they used to say, 'Okay, you've gone over a little bit, it's not a big deal.' But even ten years ago I had a project on Geffen where we went over like three grand, and this was a band who were a bunch of ne'er-do-wells who did everything they could to jeopardize the work in spite of my best efforts. I was stuck with something that was really, truly, honestly not my fault, and I ended up paying. I had to write them a check. It was really a drag."

Wallace also faced that issue while working on Khaleel's *People Watching* release (1998), which he felt was an outstanding record. "It was basically a Seal-quality record on about a tenth of the budget," he says. "It was the first time I spent five months on a record, and that was because if things weren't right I said, 'We gotta do it again. Let's try again.' It was at my own studio, so fortunately or unfortunately, I was kind of subsidizing the record because I didn't charge very much for [the studio]. We cut things, re-cut things, and I kept saying, 'We're not going to turn this thing in until it's absolutely brilliant.'"

At the same time, other issues pushed the project over budget. "I had two people fall by the wayside," he recalls. "Out of four guys, one guy ended up on crack, and the other guy couldn't play, so I ended up hiring people. I got a lot of grief on that record, in spite of subsidizing it in my own studio and really doing all I could. We lost two members, we went over budget a bit, and they were really going to nail me for it. They were going to actually charge me out of my royalties.

"Sometimes producers will spend a lot of dough," Wallace continues. "There are some guys who are known for spending a million-plus dollars on a record. They blow it on a lot of food and fun things, but I've never been that kind of guy. I used to make records for a thousand dollars, all in. So, I'm very, very tight with money. But it happens, and it's just frustrating to be taken to task for it."

Even with label approval, there are the times when a producer can be nicked for overages. Wallace recounts the experience of a fellow producer who was working with a band that wanted to record a couple of extra songs, which met with label satisfaction. When it came time to settle the final invoices, that producer was charged with the overages incurred by the extra studio time. "At that point I would say, 'Great, then I own these tracks. If you want them you can buy them from me.' Labels can follow the letter of the law and make you pay, and that's frustrating when you're a producer," Wallace says.

Nick Launay admits with a smile that he has probably gone over budget on every project he has completed. He says a label has never approached him for payback because he is up-front with them at the beginning of the process. "The rule in the contracts, and this is pretty standard, is that if you're going to go over budget then it's your responsibility as a record producer that you're going over and ask for whatever money you need. It's their decision to give you more money. In England, there is never a budget; they just employ you and you do the album. That's why albums take so long in England, because no one's looking. It's stupid over there. But here [in the United States], you have a contract, obviously, that marks down what you're getting and also says that it's the record producer's responsibility to keep the budget to what's been decided."

That said, Launay recalls a situation that he did an inexpensive album for a New Zealand-based band and then nearly got money taken out at the end. "I cut my pay by half, I borrowed all the equipment from Midnight Oil, I saved them about $100,000, and we did this album for under $80,000," he reports. "They are not signed in America, so we did this record for Australia, and when they get signed in America I will get paid the rest and get to do more, and it will all work out. But, we had a very, very, very small budget, which I was supposed to keep to, but I found it impossible. So, I rang them up and told them I'd mix it fast and compromise." The band and label asked him not to sacrifice mix quality for price, and in the end he went over the budget by $800. "They said, 'Well, you said you'd do it for…' I said, 'Yeah, I did, but it's $800.' I said, 'Look, I reduced my fee by 45,000 American dollars, and you're giving me a hard time about $800. Are you serious?' Then I talked to the head of the label, and he said, 'No, look, just do whatever you want.' So, it's this weird situation where the guy who owns the record company is thanking me and the head of A&R who has the responsibility of saying, 'Nick, you're going over budget.' I got an e-mail saying I've gone $4,000 over budget, which is nothing, but I am probably contractually obliged to pay that $4,000 myself. If I have to pay it, I'll be so surprised because this is such a weird situation."

PRODUCING ON THE CHEAP FOR THE LOVE OF THE BAND

If there is one universal truth when it comes to record producers, it is simply that each started their careers with a love of music and an idea that they would be able to help a band or artist achieve something inspirational in the studio. Often, these new producers would provide their services gratis in the hopes that a reputation would be built and relationships established. Frequently, it would work, and as the bands they helped signed recording contracts, the producers would get the chance to produce a collection of songs with the freedom of a budget. If that album is a creative and/or commercial success, the odds are high that the producer will move on to work with more and more bands.

One of the luxuries of a growing credit list should be the ability to earn more money. Success should breed success, and many producers have seen their salaries grow to substantial amounts. However, at the same time that some producers command up to a million dollars per job, there are others who bounce between salaries on projects, depending on budget and artist visibility. On those jobs, a lower advance can be made up in the long run if the producer can secure a higher percentage on the back end.

Even with a discography that includes a handful of genre-defining releases, Dave Jerden believes in working with younger bands, and he will often put his fee on a sliding scale to make that happen. "I am nowhere near the top-dollar fee for doing an album," Jerden says. "My whole thing is if the record is going to sell then the money is going to be there. I don't want to be the guy that the band's in hock to forever. I don't want them to be so far in the hole with me. The MxPx record, for instance, I think I was probably the smallest thing on the budget. I think the Alge brothers [Tom and Chris Lord-Alge] got more than I got for mixing it. I'd rather sell the record. If the record is going to sell, then there's going to be money to be made and we'll be fine."

"I do budgets for $10,000, because some people don't have a lot of money," says Mark Howard. "There is a band from Texas, they are unsigned and are called Dead Man, and I just liked some of their songs. I said, 'Okay, give me $10,000 and I'll make your record in five days.'" The difference between a $10,000 budget and the $30,000 budget he had to record Vic Chesnutt's album? "We were able to pay for people [to come in], and food," he says, "and for [Dead

Man], they had their band together and we ate pizza."

CREATIVE FINANCING

There's a big difference between finding creative ways to spend the money in a budget and stealing. "There are a lot of producers that scam a lot of things," states Dave Jerden. "For instance, they'll buy gear on the budget, charge it back to the artist, and then end up owning it on top of it. So, they may put in the budget enough to buy, let's say, a Fairchild compressor, and then they'll charge the artist on top of that or they'll make up some phony billing thing to say that they're actually renting that thing, and then when the project is done, they own it. That's a common scam. Another one is studio kickbacks; a producer will pick Studio A over Studio B. Studio B may be a better choice, but they're getting a kickback at Studio A. You only have your word and if you're caught once lying in this business, you're over."

MONEY DOESN'T EQUAL PERFECTION

It is clear that producers and artists who are working with low budgets need to work efficiently in the studio, and there might even be a certain benefit to that pressure. Sometimes when teams have unlimited budgets and time in the studio, the music suffers, because every note recorded can be scrutinized and perfected. Every performance can redone or edited, practically to sterility. "Even if there weren't budgetary concerns," says J.D. Foster, "I feel like there are definitely records that have been way over-thought, where people jumped down a rabbit hole and should have stopped."

The navel-gazing approach can stretch from the recording sessions to the mixing dates, and more often than not, that search for perfection is wasted time. In fact, that quest is one of Lou Giordano's frustrations. "It's really frustrating, because there's a point where you stop making it better. Every time I'd mix a song for Paul Westerberg [on *Eventually*, 1996], he would come in after an hour-and-a-half or two hours and say, "You've been working on this far too long. If you keep on going you're going to ruin it. Start printing it right now.' It was one of the funniest things said to me. That's just the way he is, and it was really refreshing."

11 BEFORE THE STUDIO

From the outside, record production might look like it boils down to finding an artist, building a team, putting a budget together, and then recording. It is not quite that simple. In fact, much of the work that record producers and bands do together happens before one note is played in a studio. Through the process of pre-production, a blueprint to success is designed, with songs and arrangements fine-tuned and lyrics finalized. At the same time, a delicate balance is created, where a producer can push a band to something new or leave space for an inspired performance to happen in the studio.

Pre-production is also the time when a producer will consider the band's demos and the label's wishes for songs to be developed into singles, or when a producer will take the opportunity to reel in a band that is trying to stretch a bit beyond their comfort zone. All of this work is done before entering the studio, to save time and money. Rather than spending thousands of dollars a day in a recording studio, bands and producers spend a fraction of that in a rehearsal space or somebody's home, working out any issues that might appear when the red light is flipped on.

"I basically make a rule with the band and I explain to them before we go on in [to the studio] that rehearsal time is cheap time and it's experimental time," reports Nick Launay. "The point of it is to go in and try absolutely everything we can on each song—any idea that any member of the band has that's been lurking around their mind, that they've been too afraid to say because they're maybe not the main songwriter. This is the time when we try starting the song with the outro, or we try it slower, or we try it faster, we do anything we can in rehearsal. If, at the end of the day, it really isn't any better than it was when we walked in, that's fine, but at least we've gone there, so when we walk into the studio, which is a thousand dollars a day, maybe more, we're not fucking around. We know that we're gonna play it this way and all we're gonna do is get great sounds and concentrate on the playing. If ever a new idea comes up, that's fine too."

Pre-production is also the time to make sure that the producer and band are a good match before a good amount of money is spent. Producers use that time to get to know the band members better and uncover problems that might have stayed hidden until that time.

"You can listen to the songs that are being considered for the record and make opinions about what songs are the better songs, or what group of songs would make a great record among what you have to choose from, but it's not until you get into pre-production where you find out the politics in the band," explains Sylvia Massy Shivy. "You find out how they work together or who the master of the band is, the person who calls all the shots. Is it a democracy where everyone has something to say? You don't know that until you really get into pre-production with them, and sometimes you have to tip-toe around some of the issues until you find out. You don't want to tell [one person] their songs are crap and the other guy's songs are the good songs. But that happens. My job is to make the best record, and it's not to make everybody happy in the band. So, sometimes some of the band members feel neglected or put out, and then you have to kind of massage that and make everyone feel like they're equals. You don't know all that until you get into pre-production."

THE ART OF PRE-PRODUCTION

For days or weeks, bands and producers have the opportunity to sit down outside of the pressure of a studio to pick songs that will appear on the album, work out potential song issues, get to know each other, and make sure that a plan is in place to have a successful set of recording dates. There are many ways to accomplish those goals, ranging from sitting down with acoustic guitars and a small drum kit to hear the bare essence of a song, to setting up the full band and ripping through the songs in all their electric glory. The variety of approaches in pre-production often mirrors how the team will work together in the studio.

"The most important thing going on in pre-production is song selection," explains Howard Benson. "The first day, I'll listen to everything and I will immediately weed out songs. If we're doing a twelve-song record, I'll pick my favorite six to eight songs and say, 'I gotta have these, you guys can have the rest.' Usually, the first six I pick are the ones they want to do anyway. It's the ones that are after that six that you start getting into arguments with them and it's sort of a waste of time. I just let them have their way, because it's their record anyway. So, if [those songs] are not singles, really you gotta trust that they're gonna know more than you are about what their fans are gonna like, because those are fan-type songs."

After the songs are picked, Benson takes notes during rehearsal about the structure of the songs and talks about arrangements, parts, and pieces that need to be rewritten. "It's basic stuff, real fundamental stuff," he explains. "I get the drummer playing with a click if we have to do that. You find out a lot of things about the band in rehearsal. You find out their weaknesses and strengths, so when you go into the studio you're not totally surprised. You can listen to the guitar players and go, 'Wow, I've got great guitar players,' or, 'Boy, I'm gonna spend more time on guitars than I thought.'"

More than that, Benson adds, there better be a single-worthy song by that time. "Believe me, when you walk out of pre-production, if you don't have a single there, you're screwed. Now, that doesn't mean that you can't get it, it just means that you are going to have to work harder at it. Cold didn't have "Stupid Girl" in pre-production. That was created in the studio with the combination of Scooter [Ward, the band's singer] and Rivers Cuomo [of Weezer], who did some of the co-writing of songs, and me doing some Pro Tools magic. The three of us, unknowingly amongst ourselves, had no idea that we were coming up with the single. We just kept working on the song and made it as good as we could get it. Then, the people at Geffen heard it and they said, 'That's the single.' That happens sometimes. You can't discount those types of things, but that's not really the way you want to do it.

"I know [Cold] well enough that I can sit in a room in the studio and we'll probably pull something out," Benson continues. "I feel that way about P.O.D., too. When we walked into the studio, we didn't have "Alive" or "Youth of the Nation." [Those two songs fueled the multi-Platinum success of the *Satellite* in 2001.] We had the parts, but we didn't have the finished songs. In fact, Sonny didn't have lyrics to "Alive" until we were ready to sing it. As a band, they can sit around the table and work songs out really well, and that's kind of how some of that has worked out, but you have to know your artist."

Dave Jerden's pre-production starts when he first gets a band's demo. "I listen to it first to see if it's anything that I might be interested in at all. If it is, I start over, maybe I'll pop through a few songs, maybe listen to the first song all the way through, the second song, and then if it sounds like someone I'd be interested in, then I'll listen to maybe the first minute or thirty seconds of every song after that, just to see if they just have two songs or they have enough to work with," he explains. "If they do, then I'll sit on the couch with a notebook and write down my first impressions. First impressions are really important, because a lot of things start shading your decision making after that. The reason I think it's important is because I'm in the same position that the audience will be in, or the radio-station programmer, or even the record company—it's all going to be first impressions. On the first notes, I may write down that the song needs a bridge or we need to expand the bridge, whatever, just really quick notes. Then I put that notebook aside and I don't listen again or do anything else until I go into the first pre-production or rehearsal."

During the first pre-production dates, Jerden is looking for the band to play the songs in a comfortable setting without the pressure of production. "Making a song work through production is always a stiff way to work," he says. "If a band can just play it through naturally and the arrangements work naturally, then it's going to record really well. I just want a song to flow, I want to make a statement, get in and out, and I want it to be played properly. I just want to make sure everybody's on the same page, everybody knows what each other's doing, and it grooves. So I have my first notes, then I go into pre-production to make sure it's going to be played through properly and it feels good, and then it's usually at that stage that I find out what songs are working and not working."

Those notes and the band's pre-production dates helped, for instance, when Jerden went to work with MxPx on their *Before Everything & After* release. "Their songs were all written in a real strict format—intro, verse, chorus, verse, bridge, chorus, out. Every song was like two minutes long, and Ron Fair with A&M Records wanted to expand on that, so we spent a lot of time in pre-production on that," Jerden explains. "It was fun for them to do it, because I don't think they've ever really worked that way where they took the arrangements and expanded them to four-minute arrangements."

Pre-production is important for any band, but J.D. Foster believes it is especially important for a band that has been on the road for any length of time. "I think it's really good for them, because sometimes they get out in front of crowds and learn the wrong bells and whistles," he explains. "Just because it worked in front of a crowd of semi-inebriated people doesn't mean it's going to work under a crowd of microphones. I think pre-production is really great with people who have been out touring and know the stuff really well, and it's a good time to turn in some interesting directions. It's just my personal experience; that's where it's most rewarding and surprising."

To combat the fear that bands might feel over those left turns, some producers opt to record pre-production sessions. Michael Rosen, for instance, first utilizes pre-production dates as a way to set the tone for the recording sessions. "Your shtick kind of gets going with them then, and you can start winning the little battles, like 'Try this.' 'Wow, this sounds pretty good. This guy knows what he's talking about.' Every little victory starts to add up. When you get in the studio, you still change stuff, because the speakers don't lie and I'm not right one hundred percent of the time."

That is why Rosen records the rehearsals with a Pro Tools rig. "When you're arranging, all you have to do is step back and listen to it," he explains. "The band will say, 'Oh wow, you're right, that does sound good.' Sometimes they can't hear a difference while they're playing it, but when they listen back, it becomes clear."

Matt Wallace's introduction to Maroon 5 came via some demos that singer/songwriter Adam Levine sent him. "They had kind of an urban feel," Wallace recalls. "Then there were some band demos, and then there was this other kind of thing that was, I guess, more like a rehearsal. It was kind of a different feel." With the material in front of him, Wallace sat down with the band and figured out what songs would be recorded. Then the band and producer spent two weeks working out each song. "Invariably, we'll talk about what songs we want to approach, what the songs need, and I usually spend about thirty to forty percent of the time with acoustic guitars. We sit around and play, because that way we see people's songs. It's easy to be enamored with the volume of a band playing live or a groove, but if we sit down and we play on acoustics, we can figure out what we have. Is this the song? Is it the right key? I've had bands that are in the wrong key and have to bring things down. Then we work up the tempo and the arrangements.

"For Maroon 5, one of the main contributions I brought to the band was the idea of writing some bridges," Wallace continues. "Few of their songs had bridges. If you listen to "Harder to Breathe" and "This Love," those bridges were written during the pre-production process. So, we work on the songs and I always record [the rehearsals] on my little DAT recorder and make CDs. I give them to the band, because when you're working on arrangements and you're trying to play them it's important to be cognizant of the changes. Most people don't like change, because they have to think about it. When I give them the CDs, they can live with [the changes], and if they can listen as an audience would, then they can hear it and say, 'Oh, that's great' or 'No, it's not working.' It can actually give them a bit of perspective. I find that part of the process essential."

Where Rosen and Wallace record the pre-production dates, Launay will take the band's demos, dump them into Pro Tools, and then work with them. "I do rough edits on my laptop to see for myself what's going to work," he explains. Then, much like Rosen, Launay uses the recorded sessions to illustrate his ideas to a band. "I will say to a band, 'Maybe you've worked three months, six months on your songs, and you might think they are great, but we're gonna go in nevertheless and we're going to pull them apart to see what we can do.' It's no pressure, because some bands get very, very precious about each song. Some are dying for someone to come in and rip them apart. Some bands aren't; they think very often, especially young bands, that they know it all and there's nothing more to be learned. Those are often the bands that will get surprised and say, 'Oh, I never knew that was possible.'"

There are also times when the sessions recorded in pre-production are better than what the producer and band can capture in the studio. "A lot of times, when these guys are doing demos they have these moments of pure inspiration and they get possessed to do something [in the studio] that's beyond what they've done before," says Lou Giordano. "There is usually a lot of that on the demos, and nowadays with Pro Tools it's really not a problem to use whole forms of a demo for the full recording. It has the inspiration, because that was the first time it was done and it can't be topped." He did just that while working on the 1996 release, *Eventually*, with Paul Westerberg. "We found there were quite a few songs with him where his demos were better than anything the band did, so we just used his demo and had a drummer come in and cut drums to it instead of a drum machine," he explains. "We both were listening to it, and I would say, 'You know what? Your demo blows this away; it's got a way better groove to it.' I played him the one that the band did and then I played him his, and that was it."

Certainly, sitting face to face with a band is the desired mode of pre-production, but sometimes that's not possible, as Ryan Greene explains: "Most of the bands that I work with are very low-end on the budget, and I'm normally working back to back to back," he says. "So, I try to get them to send me CDs or cassettes. I listen to them, call the band up, and make my arrangements over the phone. 'Why don't we try this and this and this? Work on it, send me another tape.' Then when they get in the studio, we'll go through the drum beats, the bass parts, and we build it up. I feel pre-production is very important. I don't get to do enough of it outside the studio." Then again, for the punk-rock style of music that Greene tends to produce, the lack of pre-production seems to work. "On a lot of the records I do, the band will show up, I'll listen to it, and say, 'Okay, let's sit down and tap this thing out. Okay, this song is now done, arranged, and all the drum beats are worked out. Let's go in and track,'" he says. "I guess with that you get an interesting energy. In this type of music where you want to keep it a little on the edgy side, I think that's a good thing."

One of the benefits to the process of working out songs with artists outside of the studio is the flexibility it gives you in possible locations. Certainly, some people take advantage of rehearsal spaces, but when Joe Henry started working with Ani DiFranco, the two spent time together while DiFranco was traveling to Australia during an early 2004 tour, and when Henry toured with her later that year. "When she was on her way to Australia she flew into L.A. late one night, and I went to her motel room in Marina Del Ray and she sat with a guitar and played me about nine new songs," he says. "That was pre-production. Then, during the tour I will be traveling with her on her bus, so that will be our chance to listen to the songs."

In addition to finalizing the musical side of things, Dave Fridmann utilizes the pre-production time to draw up an accurate budget. "I think pre-production is vital, even to bands that write in the studio. A lot of the groups I work with are pretty nebulous and really are writing in the studio, but even in those instances, to have some idea before you go in or have some plan before you go in is vital to the success of actually getting the thing done," he explains. "A more typical situation is when the band has already demoed the songs and you have an idea of how many songs there are, what the structure is, how long it's going to take, and whether or not the band is really prepared to pull it off. If you're smart, you'll sit down with a piece of paper and a pen and just start adding it up. 'I think it's going to take this many days for that and this many days for that.' In general, I can look at a rock band and assume you're going to take six to eight weeks to do a major-label rock production. A couple of weeks for basics, couple of weeks for overdubs, a couple of weeks to change your mind, and a couple of weeks to mix it. Then you go ahead and start budgeting—you have to make sure that you have a studio that's available and know exactly what it's going to cost.

"As the producer, you're the guy who's standing there saying, 'I swear, I can make this happen.' So, you have to be the first one up in the morning and, well, you don't have to be the last one to bed at night, but the last one still working when it's going on," Fridmann continues. "You also have to make sure that, day by day, you're checking off the things on those lists you made two months before you ever set foot in the studio and making sure it's getting done. If you do, then you'll be able to stay on budget. There's an element of trying to capture the magic or something that's extremely nebulous, but you have to be methodical, or it just isn't going to get done."

Although many producers declare that pre-production is the lynch-pin to a successful set of recording dates, others believe that time to be a waste. Don Gehman, for instance, reports: "I'll use [pre-production] just to help select songs or realize problems in the song, but I find more and more that it's difficult to make solutions really stick. If a band is not rehearsed well enough, then they just need to rehearse. They don't need me around for that, but the pre-production idea of actually changing arrangements and fine-tuning tempos, I've always found that I make judgments that are not accurate. There's something about trying to get all the sound through one little speaker that changes your perception of so many things. All of a sudden, this guy over in the corner who's been playing this obnoxious guitar part, you can turn him down and get him out of the way and get to the soft little guitar part that might be the hook of the whole record and turn it up. In a rehearsal, you never hear that stuff and you lose track of where the song's at, because you have no control over the balances."

Ed Cherney often avoids pre-production if he has put together a session band for an album. "A lot of times, I would just cast the band and go into the studio to work on songs, song structure, and things like that," he explains. "I would always try to make it that moment of creation where some accident would happen and I would record it. I preferred to do it that way rather than having it all mapped out before we went into the studio. I was looking for those happy accidents and sometimes, for me, pre-production would preclude that from happening." However, Cherney says that his approach differs when he works with an artist or a band who has their own songs. If it is a band, he says, "you're probably better off going and working them out in a pre-production situation," he says. "It just depends—whatever it's going to take to bring the music forward and be the most compelling."

Selecting Songs

It is one thing to make sure a song works from melodies to parts to lyrics, but if you've chosen the wrong song in the first place, all that hard work is for naught. Producer after producer agrees that, early on in a project, picking the right songs for an album—whether that means songs geared for radio, artistic statements, or fan favorites after a set of tour dates—is one of the most important tasks that will be completed early on in the relationship. Finding just the right songs depends, obviously, on what the band wants to do with the album and how realized the songs are when the band is ready to record.

The criterion for recording-ready songs is straight-ahead for Sylvia Massy Shivy. "I look for the strongest melodies in the chorus and the strongest lyrical hook," she explains. "I think vocals are probably the most important in regards to melody and chorus. I love energy and I love depth in the instrumentation, but ultimately the chorus rules for me."

When Dave Jerden gets a band's demo, he listens to it for the first time and rates the songs. "I'll use stars, like anywhere from no stars, which means the song sucks to me and there's no redeeming thing about it at all, to five stars, where I think the song is really great," he explains. "So, five-star and four-star songs are my A-list. I'll make an A-list, a B-list, and a C-list, and I'll have the band do the same if they have a lot of material. Sometimes, when I walk in with my A-list and there's a song on the C-list, they have what's on my C-list on their A-list. So, they're hearing something in a song because it gets good audience response or something that I'm not hearing."

That's when playing all the songs in pre-production becomes useful, because Jerden will listen to all of the songs the band has prepared for the release and be honest with them. "When I hear a C-list song, I'll say, 'I didn't like the song. It didn't do anything for me, and they'll say, 'Well, we like the song and it gets really good audience response.' Then they'll play it again live, and all of a sudden I can hear what they're talking about. It just didn't translate on the demo for whatever reason. So, I'll take all those things into consideration, and then we come up with a revised A-list."

Ideally, Jerden will walk into the studio with fifteen songs ready to go, with a handful of others for B-sides. "Sometimes we'll go in with twelve songs they're planning on doing and four extra songs that are going to be B-sides that are from the B-list," he says. "Then all of a sudden, a B-song is going to be an A-song. That's happened a lot. I try to record a little bit more than I need, but it's a crapshoot sometimes. You get the best songs and the best arrangements, but there are so many variables. It's really by the seat of your pants on how to do it. I mean there's no science to it."

The number of songs that a band walks into pre-production with, ready to record, varies from group to group. Jerden recalls that MxPx, for instance, had around forty songs for their *Before Everything & After* sessions. On the other hand, when Trombino went into the aborted Jimmy Eat World sessions, the band did not have enough material to fill an album. Dave Fridmann's experience is that some bands do have forty songs written, "but it's easy to get rid of the first twenty, and then it's just a few decisions after that. More often than not, the band isn't sure the song's going to go, so you try it and it works or it doesn't. You try and go through pre-production with that in mind and try to get an idea of what [the album] is going to sound like," he explains. "It usually becomes pretty apparent, and it's not usually that difficult a decision."

Mark Howard echoes Fridmann's sentiments, especially in relation to his work with Vic Chesnutt, who came to their project with sketches of 120 songs. "It's a chipping-away process," Howard says. "I picked the ones that I liked, he had the ones that he liked, and we just kept on filtering them down to the ones that we ended up with on the record," he says. Then again, there are the times when the band doesn't have quite that many. "The Bastard Sons of Johnny Cash had only sixteen songs and some of them weren't that great, but you've got to make them work."

"Sometimes a band will come in with twenty-five songs and they can't decide, and sometimes the one that's a clunker, that you're not sure about that barely gets into the top twelve, if you work on it for a couple days, all of a sudden becomes a shining star," Chris Vrenna says. "It becomes one of the stand-out album tracks. So, you never know, but [pre-production] is definitely where you narrow your field and know exactly what songs you're going to do."

Yet, when Vrenna is sifting through the collection of songs, it is not performances that he is after; those can come during the recording dates. "I try to do it by hook. Is it catchy? Is the vocal really strong? What is the guitar riff like? Sometimes the hook does not have to be the vocal," Vrenna says. "It can be the quirky drum beat. I just try to see what songs have the best hooks and what will make the best all-around album. You don't want ten out of twelve songs all being in the same tempo range or in the same keys," he says. "You want to have some slow material, you want have some fast ones, you want to make sure you've got some singles, you want to make sure you have some ones that aren't ever going to be singles. Look at Radiohead—all their stuff is so weird anyway, who knows what could be a single for them? But you've got to be able to show an artistic side as well. You gotta have those songs in there that are just cool songs for fans."

Certainly, producers look to artists to bring in a collection of songs, yet there are times when the producer will suggest choices of material for an album. For instance, when Rick Rubin and Johnny Cash worked together, the two communicated quite a bit about the songs they would record. "He would write some songs, and he would look for songs and send them to me, and I looked for songs and sent them to him," Rubin recalls. "We would exchange [songs] and then spend a good deal of time in pre-production figuring out what the songs should be."

Craig Street has made a bit of a name for himself by making unexpected song choices for the artists he has produced. Take the work he did on Cassandra Wilson's *Blue Light Til Dawn* (1993), which featured a pair of Robert Johnson songs, and a tune each from Van Morrison and Joni Mitchell. Then there's *Temptation,* the 1995 Holly Cole album of purely Tom Waits' material. Street gave the classical singer Jubilant Sykes songs by John Hiatt, Tom Waits, and Bob Dylan to sing on his 2001 *Wait for Me* release. "I just don't have any borders musically. I never have," Street explains. "I grew up in a house where there was every kind of music that you can imagine. It wasn't until I was probably out of high school that I actually understood clearly that there were different types of music. I was seventeen or eighteen and went to work at Tower Records, and I was like, 'Oh, they have it divided. There are these subdivisions. This is weird.' The radio stations I grew up with played everything and it didn't matter. So, I don't hear divisions, and I also don't hear the reason why you can't pull something from one place and put it into another place."

Street tested his philosophy on *Blue Light Til Dawn,* which was his first production job. "A lot of people in the jazz world freaked out," he recalls. "I had her and Chris Whitley doing "I Can't Stand the Rain," and there was a Van Morrison song. The main difference about it was that I got rid of all the jazzy instruments in the obvious sense, because to me when I heard what she was doing with the B3 and trombone and electric bass, it was all in the same range. She has a luscious contralto and was like, 'Hey, why don't we open this up? Let's use some acoustic guitar. Let's use some other instruments.'"

The strategy for finding songs varies from artist to artist, Street says. "Sometimes people are like, 'Oh, just find a bunch of songs for me.' Sometimes people are like, 'Well, I have some ideas, and you have some ideas.' For example, when I worked with k.d. lang on her record [*Drag,* 1997], we traded tapes back and forth for months until we finally came down with a list. I did a record with a Canadian singer Holly Cole where it was all Tom Waits material and we spent months trading Waits material back and forth. We both had A-lists and

B-lists, and then we narrowed it down to one A-list that we both agreed on. It was an interesting process, because it was her idea and the record company's idea to do Waits, but Holly really didn't know Waits beyond the early stuff, and she was just like, 'Well I don't know how much of this I can sing.' I said, 'Well, you gotta listen to the older stuff, because there are some amazing songs there.'

"I always like to get something from the artist first, because that's a really good clue as to what they like," Street continues. "I try to sense what an artist's taste is and then figure that, if they're asking me to work with them, then they're trying to push a little past that. So, I ask myself how I anchor myself in their taste, and at the same time find things outside of that. I think the picking of the songs is really simple."

When country music's Tony Brown is looking for the right songs for the artists that he works with, he does not necessarily look to take risks. Rather, he tries to provide those artists with strong options. "As you get prepared for a record, you listen to lots of songs. You send [the artists] songs, and they send you songs and eventually, by the time you arrive at the designated session date, you've hopefully accumulated enough songs for a record," he says. "Maybe you've got fifteen or twenty-five songs that you both like, and then you have to pick out ten or twelve of those that should be on the record. The thing that a producer, in my opinion, must remember is that it's the artist's record and not your record. The record company has hired you to produce a record, so the [songs] must be true for the artist, but then they have to have some commercial viability. That's your job."

HIT SONGS? RADIO SONGS?

Tony Brown's point that there has to be some sort of commercial viability is crucial. "If it gets down to two songs left, and you know that one song is a hit and the artist likes them both equally well, then your job is to convince them to cut them both, but eventually convince them to put the song that you think is the hit on the record," Brown continues. "Because the hit becomes the tool that tells the world that this artist has a record out there that is full of great songs like this one. You have to wear two hats. You have to wear an artist-friendly hat, which is the first hat you should wear, but then you also have to wear the smart hat that says if you cut a song that gets a lot of exposure as far as radio, it tells the world that this piece of music exists and that you should go out and buy it."

Matt Wallace takes the point one step further. "I think it's essential these days [that] if you're on a major label, as an artist, you have to at least be cognizant that they're going to ask for singles," he says. "If you're not comfortable with that, you should be signed to an indie label." Singles, he allows, happen a couple of different ways. "There are the ones that are really contrived and thought out and planned out, and then the label goes after it really methodically. The other ones are the ones that kind of happen by osmosis, where as a band you just do things that you really like and they catch on."

Wallace has a number of examples of the latter to his credit, including his work with Faith No More, Train, and Maroon 5. "Faith No More is the best example of where we made a record we were proud of [*The Real Thing*, 1989]. We knew we loved it, we thought it had something great, but for the first year or so Warner Bros. kept saying, 'Wow, great record. No singles. The radio's not going to play this, but great record.' We thought, 'Man, there must be some singles around here.' Sure enough, "Epic" went to Number Nine on the charts. Obviously, at that time, nothing had preceded that song that was that style of music, but I think that sometimes labels underestimate the audience. Now, with some of the newer bands like The Hives, The Strokes, The White Stripes, people are a little more open to things that aren't obviously singles."

That became clear to Wallace back in the late 1990s when he mixed the song "Meet Virginia" for Train. Although it became the band's break-out single from their 1998 self-titled debut, Wallace reports that there were not many believers at first. "If you played it for someone, they would say, 'There's no chorus.' It was never a radio single from the get-go, but I think by virtue of the fact that the band toured for a year-and-a-half and Aware Records hung in with them for that long, it became the single. There are a lot of songs that could be singles if given the nurture and the patience." Patience, though, is not necessarily a staple in many record-company lexicons. "If it's not happening in five or six weeks, the label [pulls it]," Wallace ruefully admits. "They've got other things in the pipeline. They just let it go. It's very frustrating."

American Hi-Fi and producer Nick Launay experienced just that type of angst after *The Art of Losing*, the band's 2003 release, was handed into the record label upon completion. Originally, the band approached him in the hopes that they could strip away some of their pop sheen and move toward more of a punk and aggressive sound. "They wanted to be perceived more as a real band, because they are, and when they play live, they are amazing," Launay says. "They are an amazing band. You could say unfortunately they had a huge success with a pop single ["Flavor of the Weak" from the band's 2001 eponymous debut], but they wanted to move so they could become an established band. So, that's why they wanted someone like me to come in. The plan was to come in and make a really raw rock record, so they would go out and they could present themselves as a little more edgy. We made this album, and there were a couple of songs on there that are really more punky. The whole thing was perfect. It was set up brilliantly. We delivered the album, and the record company was ecstatic. The head of the label heard [the "The Breakup Song"] and he said, 'That's the biggest hit of the year. We're going to spend a million on the video. We're going to do this, we're going to do that.' I thought that was fantastic."

Then Launay went on vacation. "When I came back, the record company was putting out the wrong first single, they're not spending any money on a video, and they're telling the band to stop doing punk tours," Launay reports. "Suddenly, I was seeing this whole new world which I have never been involved with of deliberate planning and over-planning, and over-thinking. I was thinking, 'Okay, well maybe this is how Britney Spears and Christina Aguilera and all of those pop things run. They do plan it, and they do spend lots of money. Okay, so American Hi-Fi is more in that area, I'll just sit back. It has nothing to do with me, but this is interesting.' So, I progressively watch this record company and their management company make stupid mistake after stupid mistake. I couldn't believe it."

The demise of the band started with the label dropping the ball on the first single, pulling the support for a video—which is almost more of a single king-maker than radio these days—and bumping the band off of a number of tours that would have cemented their new punk-rock sound. Certainly, the label had suffered a tremendous financial loss by the signing and dropping of Mariah Carey, and the record industry was continuing to suffer. "But they had American Hi-Fi, who was gaining momentum and it was happening," Launay recalls. "Then they tell Stacy [Jones, the band's singer and songwriter] they need to get "The Breakup Song" in a movie and he manages to pull it off, so it's one of the main songs in *Freaky Friday*. He comes back and says that Disney was willing to pay for the video and the label says, 'Great.' Then they get dropped the next week. Here's a band who have bowed down to all the stupidity of the record company, who played the record-company game, and they got dropped. I was like, 'That's it. Never again, never again am I gonna play that game, because we're basically bowing down to idiots.'"

Launay's experience only underscores the point that, even with a song that producer and band agree has hit potential, the label needs to be an ally in the process. "See this is the thing, it's almost like you're getting into a partnership with these people who don't do their end," Launay says. "The deal that me and the band struck with the record company is that, 'Yes, we will bow down to your stupidity as long as you back us up, as long as you pay, and promote the fuck out of this band to make the band look like they are the hugest band on earth before the single comes out, so when it comes out it booms.' Because, you can do it. That's how it works. It's all advertising. But you have to have the song."

Certainly, there are songs that pop out upon first listen, with all the promise of chart-topping success, yet there are a handful of producers and songwriters who insist that picking a hit song is a fluke. When Ben Harper wrote the song "Steal My Kisses," which went to Number Fifteen on the *Billboard* Top Forty charts, he was not thinking about a song with Top Forty potential. "It was just a three-chord, fun guitar song that kids and grown-ups could like. We never thought it would get on the radio with a semi-obnoxious, human beat-box high in the mix. I mean, how much beat box was really on the radio then? None," he says with a laugh. "It's obvious now that it really made waves in that arena, because it was against the grain."

Harper, for one, does not pay special attention to a song that may lend itself to radio play. "I serve each one equally," he explains. "I don't gear them towards radio at all. I won't say it's never entered my mind, but it's never entered my consciousness. I've never written or produced a song for anything but that song, and how and what made me feel the deepest communication in it and through it." So, in his experience is a hit song fluke or formula? "The beauty of that is it can be either," he says.

Dave Jerden echoes the belief that a hit song is equal parts fluke and talent. "I don't know what a hit is," he admits. "For instance, Jane's Addiction's "Been Caught Stealing" [which went Number One on the *Billboard* Modern Rock chart] was pretty much just a novelty song. It was like a B-side novelty song, and when we played the finished record for Roberta Peterson [the band's A&R rep] at Warner Bros., the first thing she said was, 'That's a hit single.' Just like that. She heard it immediately, because that's her job and she deals with that kind of stuff all the time. We didn't hear it at all. I had my favorite songs on that record. I have my favorite songs on every record I do, and a lot of times those aren't what's picked as being a single."

Walter Afanasieff, who has scored chart-topping hits with Celine Dion, Mariah Carey, Savage Garden, and a handful of others, admits he is not sure what makes a hit song anymore. He thinks the television program *American Idol* is part of the problem. "It's very interesting for me to watch, because I'm very interested in seeing how singers are being pushed and how the American people are picking," he says. "So, I'm watching the show and there are twelve kids: Half of them are pretty good, three of them are unbelievable, but there were a couple that were so bad and they were getting votes as being great. I was going nuts. Why were those people even in there? It's because the American public was voting for them, so you gotta take that into consideration. Just because I don't like something or I don't know what a hit is, that doesn't mean that everybody's not going to love it and set it up and sell it. So, my taste is different from everyone else's. It's just beyond me to know what a hit is anymore. I don't really know. I know that a lot of times we do songs and go, 'Oh, God, nobody's going to like this. It's so great, but nobody's going to like this.'"

Afanasieff took that philosophy to working with the singer Eric Benet in early 2004. "We're doing songs that we enjoy. We know that if we [give the songs] to the record company that they were never going to be singles, so it was just for us. Then, on the other hand, we're doing songs for the record company that we know they want to be his shot at having a single. We're just doing it like it's painting by numbers. You have to make things so simple, and so boring. It's like, who cares, because radio and the public over the last twenty years have made it so that that's what we need to do to compete with radio and to make songs for that—it's kind of a goofy science, backwards."

Although there have been times when Afanasieff has tried to fulfill the radio hit formula, he says there have been other times when chart-topping success was more luck than skill. Take the work he did with Celine Dion on the smash-hit single from *Titanic,* "My Heart Will Go On." "Sometimes you have these accidental songs that we think are so artsy and so, oh my God, over-produced. They're full of orchestral dynamics and wonderful things, like "My Heart Will Go On," by Celine Dion. Nobody in their right mind, at any record company, period, end of story, would have gone with that song, but it was attached to a huge film. The power of that film drove the song, and then that song became her biggest hit. If you listen to that song, it wasn't being produced to be this hit single, it was being produced to be the huge bombastic ballad inside of this huge movie."

For all his success as a producer, Dave Jerden admits that he had a better handle on what had the hit potential when he was working as an engineer. "You're more detached than when you're in the producing role. When I did *Remain in Light* with the Talking Heads, [producer] Brian Eno came in one day and said, 'The record company is coming down here and they want to hear a single, just pick one.' So, I picked "Once in a Lifetime," because I liked the song. When I did Herbie Hancock's record that had "Rockit" on it [*Future Shock,* 1983], I liked the song. Whenever people asked me what I was working on [during that time], I would put those two songs on, and that's a telling thing. As a producer you're a lot closer to it," he says. "Sometimes you're so inside of it that you just lose your perspective."

"Being a little older now, I couldn't tell you what a hit is," says Ed Cherney. "If it affects me in some way and I love it, I have to assume that somebody else will, but I've been wrong a lot—more than I've been right. I've worked on records that I felt really strongly were great, but when they came out, they just totally shit the bed. There are probably economics involved and politics involved, and all kinds of other things that you can't control from the creative end of it, but I just assume that if I love it, somebody else is going to and that's not always true. It's rarely true. All of us have made lots and lots of records that we felt there was something there and it didn't work out."

Yet, while Cherney was working with producer Don Was on Bonnie Raitt's *Nick of Time* (1989) and *Luck of the Draw* (1991), he knew there was something special there right away. "There were some songs on there, obviously "I Can't Make You Love Me" [from *Luck of the Draw*] that you knew were going to get over. When we did *Nick of Time,* the label didn't hear it, and I've said that publicly before, which is probably why Capitol never hires me for anything," he adds with a laugh.

Finding just the right songs for radio puts an inordinate amount of pressure on bands and producers. Mark Trombino has faced the situation when it seems that he's got "the" song, but takes a lot of diplomacy to get it through. "I will just try to streamline that song as much as possible. A song like that usually does it itself, I think. There's not a lot of work to do on a song that stands out," he says. "I try not to do too much to it, because bands don't like those songs, and if you put too much emphasis on it I think they start thinking that that's all you care about and they start fighting it."

Before he was fired from the Jimmy Eat World sessions, Trombino was working with the band on a song that had the same vibe as "The Middle," the breakout song from the band's 2001 release. "It wasn't as good, but it was the closest thing that they had, and there was a lot of pressure from the label to finish the song," Trombino recalls. "All [Jim Adkins] had written, structurally, was chorus, chorus, chorus. We worked on it in pre-production, trying to make it into more of a song. There was a lot of pressure on it, and I think that was one of the songs that kind of freaked him out, because he didn't really care for it but the label really wanted it. They wanted another "The Middle" and that's an example of the pressure just freaking a band out."

"If you're doing some sort of rock band and you're on a major label, there is always going to be that thing," Chris Vrenna says. "If you're doing something like a Tweaker [Vrenna's own band], there is no concern really, because unless the wind is blowing in the right way for you, Tweaker is not going to live or die by whether we get on commercial rock radio. We know we are not going to get on commercial rock radio, so why are we even going to bother to try?"

12 WORKING ON THE SONGS

The list of tasks that a producer checks off before a note is recorded in a studio is impressive, but the most important part of pre-production is fleshing out the songs, because they will make or break an album. It is at this point in the process that a producer stands at a diplomatic crossroads. An artist may be ready to record a collection of songs that, in the producer's opinion, are not quite ready. Or a producer may have to talk an artist back from the ledge of frenetic creativity that does not match the material. There are a number of ways a producer approaches this part of the job, from becoming a co-writer on songs that need help, to playing an instrument on the track, to finding some sort of technical inspiration that eases the challenges of creative roadblocks.

Often it is at this stage that a producer's reputation is built or ruined. If a producer can't help an artist help these song ideas fulfill their promise, then that producer does not belong on that job. On the other hand, producers who can bring to light a hidden gem of a song will be as busy as he or she can stand. This is not necessarily about writing songs that will soar to the top of the charts, or garner Gold or Platinum status. It's about coaxing the best efforts out of the players at the writing stage, as well as during recording. Look at career producers like Rick Rubin, Tony Brown, Nick Launay, or Don Was as prime examples. Each has helped a stunning array of artists and bands come up with their best efforts. It all starts with a song.

POLISHING ARRANGEMENTS
"A lot of times, arrangement is a delicate balance between geometry and voodoo," says J.D. Foster. "You're kind of trimming the fat and finding a balance. It's like Screenplay 101—you're trying to look for a dramatic arc with a beginning, mid-

dle, and an end. I don't think a lot of songwriters seem to think in that way. Obviously, there are really crafty professional songwriters that think only in terms of making a Brian Wilson-type vignette, but [most] songwriters tend to think about, 'Here's what happened to me.' They write in a literary sense a lot of times. So, sometimes [arranging] is a matter of putting in another chorus."

Foster added those types of ideas while working with Richard Buckner. "He's a very literary type of writer," he says. "He's a really good musician, and he's really got a natural gift, but he does his thing, which is an unusual song form. It's not like a classic John Lennon-Paul McCartney song. So, the best thing was to let him do his thing and then try to figure out later in pre-production where to put the weight to make it balance. Maybe we'd have a more musical intro. Maybe we'd add more instruments. It's always about how we can make it sound bigger or smaller, or sad, or whatever. You do whatever occurs to you, whatever will make [the song] sound more interesting."

Foster goes to the crux of the matter with his point about adding or subtracting from an arrangement. To put a song over, it might take the addition of varied instrumentation to a singer/songwriter who has depended only on an acoustic guitar and a voice. At the same time, it might be a matter of scaling back excessive guitar playing, over-complicated drum parts, or even singers who are reaching beyond the emotion of a song, as Chris Vrenna found during pre-production dates with AI.

"They came out of the jam-band stuff, so there would be these great three-to four-minute songs that took seven minutes," Vrenna recalls. "I told them, 'You can't start a song with a thirty-two-bar guitar solo. You just can't. You take one section and that's the chorus. You can't have that happen three times, dude.' I had to build trust with AI over months. After a while, they learned to trust me and they realized how to make more commercially viable songs."

That does not mean, Vrenna adds, that all of the songs needed to be rewritten from top to bottom. "Sometimes the songs are arranged, but we go in and work on those," he explains. "Maybe half the songs are perfect the way they are, but I'll always hear different ideas and want to try different things that help it stand out and help the song build and grow a little bit. Maybe those ideas will work, maybe they won't. Sometimes it's like an AI thing where arrangements need a lot of work to get them into more commercially viable things. The label loved the band, but they couldn't get their heads around what the hell they were doing. The songs were arranged so weirdly, because half of it was jam band and half was a pop song. So, we had to help curtail some of that a little bit, rein it in."

Producers approach arrangements in different ways. Some make gentle suggestions, some record pre-production and make edits to show the band, and still others pick up an instrument or sing to illustrate their ideas. "I'm pretty hands-on," reports Mark Trombino. "I can't pick up a guitar and play a riff for them, although I have done basic stuff before. I don't know how other people work, and I don't know how hands-on I am relative to other people, but it seems like I'm pretty hands-on."

Trombino believes his background as a musician helps him quite a bit. "I'm good with arrangements. I think drummer/producers seem to be pretty good at that, because they're used to sitting back behind the music, not focusing so much on the riffs and the parts, and taking the whole thing in. I'm saying this as a drummer, but [we're] a little more objective than the lead guitarist might be," he says. "I think the guitarist/producer guys seem to make better songwriting producers than drummer guys. I don't know who makes the better producer. I think each band probably requires something different. If a band needs a songwriter, I'm definitely not the guy to work with. There are guys way better than I am at that, but if they've got their songs down and they need a little help with the arrangements, I can contribute a lot rhythmically, with the emotions and performances."

Butch Walker, who is a songwriter in his own right, moves between writing songs with an artist and making suggestions. While working on The Donnas' 2004 *Gold Medal,* he rarely picked up an instrument to show the band his ideas. "I would point to the neck [of the guitar or bass] and say, 'Play that note there and see what that does.' Or I would say, 'Hey, Torry, check out this [drum] pattern and see what that does to the song.' She understood my beat-boxing, so I didn't have to get behind the kit. There was minimal work involved. It was just about making sure the right sounds for each song were used so that there was some diversity to their record, because we didn't want to have every song sound the same. There is a signature sound to a Donnas record, but you don't want it to get redundant."

While Walker and the band members had most of the songs ready for recording, the song "I Don't Want to Know (If You Don't Want Me)" was worked out during pre-production. "That, to me, was one of the songs I saw as being a big single, so we talked about how the song would start," Walker says. "When I got the demos, it was nothing but a click track and a guitar. There was no perception of how the song was going to be, so we were like, 'Yeah, lets start this one off with kick drum and claps, almost "Rock 'n' Roll High School" style. That's kind of how I get heavy-handed into the arrangement. How are the chords in the pre-chorus working? We changed a couple of chords to set up the chorus and it made the chorus pop out even more."

Likewise, Sylvia Massy Shivy dives right in with the band. "If a song has a good chorus, but lacks a bridge or a transitional part, I'll try to make that song better," she explains. "We'll even go to re-writing the whole song, but keeping the chorus. That's happened quite a bit, where we just rewrite the verses and bridge and add new parts, or combine two songs that are both halfway there and make a great song."

Ben Harper has stood on both sides of the equation, as both an artist and a producer. When he was working with his producer (and manager) J.P. Plunier, mutual honesty was the key. "He was direct, but J.P.'s always direct, which is great until you directly disagree. That's always the case with anybody. He was very direct, and it was fun to take. [Sometimes] he'd come up with an idea that may have half-worked, and I could embellish it or I'd come up with an idea that was maybe halfway there and he'd bring it home, or sometimes you hit it and it's obvious. But, boy, he pushed me when I needed pushing, and I've learned a lot from him about production."

"When you decide to produce somebody it's because you have an opinion," answers Plunier. "It's not about twiddling knobs. I don't twiddle knobs. I'm not an engineer, but that said, I have found over the years that no matter who I work with, somehow we come close to the sound that is now [for that artist]. It's a weird thing, because it's a combination of where the artist is coming from and what you instinctively think sounds good. So, there is much less calculation, like we're going to do this and we're going to be these kinds of guys. It's much more intuitive than that.

"For example, on Ben's very first record [*Welcome to the Cruel World,* 1994], one thing I knew about drums was that I didn't want them to sound like Phil Collins. No dis to Phil Collins; everyone's got their thing, but that was my opposition. I was opposed to that 'drums in the cathedral' sound. I thought it should be a lot more intimate on certain songs. It was a clear mental picture that Ben isn't just sitting on the chair singing to you; he's singing to a certain person of a certain gender in a certain room on a certain day at a certain time. Abstract as that is, without putting any names to it, he's going to respond to a certain song a certain way. So, rather than make the story big like telling it to everyone, how do you tell it to one person meaningfully?"

As for the specific direction he gave Harper, Plunier explains, "The types of things that you suggest to an artist as producer are things you wish you could do, but can't. A lot of it comes from that, or if you're hearing a basic melody go down, you're like, if you countered this or if you made him sing a part in a minor third, it might be something that would change the tone or tenor of the song and take it into a different direction. You know, some songs start out sounding like the Commodores and end up sounding like Iggy Pop."

When Harper got in the producer's chair for the Blind Boys of Alabama sessions, he was careful of how he suggested vocal arrangements. "The Blind Boys orchestrated all their own vocals, but I loved it when I could plug my two cents in and give some ideas," he says. "Some were taken and some were thrown back at me at twice the speed, because they know their sound so well. I was working in the capacity of placing them, instead of trying to steer."

TO PUSH OR NOT TO PUSH?

Clearly, producers are charged with taking each song and artist to their ultimate potential. There are times when driving artists or songs to their ultimate potential takes pushing those performers beyond what even they feel is possible. But just how much can a producer prod? Joe Henry, who can view this question as an artist and a producer, says the danger comes when an artist is either unwilling or afraid to move into new sonic territory. "I don't choose to look at [songwriting] as a fragile, fleeting thing. I'm not precious about what I do. I don't baby it. I don't worry about it going away. I don't worry that I'm going to someday wake up and not be able to write songs anymore. I think the only way that happens is people become too precious about it. Does a cabinet-maker get up one day and say, 'I've built cabinets all my life, and I just don't know how to do it anymore. It's just not in me.'? I think if you go at [songwriting] thinking that it is so important, then it evaporates in that whole moment of self-doubt.

"I remember my publisher saying to me once about a song I was writing for a film, 'They've got to pay you better, these songs don't grow on trees.' I go, 'No, easier than that. You just make them up.' If you think that you don't know where the next one's going to come from, you have to be really careful, that's just death as an artist," Henry continues. "Picasso never worked that way. You see films of him working, and he was so cavalier and not in a negative way. I think that's what's beautiful about Ani [DiFranco]. I don't think Ani came to me going, 'I need to do something different. I need to choose a new path.' I think she just does so much work—it's like she's a photographer and she's going to shoot a roll like this and see what it's like. That will be what that roll will be like. It's not like, 'What will people think? Will people think I made the wrong choice? When this goes out as a representation of my artistry today, how is it going to look? How's my trajectory going to look?' I swear, I don't think she thinks of it that way."

The key to Henry's approach is that there is always the possibility of returning to familiar ground if the risk does not pay off. "It's like demos. People talk about having to be true to what the demo was," he explains. "Well, you can always go back to that. You know what that is. I just care about what else it can be."

This attitude can either mean more pressure on the band, or, as Lou Giordano found when he was working with Taking Back Sunday on the 2004 album *Where You Want to Be*, it can bring inspiration for all concerned. "Sometimes you've got to challenge some people to push themselves beyond their own limits," he says. "There were a couple of songs on the Taking Back Sunday record where I felt like the guys ought to try some things like strings and some different musical instruments other than just what they are playing with live. We ended up using some of those. We got an arranger to come in and write some pretty cool string parts and recorded those. They knew that what they had was a good song, and then pretty soon we're bringing in a string section and really orchestrating it and turning it into a real work of art. They wanted to do it but just didn't quite know how."

Putting strings into a song from a hardcore band such as Taking Back Sunday may have been a stretch, but Giordano points out that it is his job to help bands believe that something new will work. "It's showing them some ideas that they never would have thought of themselves," he says, "that still fit the identity of the band." Giordano admits, however, that finding that secret ingredient is tricky sometimes. "There's nothing that's predictable really," he states. "There's got to be a connection with and a good depth of knowledge of the music that the band likes and how they fit in to the whole musical history aspect."

Occasionally, pulling those new ideas out of a band or pushing them into new territories puts a producer in a tough spot. Ryan Greene recalls a number of situations where he moved parts from songs that were bandmember favorites, much to their dismay. On one project, a band member complained for more than a week about a change the producer made in a background vocal track, until he heard it. "He ended up doing the vocals, listened to it, and then said, 'It actually works better, now it's my favorite part.' [My job] is all about being objective, and sometimes it's putting the parts in the right places."

While working with another young band, Greene listened to twenty-two songs on a demo before saying to the band in the studio that they would pick three songs to record. "I found one of the songs and said, 'That intro? It's gone. These vocal parts? They're gone. They're too high school, you guys are moving up to the next level.' They sat there, dodging punches," he says, "but we had to move quick, and that was how it was going to be. They finished [the three songs] and listened to it and said, 'This is us?' I said, 'Man, this is you guys. This is all you.'"

Greene feels that the level of honesty he supplied to both bands is key to successful sessions with bands who may need to be shocked out of their comfort zone, especially when the band is just starting out. Brutal honesty can also be useful with artists who may have gotten lost in the process. When Ross Hogarth sat down with Melissa Etheridge to work out some of the songs for her 2004 release *Lucky,* the veteran singer/songwriter had been working so long on the album, with so many different musicians and producers, that she had lost a lot of her objectivity. "She came out to my home studio and she played me all this music she had," Hogarth recalls. "She basically said to me, 'I'm lost, because I think some of this stuff is really good and I think some of this stuff is not as good as it could be.' We had this whole conversation about her music, and she wanted me to mix what she had," Hogarth recalls. "I said, 'Melissa, I don't think this is really mix-worthy. I think it needs to be re-tracked with more fire and passion. It feels like it's been Pro Tooled to death.'"

On Hogarth's suggestion, more studio time was booked and the two looked over the songs that Etheridge had ready. "In some ways, Melissa was the one that chose the material, but we dove into the arrangements," Hogarth says. "Some of the songs were radically changed. There are a couple songs on the record that you wouldn't even recognize from their original format. There are some songs that had been chopped to death and just needed a real live, very spontaneous approach."

There was also a set of songs, Hogarth reports, that Etheridge opted not to put on the album and he did not have any push there. "She went backwards to the stuff she had done before, because there are things that were almost too real for her, I think. It gets to the point where, in today's world, I think, people like to keep the mystique up, and if you drop the curtain down too far, you let people see too deeply into yourself. There were a couple of songs that she chose to not put on the record, that those of us who were on the project couldn't believe she didn't choose. Even Bob Ludwig [the mastering engineer] was like, 'Oh my God, come on Melissa, this is amazing stuff.' But there were a couple songs that were just so revealing, I think she was almost scared by it.

"But my job with her was to get her back in touch with herself," Hogarth continues. "For the most part, over the course of the last couple of years, she hadn't been the person driving the tracking sessions with her playing and singing. She was almost like an afterthought. So, I made it like it was all about her. The musicians were there to play with her. I put her ten feet in front of the drums [to sing]. There's one song she tracked piano and vocals on and we kept everything. On a couple of songs, we kept her guitars and vocals from the basic tracks. She hadn't done that in a long time. It was sort of retro for her in some respects, getting her back in touch with herself."

The Hogarth method of building trust through honesty is one way to handle the issue of pushing an artist. Then there's the way that Nick Launay communicated with Midnight Oil in 1983, when he started working with them on their *10, 9, 8, 7, 6, 5, 4, 3, 2, 1* release. "I remember going into rehearsal with them and saying, 'Play this song faster. I don't want any harmony there, wussies.' I kept on accusing them of sounding like The Eagles, really pissing them off," he says with a laugh. "We went in and did that album, which has great songs on it and was the combination of me being so tough on them about not being cool. I was just being honest. I'm not that heavy-handed of a person, I was just telling them stuff that I felt. I knew they were listening to The Clash, and I'd seen [Midnight Oil] in past concerts and knew all about them, and to me there was a big discrepancy between what they thought they were putting out and what they were actually putting out, because they were actually too proficient—that was the problem. They were so good that they didn't have that rawness that some of the punk bands had, but the punk bands, a lot of them, didn't know how to play. They really didn't, and that's what was really cool about them. They were doing the best they possibly could, where Midnight Oil were so proficient that they needed muckin' up."

"A lot of times an artist will see it one way and I think, as a producer, what I need to do is knock somebody out of their comfort zone a little bit," says Michael Rosen. If they say, 'Oh, I didn't look at it from there,' then it gets them a couple of steps further. Whenever they settle on something, you just push them a little bit. Then they say, 'Oh, okay. You mean I can do it like this?' From that, it gets them to other things and that's when it gets really cool. It comes back to me, too. They can say to me, 'Why don't you do it like this?'"

Hogarth says it is also important to realize that a producer is not always right. "You have to open up the door of creative trust. It's like throwing [ideas] against the wall, and if it doesn't take, it's not that big of a deal unless it's such an important point that you feel it's like the whole project hinges on it," he explains. "If it gets to that point and you have to put your foot down that hard with an artist about something that you guys disagree about, you better really know you're right, because in the end you have to trust the artist and they have to trust you. But you had better trust them almost more than they trust you, because for the most part, artists don't trust anybody except themselves. Innately, they trust themselves, but they're so insecure they don't even know what [trust] is. So, they live in this weird zone of 'Tell me I'm great, and tell me I'm good, and keep giving me acknowledgement, but don't bullshit me.' It's just a weird thing. They want their ass kissed, and they want themselves treated great, but at the same time they want to know that you're real and that you're doing that for real and that you're not just saying to them, 'Yeah that's great' when it really sucks. So there's a lot of psychology in that alone."

He breaks through that with a combination of honesty and leading by example. "I am someone who believes that proving by example is the only real way to get someone to see whether they agree or not. So, if it's an arrangement, I'll chop it up in Pro Tools really quickly and show them my idea. If it's a musical idea, I'll pick up a guitar and play it. If it's a melodic idea, I'll hum it to them and get them to sing it back to me and we'll record it," he says. "So, I try to prove by example. I try not to get stuck in lengthy conversations that become tug-of-wars about why or why not. I try to just have it be all about 'let's do'. See the job, do the job, and stay out of misery, because the longer we vapor-lock over shit, the longer it's going to take to find out whether it's right."

Like Rosen, Hogarth will illustrate his ideas to a band in rehearsal by recording those ideas to Pro Tools. "They listen to it and they may not like it at first, they may not like it ever, but at least they can hear it and they don't have to be discussing it," he says. "It shows that I'm willing to let go of shit, too. I have to try it for myself a lot of times, to see if it's a good idea. That's the beauty of Pro Tools, these days you can try an arrangement in thirty seconds. You can try an arrangement that would take you forty-five minutes or an hour in the old days—now you can do it in thirty seconds. You can chop your song up and make the chorus and pre-chorus and fly shit all over the place and check it out and go, 'Wow that's really cool. I really like that.' Now and then, a band or an artist can learn that. For me, it's kind of like in fatherhood, you prove by example. You try to say, 'Do as I do, and not as I say I do.'"

How Receptive are Artists?

Gauging the willingness of an artist or band to accept direction, whether it is gentle or overt, is something that a producer must do early in the process so that sessions can be conducted productively. Only in the rarest of situations does an adversarial relationship between the team members result in an album that is mutually rewarding. A producer needs the combined talents of all concerned to create a release that the artists can feel comfortable with supporting, and add a successful credit to his or her résumé.

Ross Hogarth found that, while working with Melissa Etheridge, the singer bounced between being receptive and headstrong. "There are some things that you don't need to tell her, like I have to say she delivers a vocal performance like nobody's business," he says. "So, you don't have to give her direction on how to deliver. Sometimes I need to tell her if she's singing flat or sharp, or if she's stretching a note out too long, but in general I probably gave her the least amount of input as a singer as I've ever had to give anybody. She was very receptive on the arrangements of some stuff, and then other things she was dead set against and she was only going to have it her way. I mean, she's a very strong-willed, ballsy woman. She's a delight on a lot of levels; she kicks ass, she really does."

Sylvia Massy Shivy has worked with some bands who are receptive to her suggestions, and others who are not. "I think most are receptive, but there are a few that come in thinking that their shit is perfect," she says. "But I'll argue with them. There have been a few times where I've come head-to-head with a band on a particular song that I think is just not quite there. I worked with this band Splyt, and they had a song with a great chorus, but a ridiculously bad verse. We wound up not doing the song, because they could not hear the song any other way. In that case, I'd rather not do the song—just let it live in their demo collection. They can do it on their next record." So far, Shivy adds, she has not lost a session with that approach. "I think bands would rather hold on to their precious memory of a song without having to re-record it," she says.

Over the course of his career, Don Was has always believed that he has been hired to offer opinions. When he went in to work with Paul Westerberg on the 1999 *Suicaine Gratification,* however, things changed. "I consider Paul a really good friend, but he really didn't want to be told what to do even though he was paying me to have good ideas," Was says. "The way I sensed that it worked after a while was we would be in a quandary about what to do, I would suggest something, and because it was the only idea on the table at that moment and he didn't want anyone else's fingerprint on the thing, he was forced to come up with a better idea than I came up with, which he was always able to do because he is a much better artist than I am. But, I was an antagonist, and cast in the role of antagonist, I drove him to feed me, and that elevated his artistry. He was fueled by competition. But that's a guy who was not receptive necessarily to outside stuff, although we did have substantial dialogue about everything.

"It is just different all the time," Was continues. "Sometimes you just don't have the time [in pre-production]. Sometimes people come off the road, they have to go in, and you got what you got. I had an hour of pre-production with Bob Seger. Then he spent a year-and-a-half in post-production, going back to Detroit and trying to figure stuff out and probably over-figuring." The producer was not involved after the initial sessions. "I don't have the patience for that, and I wasn't invited, either. That's how he makes records, and he makes really good records. That's his methodology. I knew that going in, basically. He established a pattern of recording and retreating, and then reworking and reworking. Some of the rough mixes from the days we recorded, I bet, finally ended up on the album. That's neither here nor there. The important thing is for him to get what he wants. You're there to serve the artist's vision, and anything that will expedite it is usually welcome. If it is not welcome, they let you know real quickly."

THE ARTIST'S PERSPECTIVE

Producers might be able to pull all sorts of magic from their bag of tricks, but without a willing set of musicians, it will all be for naught. Ben Harper was willing to listen to J.P. Plunier when the two worked together because of a long-standing relationship. So, when Plunier suggested that Harper scream at the opening of the song "Ground on Down" while the two were working on *Fight for Your Mind,* the singer tentatively agreed. "That was a stretch for my vocal at the time," Harper says. "I didn't sing like that, and he pushed me to do that. After I did it, I was angry with him, because I was going to have to do that and scream every night from now on. Now I can do it in my sleep because I've been pushed there."

Perhaps for the first time in their career, reports bassist Maya Ford, The Donnas were willing to listen to an outside perspective when they worked with Butch Walker—even though Walker was not their first choice. In fact, the band started the *Gold Medal* sessions with Scott Litt manning the board. "We were really excited about working with him. We had a lot of meetings, and he was really cool," Ford explains. "We love R.E.M., and everything he said it sounded like he would be really great to work with, but then when it came down to it our ideas didn't match. He was going for a different sound than we were going for, and he didn't get our references; we didn't understand each other. We were friends and started hanging out with him, but when it came to working with him, it just wasn't working out." After Litt was let go, the band was leaning toward George Drakoulias or Walker, and the label had the final say. "They said, 'You have no option, you have to work with Butch.' We were like, 'Okay, fine.' We liked them both and we couldn't choose," she says.

Once the choice was settled, the band opened the door to collaboration with Walker. "When we were writing the songs this time, we didn't have them set in stone. I think on the last album, we were a lot more, 'This is our album, we do our own songs.' We wouldn't let our producer [Robert Shimp] do anything to them, and even the slightest change we'd be really suspicious," Ford says. "This time we were just more open to little changes like doubling the chorus or cutting the chorus in half, and we worked together more."

Yellowcard drummer Longineu Parsons kept his ears open while working with producer Neal Avron on the band's breakout release, *Ocean Avenue*. "Neal has a thought towards music, which is an amazing thought. He knows where to put certain instruments," Parsons explains. "He doesn't try to change what you're doing. He listens to what you have to say and finds out why you like the song, what parts you like about the song and then he works with what you have, what you like." That said, while the two were working together, Parsons found out that Avron didn't change many of his drum parts. "If I came up with a drum groove and it was a little too much for what it was, you know, he'd give me a little idea and then I'd feed off it. If I didn't like it, then he'd let me do what I was doing. He's not going to tell me not to do it; of course, we have to play the music from here on out. "

The members of MxPx found that trusting producer Dave Jerden helped them get unstuck at times when they were recording *Before Everything & After* (2003). "Any time we had ideas and we weren't sure what to do, Dave would always know how to do it or he could figure it out," says MxPx singer and songwriter Mike Herrera. "On the song 'It's Alright,' we had an idea on a part with an acoustic guitar that we wanted to sound really crappy. It was me on an acoustic singing on the breakdown part, and we wanted it to be lo-fi. There are plug-ins you can use, but they sound fake and we wanted to do it for real. So, we recorded it through the tape normally, and then he recorded it onto a cassette and then recorded that into a mic again. It sounded really crappy but it was the actual sound. It totally sounds authentic. We even compared the real sound—let's put it through the lo-fi plug-in—and it sounded night-and-day different. It was stuff like that, where we got exactly what we thought it should be, exactly what our idea was, perfectly on tape."

HOLDING THE REINS

Although a band may become popular performing a certain genre of music, there are those times when they want to break out a bit. The change may be as minor as adding a touch of pop to a punk band, like The Ataris did while working with Lou Giordano in 2003. Or it could be a more dramatic departure—an acoustic artist looking to plug in, a la Bob Dylan; or a rock band looking to incorporate equal parts electronica and dance music into their sound. U2 received mixed reviews when they added electronic dance sounds on a pair of releases—*Zooropa* (1993) and *Pop* (1997)—before returning to their rock base in 2000 with *All That You Can't Leave Behind*. For many performers, a change stems from more than mere boredom. It may offer them a chance to grow their fan base. It may push them on the radio. It may give them that all-elusive hit song. Or an artist may be looking for a new team of musicians.

On occasion, an artist or band might move so far beyond their base that they become something completely unrelated to their past catalog. Maybe it is a hardcore punk band going too far pop. It could be an acoustic artist implementing all electronic instruments. It might even be a metal band adding country and acoustic elements to a sound that has defined them and a genre for years, such as when Metallica turned away from their metal roots to a more diverse palette of sounds on *Load* (1996). The band was crucified by longtime fans and critics for the shift, with much of the blame going to producer Bob Rock.

"Through my career, the thing that has made me be not at all concerned about that is that people change and they want to move on," Rock says. "I think that the die-hard fans will always be upset that they are not doing *Master of Puppets* and *Kill 'Em All*. Before I did the black album [1991's self-titled release that featured a black cover], I thought they were the world's best-kept secret. Then to go from two-and-a-half million to fourteen million [records sold], I look at that as a positive thing and not just in sales, but the fact that fourteen million people finally got a chance to hear what Metallica has to offer. They offer great insights on so many things, along with the power in the music.

"The fact that *Load* has been very successful as well, I have to look at that rather than the negatives," Rock continues. "I think that if Metallica or myself decided to make an album like they used to, well, I don't think that works. I don't think that it works for anybody. Maybe it works once, but I don't think that it works for a longtime career. They are going to be around for a long time, and it shows in the quality of their music and how they approach it. The old die-hard fans, if they were really fans, would know that Lars [Ulrich], James [Hetfield], Jason [Newsted, then bassist], and Kirk [Hammett] would never do as I asked them, anyway. Everything we have done has come from them trying to bring out those insights that James has as a writer, lyrically and musically. I am not adding anything new—I'm just bringing out what is already there. That's freedom for Metallica.

"Would Paul McCartney try to make a Beatles record? Why? That's where he used to be," Rock points out. "If [Metallica] ever wanted to return to [their old sound], I couldn't be a part of that. Why I want to work with them is because it's a challenge and they want to go for it."

It may not always be the band or even the producer's idea to travel to new sonic terrain; there are times when a record label suggests that a band or an artist try something new. For instance, when Craig Street started to work with Jubilant Sykes, an operatic jazz singer, the goal was to move beyond his classical music roots and provide a crossover release. To be sure, the change was major for Sykes. "He was from a world where you do not change what was written, you don't take liberties with a song," explains Street. "He's not an interpreter like k.d. lang or Cassandra Wilson. I don't mean that in a bad way; that's just not what he does, it's not his world. So, we had a lot of talks, and I said, 'Look, you're going to have to come around to this, because it's really different. The process that were going to use to make this record is going to be really different.' I kept looking for songs that I thought he could sing, and he would 'yay' or 'nay' them. The label very much wanted him to sing pop songs, but I said, 'You can not have this voice sing a pop song, because it will sound corny.' Jubilant came in with a couple of songs that were really in that zone, that kind of pop thing. One of the songs he really wanted to do was "Unchained Melody," which was a huge hit for the Righteous Brothers. I said, 'Man, it's pretty hard to do anything with this song other than what it is.' He liked it because he liked that he could do the thing that he thought he was supposed to do, which is that big-voice thing."

Street discovered during this project that it is a challenge for someone of Sykes' training to check his talents and sing more dynamically. "He was used to walking out in a place like Carnegie Hall with no mics and just letting the rafters hear what he's singing. So, that was really interesting, and like a lot of classical musicians, he's never made a record where you are actually making conscious decisions about how it's going to sound and where you are going to put things. I think he learned a lot with that. It's funny, I heard him on NPR not long after the record came out, and he said, 'Yeah, it was like a war in there with Craig. He kept getting me to sing down, and I kept wanting to sing out, but in the end it was great.' He was happy."

Not all artists are happy when a change is called for by the record company. When Chris Vrenna remixed the title track to the 2000 release, *Haunted* for Poe and Atlantic records, he says, "The label wanted to get her on KROQ [an influential Los Angeles radio station], because without KROQ you're dead. So, we did this heavier version of her song and the label loved it, the radio loved it, and she said, 'No fucking way, man. That's not who I am as an artist, and if that's the only way I can get on radio is to be represented by something that isn't me, then I'd rather just not get on radio.' She shelved the whole thing. It was really sad in a way.

"My whole approach for remixes, like when I get a Poe or I get one for Boomkat, is that I don't want to make people not like the song anymore," Vrenna adds. "I was really bummed that she felt that way, because I thought I really did her justice. My approach is to always push them sonically as far as you can to fulfill the whole reason the label is hiring you. You can take something too far, where it's not believable. That is my rule, be believable. You could picture Poe having some great, not heavy metal, but just thick like SG [electric guitar] through a Vox [guitar amp] with some grungy, big power chords. Some of the other stuff is not believable, so as we're working I always ask if it's believable. I always want the artist to go, 'Wow that's cool, but it's still believable.' I keep using that word because that's my catch phrase. So, when she was angry about it and didn't think it was her, I was really sad because I thought the mix turned out fantastic and I thought it was very believable. She didn't say she thought it sucked; she just thought it wasn't her and does not want to be represented like that. It's the only time in my career, so far, that someone has actually thought it wasn't a success."

On the other hand, sometimes a producer is called upon to reel an artist back in, if the performer seems to be straying too far from his or her sound. "That's the point when you get on the phone to the record company and say, 'Have you heard any of these songs?'" Ryan Greene says with a laugh. "If they haven't, you say, 'Well, if I were you, I would get my little ass down here and take a listen.' Get the record company involved, because they are the ones that are putting the band in the studio. If the record company says they've heard the songs and thinks it will be a good adventure for them, then you sit down with the band. If I didn't feel strongly about it I'd say, 'I don't know, guys, I think you're really venturing off a little too far. Maybe we should make the elements a little bit more like what you've had before and do part of the record like that and part of the record like this. You know, try to give the old fans something to listen to, but give the new fans something that they'll like as well. See if you can compromise, depending on how big the band is."

Mark Trombino found himself with a band in the midst of a change when he started to get songs from Finch that were targeted for the follow-up release to their 2002 *What It Is to Burn* offering. "They are consciously wanting to change the formula. I got a batch of demos that sounded nothing like the old record, and then I got another batch of demos that sounded nothing like the old record and nothing like that first batch of demos, so they just don't know what band they want to be," he explains. "It's such a bummer because they had something good, and the things that I liked about Finch they are abandoning. I don't know how to deal with that, because bands should grow, they should change, but to call themselves Finch after it changes that erratically doesn't seem right."

From Trombino's seat, it is the songs that matter. "I suppose I don't care if it sounds like a Finch record or it doesn't sound like a Finch record, as long as I like the songs. I'll make any record if I like the songs, so I don't care. The problem is that they haven't found their new formula yet. The stuff I've been hearing hasn't been too good. It's like they're just experimenting with new ideas. I'm confident that they'll find something and it will be great but, you know, it isn't right now. So, I've just been letting them write and not booking any studio time."

This puts him in the unenviable position of having to be totally honest with the band members. "I don't think I should be telling them any of that. I think the label should be telling them that," he says.

Where Trombino may feel powerless, caught in the limbo of communication between artist and label, Brad Wood helplessly watched his old partner Liz Phair swim through a sea of criticism after her 2003 self-titled album, which was produced in part by Michael Penn, R. Walt Vincent, and the songwriting/producing collective known as The Matrix. "She's trying for something specifically, and if she gets there it will be good for her. I don't begrudge her trying something different, because she's already done what she's done three times now and it's time to try something different. You know, she's put out a lot of music. Whether or not it's going to be really successful, ultimately, I don't know. But she certainly made a splash with that record," Wood says with a laugh. "I've never seen such mean things said about an album in my life. People are crazy about that record."

As a producer, Wood believes it is his job to persuade a band stay with the sound that brought them to popularity in the first place. "What brought me there almost always is the chemistry and the pieces of the puzzle that fit. No matter how misshapen the pieces are, it's still the puzzle that works. I'm there. I'm interested in it. I like it. I've chosen to work with these guys and hope that they've chosen to work with me, and so I usually have a tendency to be even more of a preservationist of what the chemistry is," he says.

13 IN THE STUDIO

By the time a band enters a recording studio, the personnel and musical pieces of an album have been gathered, and they're ready to be put together. Producer and band have worked out the songs, studios have been hired or outfitted, engineers have been brought on, and deals have been struck. To be sure, it is a heady time when promise is stronger than reality. For performers who are walking in to record their songs for the first time, it can be the realization of a lifelong dream. For those returning to the studio, it is an opportunity to bolster their catalogue with music that has often been honed on tour.

For the producer this is the time to tie up some of the last loose strings: Finalizing studio schedules, setting the vibe in the studio, discussing the use of drugs and alcohol during recording, and checking in for the last time on band dynamics. There will always be gray areas, but most producers want to resolve as many of those issues as possible before the band steps foot in the studio.

SETTING THE VIBE

It is one thing to set up a studio so that it gives off a certain vibe, it is quite another to make sure all the right people are receptive to that same attitude. "It's seriously important," says Howard Benson. "We have a great vibe, and it comes when you walk through the door. Everybody is focused. Sometimes we're laid back, sometimes we're not laid back, depending on what we have to do. We really want to make it a place where the artists want to come every day and they want to work. It's hard for me to put into words—it is what it is."

Walter Afanasieff says the way he sets the vibe in the studio is simple. "It's my personality and the way I do things," he says. "The way I talk to people and my soft approach. Keeping the vibe is so important, because I don't do anything carelessly. I don't say anything needlessly. I learned very early in my time of being a producer that it could be one word, it could be anything said the wrong way and the vibe is gone. You can't get it back. Attitudes, egos, the vibe, as it's called, are the most important thing. From experience, you really know how to handle that personality and keep their spirits high. It could be somebody who gets into a foul mood [over a technical issue] or somebody who sees him or herself in an unflattering picture on some magazine cover or sees something on TV, or somebody who sees their competition getting some fame. You just have to know how to go with it, and you have to be a psychologist."

The key, Afanasieff adds, is watching and listening to the people he is producing. "I pick up on people and their vibes very well and I deal with them. I'm always catering to their needs and making them feel better, because at the end of the day it's their record, it's their name. A lot of producers I've seen, it's all about them and how they produce. I'm always second to the artist. It's just so easy for me, I always pick up on something and enhance it when I know it's going to make them feel better," he says. "It's just being human, just being perceptive, and they are all different, they are all children, they all have enormous egos, they're all very, very, very, very easily bruised."

To be sure, bands need to feel a sense of security in the studio. "The more you make them feel safe, they trust that when you say something's good that it's good, and they're not going to be embarrassed out there," reports Michael Rosen. "They can make colossal mistakes in front of you and you say, 'That one's not a good one. That one's brilliant.' Then they start to feel like they can do both, they can be brilliant and they can be dreadful. You'll make sure the dreadful doesn't get out, so they can experiment, if they're really artists. Not a lot of these guys really care about what they're singing, but you get the ones that are special like Steve Perry. [Rosen worked with Perry while Journey recorded at San Francisco's Automat Studios.] And some of the guys who are really going deep down and trying to pull out some real stuff. When you can make them feel like it's a cool place to do it, then you're in."

"You want them to feel like it's a magical place," Rosen adds. "This is not a regular job. You're rolling in at ten, eleven in the morning, and you're going to go out, stand in a booth and sing, and make a living at it. That's like playing in the NBA. There are just a handful of people that get to do it, and they're special people. You want that person to feel like it's a magical experience. I was doing a record in Miami at Criteria, and Julio Iglesias has a room for doing vocals. It has a giant window and there's stage lighting all around so he can feel like he's performing onstage. That's cool, you know. It's magic, and that's where you get off on it."

In fact, J.D. Foster points out that one of the first lessons he learned in the studio was the importance of the mood and how every little factor comes into play. "I don't want to get too specific here, but if somebody brings in a Yoko Ono type of spin, when you get into the studio you're going to get 'Let It Be,'" he says with a laugh. "I have nothing against Yoko, but the thing to learn is how important the vibe in the room is. It transcends pretty much all the technical and musical questions at some level.

"You have to learn how to throw it down a gear and step on the gas, or run for cover when the time is right," Foster continues. "I don't know how to tell anybody how to do that. The best you can do is creating a vibe, which is a purple word. Nobody really knows what that means, but it means everything. You create a feeling that everybody's really open to create something and getting something out of it. Let's face it, if you go in with reasonably talented people who have a great song, it's gonna come out like a great song. It's really hard to totally destroy that, I think. But to make a really great recording? Boy, it takes a little sprinkling of fairy dust."

"There's an old saying that your vibes and my vibes are all the vibes that will be caught on tape," says Dave Jerden. "The vibe that I try to create is a relaxed vibe, where everything is going okay, there are no major panics, and it's all work." Jerden likens the energy a band has in the studio to a battery, and a number of factors may dissipate that energy. "It goes right to zero within a week if you don't have a good, relaxed vibe. If there's tension or anger, it just eats it all away, and personally I've never made a record or did anything any good where there wasn't a good vibe going on with the band."

Throughout his career, Don Was has seen how setting that comfortable environment is essential. "You have to be really tuned in to the people's feelings. You can't be a brute, and just because you feel a certain way doesn't mean that the artist will feel that way. You have to kind of tune in to what makes them comfortable, and when they are not comfortable you have to pick up on that right away and try to figure out what's causing it," he explains. "Also, you have to figure out if it should be fixed. Sometimes discomfort fuels a performance. So, you kind of have to know when to solve problems and when to shut up. Everyone likes something different."

Was says he learned a valuable lesson about the power of positive thinking from Carlos Santana. The two were returning to their hotel after a particularly trying rehearsal for the Quincy Jones-inspired "We Are the Future" benefit concert, held in Rome in 2004. "Carlos and I were in the elevator, and he just looked at me and said, 'You know Don, John Coltrane said that one positive thought creates a million ripples.' Then the door opened for his floor, he backed out and disappeared," Was recalls. "It blew my mind, and I haven't been able to shake it. Every time I find myself being negative I'm reminded of his remark, and it's so true that you can really change the whole vibe of the session. You can turn it around with one really positive thought. I have experimented with it. I know I've achieved it in a room where people are frustrated and willing it to be positive. You just change people's minds. It's not some mystical thing. I don't mean to sound like Rasputin. It's not quite like that; it's projecting enthusiasm and excitement."

During the sessions for Iggy Pop's 1990 *Brick by Brick* album, Was says he saw sessions turn upside down and back to right before he even knew it was possible. "We did a song called "Something Wild," which is a John Hiatt song," he recalls. "John happened to be recording in the next room, so we asked him to come in and play guitar. He worked way overtime on his thing, and we had to take a break because everyone was starving, so he came in while we were eating dinner and he was exhausted. We couldn't find Iggy, but he said to me, 'Please give my apologies to Jim [Pop's proper name is Jim Osterberg.]. I have to go. I'm so tired that I'll be of no value to you.' He was very respectful, but he split. Iggy thought he had done something really to offend John by having missed his departure and not being able to look him in the eyes. There was nothing wrong, but [Iggy] was really depressed that he had done something to a guy that he respected. So, we had to go back and we had to get the song, because it was on the schedule for the day and it was tight. [But] it was the most spiritless version of the song, because he was really bummed about it. Kenny Aronoff was playing drums, and he could pick up on that and he also knew that John was cool about it. Kenny just put this big smile on his face and started pounding these drums and playing with such enthusiasm that, within fifteen seconds, the mood turned around 180 degrees and it was a great track. All we had to do was go back and punch in Iggy's guitar and vocals for the first fifteen seconds of the song when he really just sounded lethargic and depressed. But that is a great example of a guy who turned things around, and that's why Kenny Aronoff is so popular. In addition to being an amazing drummer, he is such a positive connection."

Keeping a light mood is certainly a help when a producer is attempting to build a creative atmosphere. In fact, Nick Launay insists on it. "It has a lot to do with them knowing that I'm there for the fun. I don't have many rules, and I never go 'This is my rule,' but I do have a thing that I will say to people. I'll say, 'Look, when we are working on songs, as soon as the song becomes boring or you're not enjoying playing it or I'm not enjoying it or any of us are not enjoying it and it's not fun, we stop and go on to the next song. If the whole thing becomes not fun, I'm leaving.' I have been doing this for too long; it has to be fun," he says. "I've given up my social life for this, I've given up a lot of good stuff, a lot things that people enjoy in life, for rock 'n' roll. So, this better be fun, otherwise I am not doing it."

From a player's perspective, vibe is equally important. "It's the most important part of music and art in general," says System of a Down's Daron Malakian.

"No vibe, no art. You have to a have a comfortable vibe—everybody has to have it. I write the music, fine, but it's important that John [Dolmayan, the band's drummer] be happy when we're there. That's why Rick [Rubin] is important; it comes down to him creating a great vibe that's comfortable and fun. There's something to look forward to today, I'm gonna go record. The vibe while I'm writing, if I'm having problems or something, it's key when writing, but not in recording. I don't think a bad vibe is ever good in recording, but bad vibes sometimes work in writing. I'm crazy enough to try to make myself have a bad vibe sometimes, because it brings out some shit. Sometimes I don't leave my house for like fuckin' two weeks straight on purpose, maybe build some natural kind of depression or something that reflects to your music. That, to me, is a self-sacrifice that you make. It's like character acting, when you get into a job and you gotta put on a couple pounds. That is what I do with writing, like I sometimes purposely zone into something."

SETTING THE SCHEDULES

To be sure, the music business is not a typical nine-to-five job for musicians, producers, or engineers. Inspiration happens in random intervals that are difficult to predict, and performers hit their peaks at odd hours. Some musicians are better in the early afternoon, some in the middle of the night. That is the luxury of bands that are lucky enough to be full-time musicians, and do not have to work day jobs. So, how do producers work that out? With flexibility, for sure, as well as clear communication with all concerned.

It also helps, says Walter Afanasieff to remember who hired whom. "My first rule is the artist is the boss. They're paying for it, it's their record, it's their name that's going on the record, and it's their life. I'm going to keep producing different artists, but when you're an artist and you've got that one CD coming out with your name on it, that's your world, that's your life. So, they are the boss, but it's always within reason," he says. "A lot of singers don't like singing until late night, because their voice opens up throughout the day, throughout their activities, and they're ready to sing after the sun goes down. It could be like three or four in the morning. Music production and music creation always happens when it happens. There are no hours to it. We're here every night until two or three in the morning. Of course, we need to get our rest and we don't even start up until around noon or so.

"It just depends. A friend of mine was producing a singer, and her whole schedule started at like five in the morning," Afanasieff continues. "It wasn't because she woke up early, but this person was such a party animal that she didn't want to start working until then. It was a really hard project on him. There are other times, when a gifted, really conscientious, very responsible artist is going to come in here, do their job well within a few hours. There are a lot of wonderful, wonderful professional artists. I mean, people like Celine Dion, who takes everyone's life into consideration. She knows that there are families to be with and schedules that pertain to life, and she just does it a certain way that is responsible. She does her job so well—she just gets in there and does it. Other artists don't give up, they just want perfection, they'll stay and keep doing it and keep doing it and keep doing it."

"When I am working with a band, my time is their time," agrees Nick Launay. "I don't have any other time socially to do things, so we might as well just work the hours they will perform at their best. Now, if the band asks what time I like to work I usually say midnight to 11:00. Some bands like American Hi-Fi can't work those hours. Vue invariably got inspired late at night and was working through the night. As long as work gets done, I'm pretty happy. These days, because I'm not as young as I used to be, I do try to take weekends off if I can."

As an artist and producer, Ben Harper likes to get to work as soon as he walks in the studio. "I don't like to futz about. I don't like to come in, sit around, and chit-chat," he says. "Once I'm there, I'm ready to say hello, give hugs, and get down to business. I really like that and it's almost a fault, because I could stand to ease up a little bit. No one can keep up with me in the studio. I am just so high doing the work, so I need to work on relaxing a little bit in the studio and not be so time-concerned. But, somebody's got to be that guy, otherwise time in the studio can slip away. You watch a quarter of the Laker game, there's a bar…When I get there, I don't consider the studio a place to hang out. If I want to hang out, I'm going to hang out somewhere else, you know, with some fresh air. But once I walk in, I like to get down to business. That's my style."

Early in most of their careers, producers work frantic hours in the studio. For someone starting out in production, it is not uncommon to work fourteen to sixteen hours a day, spread through a twenty-four-hour period. That schedule could go on for weeks on end, depending on the band. "When I was younger and didn't have as many obligations, I would let the band set that more," reports Dave Fridmann. "Plus, I used to work away from my family, so the timing of things didn't have to be as straightforward as they do now. But, ultimately I don't think any band really works very well for more than two weeks in a row. At that point, nobody has the attention span anymore; everyone is just itching to be doing something else and being somewhere else.

"I just cannot see being productive, at least from a production standpoint, after twelve hours a day. I can't do more than that," he continues. "I've done it, and the truth is, it wasn't very productive. The extra four hours didn't help. If anything, a lot of times what happens is you get more tired or you get more angry or you get more drunk and mistakes happen. You just can't concentrate that well, so I try and keep things down to a twelve-hour day at this point, which allows for breaks and meals, and two-week periods. That seems to be fairly well structured, and for most of the people I work with that seems reasonable. I try not to start before noon, to keep some rock 'n' roll hours for people."

David Lowery prefers the Nashville start time of nine in the morning, but he will work at the band's whim. "It needs to go around the band's lifestyle a little bit," he says. "There are a few bands that I've got to do that morning thing. Cracker will do it from time to time. Camper [Van Beethoven] will do it from time to time." The key is to avoid the late afternoon, adds Lowery. "I don't think there's ever been a note recorded on a record that was really kept, in my experience, that was recorded between four and six o'clock in the afternoon," he says. "The phones are always ringing, people are always totally distracted. There's never anything good recorded during that time of day."

The witching hour for Sylvia Massy Shivy is midnight, when she checks out of her Radio Star Studios. "I've found that if I work past then my whole schedule gets thrown off," she says. "My engineer, Rich Veltrop, may work later, but twelve hours a day is enough for me. I'm personally rigid, but the bands can continue to work if they want. I think that anything done around four in the morning is going to be redone, no matter how great it sounds at four."

There are many considerations for producers when it comes to setting schedules, not the least of which is attempting to have some continuity with family. "I lost friends, girlfriends for years. I've been doing this for twenty years, and the first fifteen of them it was like fifteen-hour days, six days a week. On the seventh day you slept and then you went back at it," reports Michael Rosen. "I don't like doing that anymore. I've got kids. I like to play tennis. I like having a life. So, if I can help it I like to work eleven to seven, Monday through Friday. It's a little tough sometimes. I just had a band here, The Beautiful Mistake, from Los Angeles and I felt a bit of responsibility because they're coming to me and they're away from home. After seven it's like, 'Well what are you guys going to do? Oh, you're going to the movies? Alright, see you tomorrow.' After eight hours, you can't do anything."

The eight-hour day is something that Rosen learned from Keith Olsen. "When I did Southgang with him [Group Therapy, (1992)] he was gone at seven. He didn't give a rat's ass what you were doing at seven, he was gone." The lesson came in handy when he went to Los Angeles in 2000 to record the Rock and Roll Nightmare release with the Infernos, because he could only get in the studio during those hours. "I was on a mission and it was killer, because I got in there at eleven and started working full on. We had a half-hour for lunch, and there was no fucking around. I was out the door at six, and I found that I was actually going home and listening to my stuff and taking notes for the next day. If you're working until twelve, you're not listening to that stuff. You're going home to watch some TV, read, and then go to bed. You wake up and you go back to the studio. So, I kind of like going at it really hard and then going home."

CLOSED STUDIO OR ANIMAL HOUSE?

Granted, the studio is a creative environment, but there's still a job to be done for musicians, producers, and engineers as they work to make art that doubles as a commercial product. So, some teams prefer a closed studio that's all work, where a premium is placed on concentration. Others, in order to catch a certain relaxed mood, open the doors to friends for a party atmosphere. Obviously, the rules need to be determined on a case-by-case basis.

"I want everyone in there," says Rosen. "It's [the band's] world, and it helps me determine who they are and what they're about. The best records are the things that take the best part of that person and blow it up bigger than life. So, I want to know what kind of sense of humor they have, what their passions are, what their politics are, what makes them tick. You don't get to do it unless you meet their people. For example, if the guy is like this crazy passionate dude about something and he starts singing and he's like a wet noodle, I can say, 'Wait a second, dude. I just heard you arguing with Louie, Dewey, and Chewey over there. You were ranting and raving, then you get on the microphone and you're like a wet noodle. I want that, give me that.' So, it kind of helps you with the psychology of knowing how to get to them.

"The only thing I won't listen to is, 'Well, my friend likes it.' So what? Your friend's not going to buy the record, so I don't care what he thinks about it," Rosen continues. "I've definitely pissed a few bands off. 'Fuck your friends. Go find me ten guys who you don't know and play it for them and tell me what they think. That's what I care about.' If they come back with that friends thing, I say, 'You've got a million buddies and they're all willing to put down ten bucks a pop? Yeah, right.'"

Ross Hogarth agrees that the choice whether to open or close a session belongs to the artist. He spent much of 2003 in the studio with John Fogerty, and those were all closed dates. When the doors are thrown open, though, he has a few rules. "If someone is singing and there are people walking around the studio, I'll shut that down so quick you won't even be able to blink your eye," he says. "And no cell phones. There are certain rules, because I can't put up with the distraction. On the other hand, I think artists and bands have to be part of their music; they have to feel like they are part of the process, so, if it's got to be the more the merrier, and if I can't put up with that for some reason because it's too crazy, then I'll just express it."

Many producers agree with Hogarth that vocal sessions are the most sensitive. Howard Benson, who is known for detailed and layered vocals, moves everyone out of the room. "Nobody is with me, not assistant engineers or seconds," he says. "I'll walk into the control room and say, 'Alright, everybody leave.'" Other than that, it's up to the band. "Hoobastank is the most boring band I've ever had in the studio," he says. "They couldn't be more boring. They went in, played video games, did their parts, worked their asses off, and then left. When P.O.D. comes in, half the country walks in there with them."

One benefit to opening the studio when Nick Launay worked with Vue on *Down for Whatever* (2004) was having the band's friends and fellow musicians Black Rebel Motorcycle Club drop in. "It was great having friends who are musical and inspirational," Launay recalls. "When their friends came down, they actually performed better because they had an audience. I tend to like having it open. I like to have fun. I don't like the anal retentiveness of, 'This is a closed session and nobody is allowed in.' Everybody is in a bad mood and everybody is uptight. I don't like that, it doesn't work, it's not what it's about. I haven't done many records like that, but I have visited friends who are working on sessions like that, and there's a sign on the door that says, 'Keep Out, Session In Progress' and 'Hold All Phone Calls.' The producer's having a go at the engineer, the engineer is having a go at the assistant, and everybody else is to blame. I just look at it and I go, this not my idea of fun."

"I prefer a closed studio for the first forty-eight hours, and then it's always semi-closed," says Ben Harper. "That's how I prefer my backstages, too. The second you know this guy from this band and this famous guy, you're not the same person. You're a watered down version of yourself. So, I always want to be my whole self in my music and in my life. I keep it tight. I prefer it to be closed and then highly exclusive."

Jerden also tries to keep guests under control in the studio. "If the band has friends come by, the control room is the sanctuary. That's where the work's being done," he says. "I'm working eight hours and I'm doing parts, and there's no room for people who like to hang out and party. If they have friends who want to come by, come into the control room, be quiet, and not say a damn thing, then it's okay. But if they say anything, they're out of there. It's just not a party situation where I work. It's all business."

DRUG AND ALCOHOL USE

A generation has now grown up with the idea that musicians spin around the triple treats of sex, drugs, and rock 'n' roll. The legend has been so ingrained in fans that they can only imagine that recording studios and backstage areas are dens of inequity and temptation. There's certainly some truth to this legend, yet many say that the climate around musicians' substance abuse has changed over the past decade. Not that there's a temperance movement shaking the music industry, but producers who have been hurt by musicians' substance abuse problems in the past are more cautious when someone comes in to record under the influence.

"In my sessions I haven't seen anybody use anything harder than alcohol or pot, ever. I'm not a big fan of anybody who drinks and smokes pot while they're playing," reports Ryan Greene. "Am I going to get a great performance while we're playing a song that's 210 beats per minute when you're drunk? Are you going to be able to play the guitar tight enough? Doubt it. Are you gonna play it better when you're not loaded? Yeah, probably. You may feel that you're playing it better, but the reality is you're not."

It is not that Greene lays down the law with bands, but he fosters an attitude where he and the musicians he produces have a high regard for the team. "That's why I'm able to do my records so fast. We're in tracking for maybe nineteen days and then mixing for four. Because of the budgets, we move very quickly, and everyone knows what they have to do, and everybody respects not only themselves, but also the project," he says. "Nobody really wants to let anybody down, me included. They know that they have this amount of time to do this many songs. We have to go in, we have to be focused. We can still have a great time, but getting drunk or getting wasted is definitely not part of the picture."

In the heavy metal world, Ross Hogarth says, "I wouldn't say [drugs and alcohol] are prevalent, but they are there. You have to be accepting of it, because it's not my job to be an AA leader or the guy that counsels them or get someone sober if they have a drug problem. I'm not someone's father. I'm not a police officer. I'm a producer and engineer, trying to get the best music out of them as possible. If they come in fucked up and that's going to waste a day, then I'll maybe talk to the artist about it. Or I'll talk to the manager about it and say, 'Look your guitar player came in jacked up and couldn't get his parts and wasted an evening. I can't have that happen again. It's their budget, it's coming out of their pocket, you've got to take it seriously, you got to have a talk with them.' I generally don't like to be that kind of heavy. I've tried it in the past, and it really sucked. I have my morals, I have my values, I have the way that I live, but if I'm talking about that, then I'm not talking about music."

Howard Benson, who also works in the heavy metal genre, says, "If that's happening, then they're doing it really well behind me. I don't see it, and part of it is because I don't even care one way or the other. Usually if people are going to walk into the studio with me, they're going to be respectful enough to do what they have to do to get their parts. Whatever they do outside of the studio, I don't care. I'm not their mom or dad. I'm very respectful of their lives and I respect them as artists, and they respect me. If they are respectful, there shouldn't be any problems, really. I don't make a big deal out of it."

Sylvia Massy Shivy views artists with that same attitude. "Bands can do whatever they want. I'm not going to restrict their fun. If they're used to drinking vodka every night, I will encourage them to continue that routine. Or if the singer smokes pot every day, he had better bring some with him. He's not going to quit pot during our sessions. I'm not going to get a performance out of a guy who's wound up and uptight because he hasn't smoked a joint in a week. That's a nightmare. They do what they want to do and that's their own business, but personally I'm done," she says with a laugh. "I stopped partying in 1989. I find I can get a lot more work done that way."

The pop music world, according to Walter Afanasieff, is fairly safe from substance abuse. "With everyone that I've worked with, from New Kids on the Block to Savage Garden, Michael Bolton, Mariah Carey, I have never had one incident or even seen any drugs in the studio, not once. The only times I've ever seen the usage of alcohol in a recording sessions is when [an artist] will have a drink to calm the nerves. Sometimes it's a very intimidating and very nerve-wracking experience in the studio, being in front of a microphone, being in a new place and a new time, singing a very, very difficult song. So, there's been a glass of wine or two here and there, but I've not been in that part of the recording industry business where I've seen any drugs.

"I've been to plenty of parties," he continues with a laugh, "or music-industry events where I've seen that, but I think that in the working environment people have a very stereotypical kind of way of thinking about the music business, and I'm sure that there are a lot of people out there who have seen drugs or marijuana being smoked at sessions or whatever, but I personally don't allow anything like that. I don't have any cigarette smoke allowed either."

It comes down to making sure that quality music is being made, Afanasieff says. "I've worked with people who are famously involved with drugs or alcohol, but I gotta tell you that I don't think that when people are working they take their work very seriously. So, I've personally never seen that, but I'm sure that if you go back in the old days at a Bob Marley session, you would not even see anybody in the room from all the smoke. If you were hanging out with Rick James when he was doing his music, I'm sure there was going to be a ton of blow. I think that over the past ten or fifteen years it has cleaned up."

Even given many producers' *laissez faire* attitude, there are a number of producers who have battled the insidious affect of drug addiction in the studio. Dave Jerden's experience with the late Layne Staley of Alice in Chains put him on that front line during the recording of the band's 1992 release, *Dirt*. "When we did that album, Layne came in loaded on heroin when we first started doing vocals," Jerden recalls. "He was singing all out of tune, and I got pissed at him. I said, 'Layne, you can get high on your own time. You're on my time, don't use, because you're not doing anything that's useable.'"

Trying to rescue a session from the ravages of drug addiction is practically impossible, adds Jerden. "It's such a wacky thing, the dynamics of it. By definition, the whole problem is that you never know what you're dealing with at any given time. There's no proper way to deal with it, no smooth way to deal with it," he says. "I've worked with drug addicts, and you do your best to work around it. I've worked with artists where I've literally had to give them money against my better judgment so they could get dope and they could keep working. I don't know if people that use drugs are good people or bad people, I just think of them as sick people. So, the only problem I have with giving someone money for dope is that I don't want them to die on my dime. I'd hate for them to overdose. It's hard; I mean unfortunately drugs and rock 'n' roll have always gone hand in hand with the stresses involved. I saw Layne go down. Layne went from this really edgy kid that had a lot to say to being a zombie. It was sad to watch."

"People are way more together now," Jerden says. "People that are drug addicts in the band are usually kicked out of the band, unless they are the main person." Michael Rosen concurs: "I've discovered over the last half-a-dozen years that there's not much [drug usage] anymore. The level of partying has subsided quite a bit. It's not gone and it's never going to be gone."

Rosen also knows this issue from personal experience, having worked in studios in the 1980s with a pair of singers who ingested excessive cocaine and alcohol. "It was a race against the cocaine," he says. "Killer-sounding voice, but it was just awful." On one session, he recalls, "We did an eight-ball of blow, a bag of weed, and a case of beer every day. It was stupid. Nobody could work. You start doing that much blow and you're just waiting for the bag to open again. The music suffered, it was awful. Looking back at it now, I have no idea how anybody made any records worth a shit when they were high on cocaine. That's probably why things took so long—they'd do something once, get up and do more blow, and go back and do it again."

David Lowery points out that for artists who can handle it, controlled substances offer one way to get out of a situation where a band is stuck. "Not that I recommend this for everybody," he says, "but sometimes it's like, 'Hey, maybe you should get high. Maybe you should have a drink. There's a bar across the street that has very liberal servings.' So, sometimes we send people over there. 'Go hang out, talk to some college kids that are there, listen to some alt-country and drink some beers.'"

Matt Wallace agrees. "Some bands need a den mother or someone to corral them and say, 'Alright, let's pull together and make this record.' There are some people that are so anal and in their own brain that I've actually made them smoke pot or drink beer," he says. "It really depends on the personality; some people are so wound up or just can't let go, and have mental blocks. I've kept alcohol and drugs from people and I've given it to them. It depends on the person and the situation. I just do whatever works to make a great record and hopefully not have anyone harmed in the process.

"The bands that I've found that are the most successful are the ones who really focus on keeping together," Wallace continues. "I've worked with bands that drink all the time, I've worked with bands who don't, and guys who once we're done recording will get completely loaded, but while we're working they stay completely focused. Those are the ones that I have found that make it, because whatever personal problems or demons they have, if they are small enough that they can keep them in check while they're working, then that's not going to affect the rest of your life. So, obviously, they are a somewhat stabilized and a somewhat together person. If you have to do drugs or alcohol to get through the day all the time, then that means there's an underlying personal psychological problem that's going to be there until you address it. Drugs and alcohol are fabulous Band-Aids that help you get away from it for the short term, which can be completely necessary, but ultimately you're going to have to deal with it."

DEALING WITH BAND DYNAMICS

If Hollywood were providing the script for the lives of young bands, they would live a privileged existence: Everyone would be best friends, money would never be a problem, creative conflicts would be nonexistent, and every album would top the charts. The everyday reality of most bands is something quite different, and producers are thrown smack in the middle of all sorts of band dramas about anything from girlfriends to guitar solos. Experienced producers can navigate these tricky waters.

Ryan Greene sits the band down in the studio to hash things out. "You're pounding and pounding every day, and tensions are going to start running high," he says. "So, let's get everything out on the table and say whatever you need to say. I'll tell them, 'I'm going to be here as the mediator and let's get it all out, discuss it, and be done with it.' That's the way I approach every project. I'm very straightforward, very honest. If I don't like something I'm going to tell you, and if they don't like something they have to tell me, then we'll put it out on the table and work it out. You can tell if somebody is upset about something in the control room and I'll pull him out of there, tell him to lay down on the couch and tell me what the problem is to see if we can work it out.

"It's about choosing your battles and compromising. You try to make everybody happy, but also do what's best for the project," Greene continues. "When bands have problems with anything, even musically, it's what's best for the part, and working it out and trying to make that person understand. If that person just doesn't understand now, then they'll understand after it's on the record and they've lived with it for a while. You can bend so much with everybody, but there's got to be a point where you say, 'This is how it's going to be, deal with it.'"

Michael Rosen finds that the key to dealing with band dynamics is knowing who the band leaders are. "It does you no good to have allies like the bass player and the drummer if those guys have no decision-making ability." By watching the band onstage, he says, "I can tell who the main guy is and who's just there to get chicks. Every band has to have one. That's the funny thing, if they're all even it's probably going to be a miserable project. Too many Indians and not enough chiefs—that's not a good thing. Every tribe has to have a chief who says, 'We're going that way.' I prefer the bands where there's somebody who's got a vision for what they want to do. Some of them fight it, especially back when I was doing metal albums. They all had guys who wanted to solo, so they would literally divide it up. That's not what a song is about. A song is about what's right for the song, whether you got your solos or not."

Band politics, Mark Trombino says, "can be pretty bad. There's usually a leader, one songwriter guy. He's usually one you want to cater to the most, but because it's a band you can't really do that because the bass player or the drummer or whoever will get bent out of shape. So, you've got to pretend that that's not really the way it is. There are a lot of bands that are truly democratic and everybody does contribute, but it takes awhile to figure out." Trombino works his way through that by listening and giving each member a fair shake. "I think coming from a band myself, I understand that. I treat bands the way that I would have wanted to be treated, so I think that's a strength of mine."

Dave Jerden points out with a laugh, "You have the alphas, the betas, and then the drummers. I tell everybody from the first meeting that I'm going to treat everybody equally. I'm not going to have any favorites. Some producers end up having favorites and they'll actually pit people against each other as a policy, and I don't do that. I treat everybody equally, and I'm not more of a friend to one person than another person. And when it comes to the bass player's parts or the drummer's parts, I will be in the control room for every note that is put down. They get my full attention, but nobody else from the band can tell the guy what to do. I don't allow that at all, because they know their part and they have their ideas. If you're the bass player or the drummer or the harmonica player or whatever, you feel really strongly about your parts and your contribution to the band. Then, to be cut off at the legs at the eleventh hour and to be told by somebody else what to do causes morale problems. If you want to know truly how to get the best out of somebody, you give them space to create."

By offering that space, Jerden adds, he gives each band member an equal voice and an equal amount of participation in the process. That way, band politics can be taken out of the equation. "When I worked with The Offspring, Dexter [Holland, the band's singer] writes all the songs and he's the main guy in the band, but I still gave everybody consideration," Jerden recalls. "Invariably, they thank me for giving them the opportunity, even though they have a guy that normally tells them what to play in rehearsals when they're working out the songs. When I enter the room, they know that dynamic isn't going to be the same. It's going to be, everybody is going to get an equal share, and everybody has an equal voice."

DEALING WITH DIFFICULT PERSONALITIES

If a an artist has made it this far—ready to record an album—the odds are that the combination of moxie and stubbornness that got him or her to this point is not going to disappear in the studio. In fact, the odds are producers will probably face some degree of resistance as they attempt to shape songs that have already been honed, suggest new recording techniques, or ask for latitude in selecting songs or session musicians. Many artists are open to an outside point of view, but some are downright difficult. The same way they must find a way to work around band dynamics, producers have to be flexible in their approach to "temperamental" artists who may not want to compromise.

For instance, when John Porter was working with Ryan Adams, he ran up against a wall. "Ryan is brilliant, really. He's very talented and he's very charming," Porter says. "Besides what he is and what he does, he has very little ability to focus, or else he'll focus incredibly. He'll write a song and that song may be seventy-five percent brilliant and twenty-five percent not brilliant, and in his case it's very difficult to get him to rework anything. His initial idea, quite often, is it. Even an hour after that initial idea, he's not as interested anymore. I really dig Ryan and I think he's capable of really, really great things, but I don't think he's come up with really great things yet. I think the reason he hasn't is because of his unwillingness to be able to rework them. I don't think he does that enough and I hope that will come with time." The sessions that Porter and Adams worked on were initially shelved by the record company while the singer went on to record and release *Rock N Roll* with producer Jim Barber in 2003. The next year, the label released two EPs under the *Love is Hell* name, which would have been the album Porter produced.

When Michael Rosen was working at the Automat in San Francisco, he learned a lot about personalities from observing artists like Steve Perry. "They're the stars, really. You have to know where you can push, when to push, and how to push," Rosen says. "With some of them, you've just got to get out of the way. With some of them, you're not going to win, so you run the risk of alienating them or pissing them off and losing your gig. Hopefully if they're like that, they're right. When you're Steve Perry, you get away with a lot of shit because when the guy opens his mouth it's incredible. Was he right? Probably not all the time. He was as far as his singing, but all the other stuff around the singing I would say he was wrong. I would say the worst is Carlos [Santana], because I don't think he has the goods to back it up. I think that he's got intimidation and the fear. Some guys, like Billy Joe [Armstrong of Green Day], it's his show. He's the man. You're not going to win going up against him. You hope that when you get one like that, that you're getting paid a lot or that they're right. You do the best you can to throw in what you think is right and help it along, but at a certain point you push and they look at you like, 'Okay, enough.' You just hope they're right."

Sylvia Massy Shivy starts any sessions with a historically difficult personality by studying the artist to find out what makes them tick, and then using that information to get the best performances. There are times, though, when the artist is so mercurial that it is difficult to get a read—Prince, for example. "He's the most talented musician I've ever worked with," she says, "but he's a real trip. He's hard to work with, and you're on a leash with him, because he'll keep you busy all day and all night and you won't know what the heck is going on. He's in and he's out, he's gone for a day and you're sitting there waiting for him and he ends up in Europe somewhere. You have no idea where he is or what's going on. They keep you really uninformed, but you're always on a beeper and you're being called in the middle of the night to come in and work. It's crazy.

"But, there's nothing like you and Prince in the studio." Massy Shivy continues. "He's playing all the instruments and you're recording. He's grabbing a bass, grabbing a guitar, spinning, dancing, and singing. It's just you and him, like your own private show. It's amazing. It was awesome. I loved working with Prince, but boy it's tough because he likes to mind-fuck you. He'll ask you really twisted questions and have you do things that later you go, damn, that was so evil. I think he just enjoys it. He enjoys manipulating people."

The best you can hope for, sometimes, says Matt Wallace, is that the artist will give you a bit of respect. When Wallace and engineer Trina Shoemaker worked with Blues Traveler on the *Bridge* (2001), some of their requests, like no smoking in the control room, were ignored. "I don't mind people smoking anywhere they want, but in the control room where I tend to spend most of my time, I'd rather it not be in there," Wallace says. "Even Trina, who is a smoker, wouldn't smoke in the control room, You'd say, 'Hey, could you smoke somewhere else? It's just too hard to be in this room twelve hours a day with the smoke.' [John] Popper basically said, 'No, I'm the big dude, I'm the star here, and I'm going to do whatever the hell I want to do.' It was really bad, too.

"I have to say that he's an incredibly talented singer and a phenomenal harp player, but he's got a lot of guns, which is just not my cup of tea, and he was always packing a gun. It was always loaded, and it was always cocked," Wallace continues. "I'm not comfortable with that."

These were not the first challenging sessions for Wallace, who earlier in his career had worked with Paul Westerberg and Mike Patton of Faith No More. "Every one of these guys has their own idiosyncrasies and things that make them unique," Wallace says. "Sometimes that kind of comes back to bite them. Paul would get insulted with a compliment. I worked with him on two records. [Westerberg's solo releases in the early 1990s, *14 Songs* and *World Class Fad.* Wallace also worked on The Replacements' *Don't Tell a Soul,* (1989)] "It was very, very, very difficult with him, and the rest of The Replacements guys started to beat me up all the time. Those were some very, very difficult, difficult records. You get someone who is apparently arrogant, but it might be because it's out of total fear or it might be because they do think they're the best in the world. So, you never know. The personalities are difficult. They're challenging. They're also what makes the process interesting and unique.

"Mike Patton from Faith No More was very, very strange. Very talented, but…There is something that really creates a lead singer, and it's years of irritation and agitation," Wallace continues. "It's like the grain of sand in the oyster's shell that makes this beautiful pearl, because these people are either hypersensitive to the world around them or so tuned into their emotions that they can write about these things. It makes for great artistry, but it makes for people who are kind of tough to be social with at times. I think it takes an interesting person to write about very personal things, then get up in front of a stage and sing about it. That's just the nature of the beast. It's also what makes great art. I'd never want to marry a lead singer, but I would love to buy all their records."

Quitting is always an option if a producer feels like the situation is too uncomfortable. Wallace has had to get out, but early in his career, he did not realize that was a possibility. "Unfortunately, I never had the wherewithal to bail on difficult projects when I was younger and I always kind of rode them out, because I thought I would just hang in there for it," he says. "But, I worked with Poe and I don't know what was going on with her. Something was not working and she'd disappear for days on end. I was trying to do my job and say, 'Hey, we really need to work on the chorus of a song,' and she'd be upset. I actually tried to quit a couple of times. Same thing with Courtney Love. I worked with her when she was doing demos for her new record. I said, 'I just can't do this anymore. I don't want to do it.' It's taken me a long time, but I've learned to remove myself from the situation because there's no amount of money or fame that's worth it.

"In retrospect, I would never have done The Replacements record again," Wallace continues. "The cost that I had paid for what I got was just not worth it, because they were constantly threatening to do things and were very, very difficult to work with," he continues. "They drank all the time. I was ready to quit every day for the first two weeks, and once I got past that, I just decided that I was going to make the record. If they all died in the process, I would make the record. Once I got to that place, I was fine."

Another option is looking for that hidden key to making it work, as Massy Shivy suggested. Mark Howard found his own way to work with Lucinda Williams on the sessions for *World Without Tears* (2003), though he knew going in that Williams had a reputation for being hard on producers. "I didn't know how long I was going to last, but I hooked into this rhythm with her," he explains. Part of it was catering to Williams' desired schedule, which put her in the studio at around seven o'clock every night. "She doesn't wake up until noon, then she's got to go to the gym and has a huge schedule of priorities before the studio. The original schedule was that she would come in at four o'clock. Well, four o'clock would roll around and the band would show up, but she wouldn't come in until around seven. It worked out, because I had from four to seven to work out the arrangements with the band, and when she walked in the band was cooking. I would tell her, 'Okay, we've got this arrangement.' Before she would even hear it, I would get her a glass of Grand Marnier and a coffee. When she came in, it was all about sitting down, talking, and making her feel comfortable. Once I got her comfortable, I would say, 'Why don't you slide over to your chair and let's go for a couple takes?' But she had to have a drink and a coffee so the chemistry was right. Once we had the chemistry right, it just came out of her."

Howard would get three takes out of Williams, and then the entire crew would break for dinner. "Then we'd go back in and listen, and sure enough, there would be that take that was magical—the vocal that just tore your heart out," he says. Williams, however, would comment that those tracks were just scratch vocals and that she would go back and redo them later. A Friday-night listening party, where friends would gather to listen to the week's work, changed her mind. "Her friends would listen and go, 'Lucinda, this is amazing.' She'd ask, 'You really think so?' They'd hype her so much and she believed it so much that it gave her the confidence that those were the vocals and she never sang them again."

The key, Howard adds, was finding the right emotional space for her to sing. "It was like clockwork. She would come in and say, 'I feel ugly. I'm ugly.' 'No, you're beautiful, sit down.' You just try to make her feel comfortable. One day she got in an accident and she was a wreck and angry, but put a little drink in her and "Those Three Days" comes out. I just found the right kind of spot to get it out. I tell you, though, you go too far and it gets ugly. I think that's the problem that other producers have had with her; she just hadn't trusted anybody and was fighting the whole process."

Knowing her history, Howard thought about turning down the assignment. Yet, he says, his friend and mentor Daniel Lanois gave him a boost of confidence. "He said, 'If anybody can make a record with her, you can. If anybody can pull it off, you're the guy.' That gave me a little bit of confidence; that, and her songs were incredible. It's all about the songs for me. If you've got a great song, no matter how shitty the record sounds, the song is going to overpower any sound. You can have the best-sounding record in the world, but if you've got a really bad song behind it, it's not going to last. Or it's the reverse; you have a great song but things don't sound as good, that song's going to win out. If you can get the sound great and have a great song, then you've got an even stronger record."

14 RECORDING THE SONGS

All of the work and all of the decisions made over the preceding months lead up, of course, to recording and mixing a collection of songs. This part of the process, where all of the creative ideas come to fruition for artists and producers, can take anywhere from a handful of days to a few weeks to a number of months.

If things have gone according to plan, producer and artist are in sync with each other and the songs are in a workable shape. That is not to say, however, that the direction of the music won't change once the recording sessions begin. In fact, many producers feel that their best work in the studio comes when the team takes a song into uncharted territory.

For instance, the off-kilter slide guitar introduction to the Ben Harper song, "Roses from My Friends" on *The Will to Live* (1997) came as Harper and J.P. Plunier experimented by recording the guitar tracks conventionally on analog tape, turning them upside down, and recording them again.

When Nick Launay was working on the song "Maralinga" with INXS in 1984, he found a guitar part that was not quite working. "It just annoyed me, because it was so high and it was kind of moody. I asked him if he would play it lower, but it still didn't sound good. So, I said, 'Why don't we get it to sound lower by me speeding the tape up and you playing it faster and higher.' Given that they could play that fast, we'd do it and then we could slow the tone of the guitar back down," he explains. "He was playing the same notes that he wanted to play, but the tone of it was different and it suddenly sounded really interesting."

Dave Leto of Rye Coalition reports that producer Dave Grohl influenced their release in a number of ways. "During practices we definitely gave it a lot, because it was our first time hanging out with Dave, and it was our shot to make a great album," Leto says. "It was the door-opener and the introduction [to the band] for most people," he says. "We were working on the slowest song on the album and it had all of these parts, but they never made sense. Dave's sense of songwriting helped us craft it into a song, which is something we needed. Then in overdubs, we added some things that we never would have thought of, like guitars going through Leslie cabs, and it turned into a different song. It was a surprise when I heard the final thing. It's still the same song, but it's different."

A producer may leave a recognizable stamp on an album, or that influence may be more transparent. For instance, Sylvia Massy Shivy says, "If it's possible to capture the band's live essence, then that's what I'll do when working with a group. If they play together live, there's an energy that gets lost in the studio usually. So, I'll try to make it as comfortable as possible and have everyone playing at the same time to capture some of that energy."

Energy is important, to be sure. So is the groove, the feel of a song. "Rock 'n' roll, for me, has got to breathe," says Dave Jerden. "It's got to have feel. What I do when I record basic tracks, I usually have the guy play to a click track that I can take in and out. I can also change the meter within a click, because a lot of drummers speed up too much or slow down too much, and what happens is if the take isn't breathing right, people listening don't know what's wrong with it, they just know it doesn't sound good. You can ruin a perfectly good song and a good arrangement by not playing it properly. So, what I do is give a structure that the drummer plays within, but I don't demand that the drummer play it click-accurate. I want to use that as a guideline. So, I'll get the song started with a click, and then I'll take the click out to make sure we start at the same tempo. The other thing is that a song usually has its resident sweet spots as far as tempo goes. Let's say a song sounds really good at 120 BPM, but if you try doing it at 130, it kills the song. That's something I'll do in pre-production, find the right tempo for the song. That's real important."

There are some fairly standard ways to record tracks. Many will record the basic tracks—drums, bass, and guitar—along with a scratch vocal and then concentrate on overdubs to fix any missed notes or flubbed performances. Others will utilize a digital audio workstation or hard-disk recording system to get the tracks down a number of times, then cut and paste to get the final track. There is no hard-and-fast rule about laying down tracks. It comes down to what's comfortable for both producer and artist.

"There is nothing that works all the time," Don Was says. "The only method is to stay on your toes and be flexible. The best lesson I have learned about this stuff was from Keith [Richards] when I first started working with the Rolling Stones doing the pre-production for *Voodoo Lounge*. I went to listen to the fragments of about forty songs. I didn't think any of them were complete and I left, I thought, with the agreement that we were going to have some written songs so that one could interpret what the songs were about and that the music would reflect that. I got home from Dublin and I got a fax from Keith like two days later saying, 'Alright, be in Dublin next Tuesday, we're starting.' There was no way they finished even one of the forty songs in that period of time, so I faxed him back a note asking about the songs and what we were going to do. He sent back a fax saying, 'What are we doing? That's for me to know and you to find out. Just remember, when we get to Dublin we will improvise and overcome. Don't paint yourself into a corner.'

"I was just as bummed as anything," Was continues, "and after a couple of weeks I realized that these guys only build out of chaos and if we had imposed structure on them, it would have taken extra time to undo the structure—to tear down that structure and then allow the proper one to be built, which you can't even guess what that might be. It is different for them all the time. So, that lesson has applied pretty much to everything: Just don't go in with any preconceptions. Whatever worked for you the last time and sold ten million records, it doesn't mean it will work again."

GETTING PERFORMANCES

Even in the era of sonic perfection, when digital tools give producer and artist the ability to polish each performance to a gloss, it's still crucial for an artist to deliver an inspired performance. "You cannot make a groove," repeats Dave Jerden. "For what I do in rock 'n' roll, you can't. I think a good performance is still a good performance. Yeah, you could fix stuff, and occasionally I use pitch correction [plug-ins], but I still get a good vocal performance and it's sung right. I'll spend the time, even if the guy can't sing, trying to get him to sing it right, sing it on pitch, because I can hear all that [digital processing]. To me, it just sounds phony, and I hear so many records that are spot-on precision-wise, but something's been lost."

Was says he focuses on the emotion behind the song, and will adjust his approach to what works best for each artist. Working with Mick Jagger, for example, he becomes almost like a film director. "Mick likes acting because it breathes some life into something that he has been doing for a long time," Was says. "He likes to have an almost director-actor relationship. Not that I go out there and say, 'Can you sing it like this?' I would never presume to do that, but we will discuss the emotional content of each line if need be."

While recording the Stones' *Bridges to Babylon* album, Was had to regroup with Jagger while they were laying down the vocal track for "Anybody Seen My Baby?" "It's about a guy who comes to a realization that his chick has actually left him," Was explains. "The interpretation gets more intense as the song goes on and it becomes clearer. In the first bridge, he is kind of dazed and he is a little stunned by the realization that she is really gone for good. Mick came in singing it with a lot of energy, and I asked him, 'Is he mad at the girl here or is he stumped?'"

Jagger referred to a notebook to check his motivation. "I had never seen anybody else doing that, it was a really unique experience," Was says. "He had written what I would call a ten-page treatment of what happened leading up to where the song begins and what happens afterwards. I don't know if it was a true story or what it was based on past that, but he sat down and read this thing and said, 'No, alright, he is not angry in the first verse, he is actually kind of wistful.' So, he went back and gave the character a wistful voice," Was explains. "That's what he thrives on, that acting. I don't know how else to call it, even if it is a true story, even if this really happened to him and he doesn't have to pretend. I believe that his songs aren't third-person songs and when he sings from emotion, that comes from him. He still likes making sure that he is writing truth."

A similar scene occurred when Was worked with Bonnie Raitt on the song "I Can't Make You Love Me," which appeared on her 1991 release *Luck of the Draw*. "I didn't pry and I don't know what the incident was in her life, but clearly when she heard the song she was able to relate to it," Was explains. "She came right out of the actress school of method acting and she tapped into something that caused her to feel that way, and when she performed the song she returned to that emotional place. She didn't need any coaching to do that. She already knew what she had to remind herself of. My job was more to create an environment where she could feel safe enough to break down and cry. The only lines we had to punch on "I Can't Make You Love Me" are the ones where she was sobbing. She just had to have an environment where she felt comfortable going to that place and knew no one was going to be taking pictures of her. We didn't actually discuss the emotional content—if you've got it, you've got it. My job is to mostly make them comfortable."

From that level of comfort and trust, a producer can elicit performances that would not be possible otherwise. For instance, when Matt Wallace was working with Blues Traveler in 2001, he was faced with the daunting task of recording "Pretty Angry," a song that John Popper and the band had written for their former bassist Bob Sheehan, who had died from a drug overdose the year before. Finding the right time to get the band in the proper emotional space was tricky. "I had been thinking and planning [when to record that song] for so long, because I knew it was a difficult track. I had a feeling that the whole band was not that excited to jump onboard that song, because we wanted to do it well enough for Bob and we didn't want it to be over-sentimental, but we wanted it to have power. We'd been there doing a week of tracking, and it was the one year anniversary [of his death]. They went out in the [San Francisco] bay to dump the remains of his ashes and I could feel it. I talked to Trina [Shoemaker, who engineered the project] and we were all set. When the band walked in, I could see they were all really moved and somber about the whole experience. I said, 'Let's go cut a track.' We captured that feeling, which is what it's all about. It's capturing the feeling and having people listen to it and be moved by it. Being a producer is just sometimes being able to disarm artists just long enough, or let their guard down long enough for them to do something great."

"I think making records can be boiled down to a very simple statement, and that is, we're really just selling emotions." Wallace continues. "If we could do away with all sound and all lyrics and you could just convey the emotion, I think we'd do it. But because emotions are so deep and broad, and sometimes so mysterious, the only way we can deal with them is to either dance, paint, or sing about them. I tell that to all the bands, 'Hey, we're just selling the emotion, so whatever we do has to kind of support or reiterate that emotion.' Often, I'll have the songwriter tell the musicians what he or she was thinking when they wrote the song. They'll start talking, and then the people in the room hear it. Usually that does a lot. I think it's a really effective way to do it, because then people get an idea of what we're trying to convey. Once you know what you're trying to convey, then it's pretty easy I think for people to play. If we know what we want to do, I don't have to say, 'Okay, now play this part here. Do that over there.' I have a lot of faith in the people I'm working with. I know that they are capable and talented, and given some decent direction and support, they can do great things."

For Nick Launay that emotional peak can only come with getting the whole band in the studio and playing together. "I always record whatever the band is live. If it's two guitars, bass, and drums, that's what I'll record and I will go for complete takes. We'll do complete take after take after take after take, and I'll do lots. I will do it until they hit their peak of recording that song and that arrangement, and when they start dropping it and it's not happening anymore, that's when I'll stop. Basically I will do as many takes as it takes, and then I will listen to all the takes and I'll make notes as they go down and I will chop between the takes," he explains. "So, I basically try to get the best performance that that band can possibly do at that time in their lives of that song. That invariably involves all kinds of different methods, like doing the song a couple of times without a click, doing it with a click, doing it with a click that speeds up and slows down as I feel it. You know, have the drummer listening to the click and no one else or whatever it takes. Sometimes I'll do something like putting those Christmas lights in the studio and they'll be on a blinker that's in time with the tempo, so they're not hearing clicks in their headphones and they'll be looking at the lights. That is very cool."

"Some people are really mathematical about the way they think about stuff. A lot of times for the rhythm section it's not inspiration as much as they need some quiet concentration," says David Lowery. "I think some people do their best takes after they warm up. They need to play for a long time, and everything needs to sound right. But, a lot of times, for the lead guitarists and vocalists it's a really emotional thing and it could be anything. Do they need a drink? Do they need to smoke pot? Do they need to go for a run or swim? I think it varies according to every artist. I will say the lead guitarists, though, are particularly difficult. Sometimes they have to ride a real emotional high to play their parts. So, lead guitarists tend to get stuck out in the room with their amps with their headphones taped on their head or with the monitors blaring and blasting and the lights are turned down low. A lot of them play better that way. Not all of them."

Daron Malakian, a lead guitar player himself, describes how Rick Rubin advises the band: When pressures rise, just relax. "When a guy is giving a performance and he is struggling a little bit, stop trying because when you're trying it sucks," Malakian says. "'Come on in, let's hang out for like ten minutes. Let's go take a ride.' Get your mind off the performance. Get your mind off the damn song. Maybe even move on to another song. That works, too. You might not be in the mood to work on that song. There are a million things, because there are millions of characters that you're working with," he says. "When you're producing a band you're usually dealing with four or five different characters, so every one of them you gotta deal with in different ways. It's like being band psychologist."

When Malakian produced the Bad Acid Trip 2004 debut, *Lynch the Weirdo*, he took the lessons he learned from Rubin and added some of his own. "They were such a thrash band, they didn't bring out some colors that existed and I saw. I understood what they were playing and I'm a fan of that music, but I [knew I] could bring out colors that didn't exist. So, I got Dirk [Rogers], who before this album had never, ever sung. I had him sing in three-part harmonies. I even stood there and taught him how to sing, and then when he could do it I'd press record. Five minutes later he might have a little bit of a tough time, but I tried to capture that fuckin' moment, and next thing you know I got the guys singing in three-part harmonies. We took that and then he'll build on it, and he'll actually learn how to do that more naturally from listening to his album."

When Linda Perry and Pink were working on the songs for *Missundaztood*, the artist's mood ruled the day, especially when they were making "Eventually," the first song they worked on together. "Basically we were looking at each other and I asked, 'What kind of mood are you in?' She's like, 'I'm in kind of a mellow mood.'" Perry recalls. "She was sitting on the floor, and I just grabbed my microphone and stuck it right where she was sitting, and I went to my piano and put up a rough beat and started playing piano and she started singing. She's like, 'What should I sing about?' I said, 'Just ad lib. Sing whatever the hell you want to. Don't worry about feeling stupid; it's just you and me. You're going to say some really stupid things and you're going to say some really brilliant things, but don't worry about it.' Basically, her whole ad lib was pretty much the song. It was really great. That's pretty much how we worked. It started off with what kind of mood are you in today, and then I would give her the vibe of what I thought the song should be, and then she would just go with it."

A Few Tried and True Tricks

Some producers get a singer to stand in a booth and sing along to a track the band has already recorded. Others set up the band in the studio and have them play facing each other for a heightened level of communication. Those methods are pretty standard. But other producers, such as Sylvia Massy Shivy and Garth Richardson, have a few tricks up their sleeves to extract inspired performances. These might not be for the faint of heart, but here are a couple tricks that those two have used in the studio.

When a drummer is laying down tracks, Richardson may put a touring P.A. behind him. "It makes them feel like they're actually playing live. People bring in bands [to the studio] and they make them put on these tiny little head-phones. They are so used to playing in these big halls, these big monster caverns," Richardson says. "Then they get in the studio and the band goes, 'It does-n't feel like I'm playing live.' The guy that taught me that was Bob Ezrin, who did *The Wall*."

Massy Shivy employs a unique approach to working with singers. "Maynard [James Keenan] from Tool is a comedian, and then he's also a very dark, but artistic, personality. So, in order to get a real aggressive performance out of him, because he could just be goofy, I'd purposely antagonize him. At one point I wasn't getting the performance I wanted out of him, I wanted him to be blood-curdling and hit some notes that are at the top of his range, yet have a real emo-tion, so I told him to go outside and run around the block three times. He was so pissed off," she says with a laugh. "But, he did it, and he came in and he hit those notes. He was so angry, but he hit those notes and it was fantastic. That was the performance. So, if I can find out where their buttons are, if I need to push them, I'll push them." The song that resulted from Keenan's bit of exercise was "Crawl Away" on the 1993 release, *Undertow*.

If she can't find those emotional buttons, Massy Shivy will go for something different. Take the time she had Econoline Crush singer Trevor Hurst lie on the couch to sing the song "Razorblades and Bandaides." Then there was the bizarre technique she used with System of a Down's singer Serj Tankian on the band's eponymous debut. "I had Serj hang upside down to sing a part," she admits with a laugh. "I thought maybe there would be something we could get out of that, because I'd heard that John Lennon hung upside down to sing some parts before. Poor Serj, he hit some notes and his head almost exploded. All the blood rushed to his head, and I felt like I may have put his life in danger."

Time for Inspiration

Most producers say that the goal of pre-production is to have every song lined up, so that the only thing left to do in the studio is record. Yet, there's a handful of producers who leave extra time in the studio for those last-minute inspirations. For example, Don Gehman found he had to be more flexible than usual during his work with R.E.M. on *Life's Rich Pageant,* (1986), because they needed more time to finish the songs. "Previous to that time I was so used to the whole process being very ordered, that you had parts and put things together and then it kind of came out over here. R.E.M. really taught me a valuable lesson in how things really didn't need to be that focused," Gehman says. "I taught them a lot about how to make records: [Things like] choruses had to have things come in and lift, and all that Producer 101 stuff of doubling things, making shifts and color changes throughout the song. It was the first experience they had with that, but they really taught me about chaos and how you can let a lot of it go and still come out of it in the end with a viable commercial product, but it will have a level of magic it would never have had any other way.

"We had a wonderful time, it was very creative," Gehman continues. "I remember wondering, 'I'm not sure what's going on here.' I remember arguing with Michael [Stipe, the band's singer] about what the lyrics meant and why he was writing lyrics so late. He'd come in every day with another set of lyrics and I wouldn't know what was going on. It was just so helter-skelter. I remember at the end of the process being so pleased with the results that I looked back and said, 'I should be doing things more this way. I don't need to be so rigid.' I always look back at that record as the moment where I learned Zen producing."

Sunny Day Real Estate came into the studio to work with Lou Giordano on *The Rising Tide* (2000) with some work left to do. "There was a fair amount of lyric and melody writing that happened in the studio and it was fun, because they really had a method for doing it and it was a very natural method. Jeremy [Enigk, the band's singer] would go in and kind of sing his way through a song with whatever came out," Giordano recalls. "I would just roll the song over and over again, and he would start to form some words that really didn't mean anything, but they were kind of placeholder lyrics. He'd get a melody going with that, then all of a sudden, we'd have something that was really good, and all we'd need is finished lyrics. So, we would make a quick rough mix of that and give it to Dan [Hoerner], the other guitar player, and he would go off and he'd write some lyrics that meant something. He'd come back, then we'd edit them some more and pretty soon, we'd have the finished lyrics. Then we'd record the vocals for real. The songs weren't finished, but we had a real method for coming up with the lyrics and melodies that worked, it just took a little bit of time."

Joe Henry does not need to be sold on the idea of musicians using studio time to get creative. He has seen it work while recording his own albums, as well as the album he produced for Solomon Burke. During the Burke sessions, in fact, Henry saw how having that space and committing the musician's risks to tape inspired a daring rendition of the song he contributed, "Flesh and Blood." "The demo [of that song] was just piano and vocal. We'd already done a bunch of songs, but nobody talked about what this song was going to be," he recalls. "The only conversation that happened leading up to counting it off was Solomon asking David Piltch, the bass player, to switch to electric bass because he'd been playing upright [bass]. I walked into the control room and heard David playing electric and I said, 'Dave are you hearing electric bass on this?' He said, 'Solomon just asked me if I would switch.' So, I said okay and we just counted it off thinking, 'Let's hear where this starts.' We started digging in and then it happened, just as you hear it."

Henry says the line-up had a similar experience while working on the Tom Waits-written song, "Diamond in Your Mind." "By the third take Solomon was more confident, and when that take started it was already the song. I could hear it from the intro. I said, 'Here we go. Unless somebody just crashes and burns and we stop ...' It was just the song."

While Henry utilized the live-in-the-studio approach with Burke and Aimee Mann for her *The Forgotten Arm* release (2005), he acknowledges that the method is not for everybody. "I mean, Janet Jackson wouldn't make a record that way. I don't know why she would. I think she could make a beautiful record that way probably, if she would embrace that as an idea," he says. The idea did pique the interest of Henry's cousin, Madonna, who had stopped by the studio on the Sunday afternoon that the team was mixing the record. "I played a bunch of stuff for her, because we were excited about it. I remember she kept asking, 'These people were playing and he was singing at the same time? This band sounds great.' I said, 'These guys could make a record with you as easily as they made one for him. It wouldn't sound anywhere the same, but these players could step into your world as easily as they stepped into his, and it could be authentic for what you're doing.'"

HITTING PROBLEM SPOTS

In an ideal world, everything goes according to plan in the studio, and performances pour out of musicians and singers at a stunning pace, technology cooperates, and songs come to fruition as originally designed. However, more often than not, something goes wrong.

When Butch Walker and The Donnas started working on *Gold Medal* (2004), the band was forced to record Torry Castellano's drum tracks at the end of the sessions. Castellano had suffered an arm injury after years of touring and playing with improper drumming techniques. "That was a little tricky, but The Donnas are The Donnas. You don't tell one of them, 'Hey, you can't play on the record.' We were pretty intensive with her therapy and recovery and practicing. She kind of changed up her technique a bit as well, just to make it work," Walker says. "It worked in her favor, because the way she changed her technique fit the style of the band and the way the music was going. It made sense [to record her drum tracks at the end of the session] because of the recovery time. We didn't exactly play to a click track, because that would have felt terrible by the time the other tracks got done, but we temped in some drums and then we had her go back in and re-play them with more tender-loving care. We were being real careful with her, making sure she took her time and didn't rush it."

Three songs into Rage Against the Machine's self-titled debut in 1992, producer Garth Richardson ran into a bit of a problem when singer Zack de la Rocha lost his voice. "The best thing to do was to let Zack take some time off while we carried on," he reports. "We got about three songs live on the floor, and the rest we had to go back in and fix later. I got him in front of the control room console, moved everything out of the way, and I blasted the mains as loud as they could go. I gave him a Shure SM58 handheld mic and said, 'Go.' I was sitting over on the side of the room and he was singing. I really wanted to keep that live vibe."

SURVIVING DIFFICULT SESSIONS

There are also times when a session is just downright difficult. J.D. Foster chalks it up to the pressure of the red light. "There are some artists that have this really over-amped value on recording. 'Now we're doing something. We're documenting here for history.' So, people get uncomfortable sometimes and that's hard to fight," he says. "When that happens, I think the most productive call is to say, 'Okay, let's go get a bottle of Jagermeister or whatever.' My little two cents as a total amateur psychologist is that a lot of people being resistant and aggressive comes directly from fear, and I kind of run into that sometimes."

Foster struggled with a tense artist while he was working with songwriter Richard Buckner. "We had this incredible session where it was like, 'Are we on the same page here?' We were really having a big disagreement and I said, 'Should I just go home? Now?' I didn't realize how much tension there could be," he recalls. "It was both of our first major-label attempt. I think the record turned out really, really well. It's just so funny how it can go from so dark," he adds with a laugh, "to so fine and dandy."

The two got around it by going home for the day and then regrouping to talk it out. "I came back and worked on some stuff of my own afterwards and then played it for him," Foster recalls. "I think it had to do with the both of us proving that we had each other's interests in mind. Music is definitely tension and release. Sometimes what seems like the worst day, when you think that it's just not happening, in retrospect is great. That's another thing about recording, it's something that's going to live for as long as it's going to live, but it's so much bigger than the moment. Sometimes that's hard to judge."

Foster ran into an even tougher situation while working with The Damnations on *Where it Lands*. That album was so troubled that the band bought it back from the label, Sire Records, and released it on their own label, without the Foster-produced tracks. According to statements that singer Deborah Kelly made in the press, the band had to pull Foster back at times. "That's an interesting perception of that, because I was not able to do my job well there," Foster says. "Even though it wasn't put this way, I think there was some division in the band, and I couldn't find the middle ground, unfortunately. There was some stuff that Amy Boone, one of the songwriters, wanted to do that we went into and I thought was the best thing they recorded, but the guys didn't really like it.

"I was told once that the band wanted to go in this direction, and so I went there and I thought it was great, which basically the thing they hire me to do is to give them an opinion," he continues. "Then everybody didn't want to go there and it just got to kind of a weird point. I was a little bit less than happy with the outcome of the record, and the record that I made didn't come out. Part of that had to do with them getting dropped. So, the record that came out is definitely different than the record that I thought was what they were trying to do, but I wouldn't put it that they wanted to do one thing and I wanted to do another. It's more like my perception of what they wanted to do and what I thought would be the best for them to do with what they gave me."

While Craig Street is quick to say, "Making records is an incredible amount of fun," he also knows the pain of working with a difficult artist. He won't name names, but he says that the artist in question was an established singer/songwriter who approached him to make a record. "They didn't have a label at the time. It was a very, very small project, and I knew how this person had been making records," he says. "They had been making very, very clean precise records. Great musician, great songwriter and I said, 'I don't think I can help you. You do something that's really different than what I do.' They said, 'No, no, I really want you to help with this.' So, I did. I brought some people in that I thought would be really great and the person turned out to be very, very, very disturbed. I don't know where that came from. I can imagine where it might have come from in that person's life, but their issues became everybody's issues. The artist did not, in fact, want what they said they wanted when they came in. They started picking on people, started by picking on the engineer in a really abrasive, horrible kind of way. They wouldn't let the musicians off of the leash, which was the whole deal.

"In the end it was really difficult," he continues. "In the middle of this process, the artist got signed to a label and it's a label that had people that I'd worked with before, so I called the A&R person up just as we were getting ready to mix and said, 'Fire me.' I went into a closet at the studio we were in, because it's the only place I could get privacy, and asked him to fire me. He started laughing and said, 'I can't, I didn't hire you.' What he did, and this is an example of a record company working in a great way, is say, 'Look I will get the artist off your back. Finish the mixes, turn them in, you will not have broken your contract.'"

Street also went to his manager and said that he did not want the credit and was not worried about the money. "She said, 'You did a great record, this person doesn't appreciate it, and whatever happens with it is fine, but you are going to get paid and you're going to get your points.' Then she asked me why I didn't want credit. Basically, my thing was really simple. I was definitely proud of the work, the work that was fine, but I know a lot of journalists and I didn't want someone to call me up that I knew asking me what it was like and I didn't want to say, 'I'll tell you what it was like...' But that was just an artist who had a personality problem."

MIXING THE SONGS

More and more these days, producers are active participants in the mixing sessions. It's understandable that a producer would want to see a project to the end, especially songs that he or she took so much care to help shape and record. Often, however, record companies looking for a certain sheen on a potential hit song will turn mixes over to a dedicated, successful mixing engineer, such as Jack Joseph Puig, Tom Lord-Alge, Chris Lord-Alge, or Andy Wallace.

When mixing responsibility is taken out of a producer's hands, it can lead to considerable disappointment. After finishing the recording for the MxPx release *Before Everything & After,* Dave Jerden was all set to start the mixing process. "I've mixed every record that I've ever produced," explains Jerden. "I mixed that record and Ron Fair didn't even listen to it. He immediately went and hired the Lord-Alge brothers to mix and paid them a lot of money, too. So, I was really frustrated working with Ron on that."

Before Mark Trombino was let go from the Jimmy Eat World session, there was a decision to have someone else come in and mix it. "We got demo reels from a bunch of people, listened to them, and didn't like anything. In the end they decided they wanted me to mix it, but it was weird because it made me think a little differently when I was recording because I knew somebody else was going to hear my tracks," he explains. "I don't know if that made me work harder or what, but the raw tracks on it were pretty good."

Matt Wallace bounces easily between mixing his own sessions and using an outside mixer. "If I'm not the guy that mixes it, great. I'll be the first one to make recommendations for other people. Over the years I've lost my ego in that regard," he says. "Like with Caleb [Kane, whom he produced], I think I am mixing it, but if someone else wants to do it, great. I've made recommendations who I don't want to mix it and who might be cool to mix it. If people can just get rid of their ego for a minute and look at the greater picture, that you'll improve the record and you obviously want all your artists to have a better record. I think it's smart."

GETTING READY TO MIX

Whether or not a producer is going to mix a project, he or she is still in charge of getting the tracks ready for the mixing process. "I never really know if I'm going to mix it in the end, because the labels are so crazy. It's almost like the better the record is going to do, the more they want someone else to mix it," reports Ross Hogarth. "They'll hire me to mix something that I haven't produced, and they'll hire someone else to mix something that I produced, so you never know what's going to happen." That said, Hogarth makes sure he has made a mark on the tracks he produces. "My ultimate vision in the recording has to come out in the recording," he explains. "So, when it comes down to the mix, whether it's by me or anybody else, there has to be a certain type of vision that has to be intact with the choice of sounds and arrangements."

Hogarth's attitude is informed by his experience working with producer Giorgio Moroder and artist John Mellencamp. "Giorgio's production philosophy was everything and the kitchen sink. You wouldn't decide now whether you wanted eighth notes on the second verse, so you put it through the whole song, then you decided when you mixed where you needed the eighth notes. That's certainly an interesting way to produce—it leaves the door wide open all the time," Hogarth says. "John would erase everything that he didn't want to hear again. So, I have both of those schools going on in my thoughts all the time, because there are things I'm not going to decide right now. So, I'll record a bunch of drum mics and a bunch of different sounds, or maybe a really distorted bass, a really clean bass and then a normally kind of compressed bass. Say down the road I don't like the sound of the distorted bass, I'll have the cleaner bass that I can work with."

Leaving the door open is the key, Hogarth adds, whether he's going to mix it or not. "There are things that are my imprint on the arrangements that will be completely obvious on someone else's mixes. Now, if they choose to make it otherwise and I hear it while the mix is going down and they disagree with me, that's the way it goes," he says. "But, I try when I'm making records to have the end result in mind."

Sometimes Wallace will look forward and set sounds a certain way for the mix, and there are times when he'll offer several options. "Sometimes when we're getting the sound right, I'll commit it to tape exactly as I want it to sound," he explains. "I get the sound effects and EQ down. Sometimes I'll definitely go all the way with that, and other times, we'll leave it open-ended. I don't think I've ever gone into a record knowing exactly how every piece of it is going to sound exactly in the mix, but I pretty much always go into making a record knowing what I think will be the general, fundamental sign posts, and what is acceptable and what is not acceptable in making the record. I like to be able to be open to the possibility of happy mistakes, though, where things happen all of a sudden. I'm focused and I know what I want, but I'm also open to things changing."

Throughout the recording process, Howard Benson and his team turn out rough mixes to make sure the songs are coming out as originally planned, and help all the players visualize the outcome. "Then we'll give our roughs to the mixer, and if he can't beat the rough, then we're using our mix," Benson says. "Our roughs are really good. We've been having a little bit of trouble with that lately, mixers trying to beat our roughs. They just can't do it. So, we're kind of like in a weird zone right now with mixers. We're trying to help our mixers do the best they can, but by doing that we are almost mixing it for them." Benson also provides mixing engineers with any drum samples that might be used to sweeten the drum tracks. "We are just making sure that they have everything, and when they get everything, if they can't mix it, then something's wrong. Our sounds are good, so if they can't mix our stuff then something's absolutely screwed up. But that's good for business; it's good for everybody that things sound better. I would say we want our mixers to mix and not fix. I don't want them to spend time fixing my projects."

Sylvia Massy Shivy concurs, adding: "I try to lay out all the tracks and record them with mixing in mind. Absolutely. I try to clean up anything that's not going to be in the final mix, so that it mixes itself, hopefully. I try and create the mix as we're going along, which is really easy to do in Pro Tools."

THINKING ABOUT MULTI-CHANNEL FORMATS?

The burgeoning market for surround sound home theater systems has prompted some labels and producers to begin releasing multi-channel music. Interest in surround sound began with movie viewing in mind, but the demand for music to play through these 5.1 systems has grown. Music companies are entering this new market cautiously, of course, and are slowly introducing SACD releases from a select portion of their catalogue.

Some producers are optimistic about the future of multi-channel music. Others believe it will never take off. "I can't stand 5.1; it's just the worst idea in the known universe," states Matt Wallace. "The reason I say that is that because 5.1, for people to really get it, there's only one great seat in the house. If you've got it in your home stereo, there's one spot right in the middle—there might be two, right next to each other—where the sound is. The problem is, very few people nowadays sit down in their house and dedicate hours or an evening to listen to music and appreciate their surround sound. Most people use music as wallpaper. The 5.1 stuff I have heard always sounds completely incongruous to me when you've got the kind of the band in front but then you've got instruments kind of left and right, and you've got background singers behind you—that would never happen in a million years unless you're standing on the stage with the band or you're standing in there during pre-production.

"I still think stereo is absolutely fabulous," Wallace continues. "We all have two ears. I don't think 5.1 is ever going to be for everyone. Put it this way, you can't put it on your iPod and listen to it with headphones. A whole other thing is that 5.1 takes some serious dough and some serious time to sit down and really listen to the minutia and the details in a recording. The only people that do that are engineers, producers," he adds with a laugh. "The rest of us just throw something on. If you go to somebody's home and pick up a CD, there are scratches all over it and they're in a stack somewhere. The speakers are out of phase and the loudness button is on, the treble is off. People don't care. They just want to rock, or be moved. I personally believe it's gonna go the way of quad, because I just don't think it's essential. Does it affect the emotional impact of what you get from music? Not a chance in hell. I'm sure there are a lot of people who completely disagree with me because I've had discussions with other people about it."

Dave Fridmann is one producer who sees a future in multi-channel. "God, I hope so," he says with a laugh. "I just wrote a check to upgrade our studio for surround sound. There are certain elements of it that I think are going to become more prevalent, and certainly since I'm going to have it at my disposal, I'll be looking at it more and more."

Fridmann was part of the team that worked on a 5.1 remix of The Flaming Lips' *Yoshimi Battles the Pink Robots* release, but he is not so sure it would work for every release. "I'm not going to record six tracks of guitar so they each have their own surround sound presence. I don't think I'm ready to go that far and deal with that many tracks," he admits. "That requires Pro Tools, and even then if you start looking at assigning five or six voices per instrument, you're going to run out [of tracks] pretty quick. I think it's slowly becoming more acceptable, and obviously, it's a sales-driven thing. It has to be in people's homes and their cars before there's any reason to create the music for it, but I think it's going to be great.

"Personally, from a production and musician standpoint, I think it's infinitely more expressive. Normally, if you want to isolate some instrument and make something special you have to throw it all the way in the left channel or all the way in the right channel and there's a big difference when [the sound] actually comes from behind you or from the left, or when the lead vocal is hovering over your head instead. Creatively, I think you can convey even more complex scenarios and emotions by having surround sound available."

Ed Cherney says he can imagine the day when musicians start to compose with 5.1 in mind. "It may be next year or in ten years, but it will be a multimedia experience and artists are going to have to be multimedia artists," Cherney says. "The challenges are the same—make it sound great, make the music compelling, make people want to lean into it and turn it up and hear more of it. I think it's a little bit easier to mix it in 5.1, because you have more space. You know, with stereo records you're typically trying to get twenty pounds of sausage into a ten-pound casing. When you try to do that, it makes it smaller and smaller. Certainly there's a time and place for that, but with surround you can really open it up. You can hear the instruments clearer, you can hear harmonies clearer, and you can hear a sound field that goes beyond the speakers. You can almost make the speakers disappear and make the music appear in the room with you."

Cherney has remixed albums for Bonnie Raitt and the Wallflowers in 5.1, and he worked on the Rolling Stones' DVD, *Four Flicks*. The Wallflowers, Cherney says, "came in and heard their record in that format. They were totally energized by it and fell in love with their record again. That was really great having them come in and be able to hear it in that environment." Even with that experience, Cherney does not have surround on the brain while working on a project. "I'm just trying to make a hit in stereo," he says with a laugh. "I'm still thinking in terms of great music and making hits."

15 POSTSCRIPT: THE STATUS OF THE MUSIC INDUSTRY

Read virtually any music-business trade magazine from around the turn of the 21st century, and the tidings for the music industry will appear grim, to say the least. You'll find stories bemoaning the high costs of signing and marketing major-label artists, of recording albums, and the negative affects of label mergers on non-Platinum artists. But the most consistent complaint, from all parts of the business, will concern the "scourge" of music downloading and piracy. Some say the business has suffered because the rash of music theft is depriving artists and labels of their livelihood. Others insist the problem is that labels have failed to "adjust" to the new technology and new economics of Internet music. The truth, most likely, is in the middle.

Brad Wood does not buy that major labels are solely to blame. "I've been fleeced at the tiniest of indie labels to medium-size indies to the big indies, and the good majors and the bad majors," he says. "I've been fleeced by them all. I think those kinds of people are in any industry, from the guys that don't manufacture the O-rings to spec so the Space Shuttle blows up to the guys at Enron. There is nobody in a major label as evil as Kenneth Lay and those jackals. I mean, jackals and thieves are in every industry. The music industry allows a broader and more colorful variety of every kind of businessperson and artist, because it's much looser. I think that we kid ourselves in the music industry to think that the bad guys in the music industry are a particularly virulent strain of bad guys. You can't get worse than Kenneth Lay and Dick Cheney. Those are just evil bastards to the core.

"I don't buy that this is a vile, evil industry that is soul-crushing," Wood continues. "I think every industry, when it gets to a certain size, invites a certain level of bone-crushing, soul-stealing behavior. I'll bet you the percentage of nasty people in the music business is probably lower than the percentage that is in the energy business, or the rebuilding-crushed-foreign-states business. I just don't see the evilness. I think that my biggest disappointments and most flagrant rip-offs came from indie labels. When you do the work [for an indie] you don't always get paid, because their bottom line is much more sketchy and their checking account might be bare and they might be lying to you. Indie doesn't equal angel, just like major label doesn't equal devil. That doesn't equate. That's a naïve assumption."

David Lowery, however, does take issue with the major-label world. "I think the music business is incredibly nepotistic and a lot of people have their jobs because of family connections. It's really bad. I really can't stand that, because I felt like I really pulled myself up from the bootstraps," he says. "So I have some contempt for a lot of people there, but I just don't think they're a very good way of finding talent and they're not a very efficient way of marketing talent any more. I think finally what happened with the Clear Channel conglomeration is that the record labels finally got what they had always wanted—a top-down sort of approach where they could take a record and shove it down people's throats to make hits. It's like payola in the Seventies."

Major and indie labels alike must accept the fact that the entire industry is contracting, and that, says David Lowery, is making things very political: "A lot of my perspective is based on the last eight years in the music business, which has been the incredible shrinking business. I think you have people doing things who just can't have any stain of failure or fault on their job, so they just absolutely won't help you out in any way at all if you're getting stuck or you need more money. It's just like they don't want to be around you. They don't want to have made the wrong decision."

Often, that fear of making the wrong decision affects the creative process. An A&R rep and producer may decide upon the direction of a song, but once the rep talks to the band's management or higher-level management at the record company, suddenly the decision is changed. "So, I will have gone off in the direction we talked about and then they change their mind, so it's my fault and I get fired. It's pretty ugly," Lowery says, "but that's kind of just what the job is. If you didn't want the job, you shouldn't have taken it."

From Dave Jerden's point of the view, the flailing industry boils down to the lack of originality in music. "People don't talk about sound anymore. It used to be back in the Sixties you talked about the sound with the song, people don't talk about a sound anymore. It's just assumed what the sound is going to be today. It's like what you hear on KROQ [the Los Angeles radio station], every song sounds the same and that's going to be the sound. That's the problem I had with Ron Fair; he wanted every song [on the MxPx release *Before Everything & After*] to sound like "Everything Sucks (When You're Gone)." He wanted it to sound like Jimmy Eat World. That's what he wanted and that's what he got, but to me the original version of the song was a much better version of that song. The marketplace told him the song was not a hit the way it was mixed. It sounded so much like everything else out there. It had no personality when it was done.

"When you listen to stuff from the Sixties, for instance, or even the Seventies, when you listen to a band, you can tell immediately who they are," Jerden continues. "They all sound different. There was only one Janis Joplin, there was only one Jimi Hendrix, there was only one The Kinks. You could tell immediately who Led Zeppelin was, and now it's as if everything sounds like Led Zeppelin. Who cares? There's one Jimmy Eat World. Great, leave it at that. With a lot of these bands, I cannot tell the difference. For the last five years, it was all falling into this one sound—real dry vocals and it was a formula. It's really boring and I don't buy records anymore."

Further, Jerden understands why people are using file-sharing programs to distribute music without paying for it. "They'd rather just buy the single of the song that they like, because all the rest of the songs on the record are going to be a version of the single anyway. There's not going to be any personality," he says. "I think music needs another big kick in the ass myself. It needs another punk revolution, it needs something; it's all boring and it's all been done before. Josh Freese [a popular session drummer who has ghosted on hundreds of albums] plays his drums and the Lord-Alge brothers mix it. The reason record companies are doing that and promote that is because they're scared. It's easier to fall back on a formula that works instead of trying something new."

Part of that formula involves pushing songs onto the radio. "You have to look at why things are so shitty right now," says Garth Richardson, "like a bottle of wine. In the music business today it's like the grapes get picked on Monday morning, Monday night they get stomped on, Tuesday morning they get put into the bottle, Tuesday night the bottle is corked, Wednesday you buy that bottle of wine. In the old days, when a band would sign, they would get four or five records to learn how to make records and to learn how to write songs. Then they would break and it was huge. It was like the bottle of wine got to mature. The problem today is that the record labels want that first-quarter, second-quarter, third-quarter money. So, they put [albums] out and if it doesn't fly in the first week, it sucks."

Richardson has a solution. "Our job now is to find these young bands, teach them what a song is, help them write songs and show them, so that when they finally sign to a big record label they have already had three or four records out," he offers. Richardson adds that he knows of many other producers who are taking that philosophy to heart and are out looking for bands.

How is Piracy Effecting Producers?

Thanks to Lars Ulrich of Metallica, just about every music fan in the world knows how the issue of piracy has affected him and the rest of his musician brethren. Music that is downloaded without payment, Ulrich argued, robs musicians of their earned royalties. From this logic, it follows that producers would also lose big at the hands of Internet thieves. After all, musicians are not the only ones who earn royalties on albums sold.

According to Matt Wallace, piracy is affecting his livelihood, as well as recording budgets. "I think it's one of the reasons why our budgets are diminishing and [labels] are more reticent to put out so many records," he says. "It's a tough thing, but I understand why it's happening. I think the record labels have a lot to be responsible for. We've seen this thing coming for a good ten years. The fact that Steve Jobs has put something together is great, but the record labels, I believe, should have gotten together five years ago and said, 'Okay, here's what we're going to do. People are going to pay a fee per month, and they can download as much as they want.' You know what would have happened? They would have actually had more customers than they could have ever dreamed of. Instead, everyone operated from a place of fear, that they were going to lose their little piece of the pie."

Wallace concedes that he's happy that people are listening to the music that he's produced, "but I'd prefer that we'd get at least a little bit of dough," he says, "even if it was just pennies on the dollar. I just want it to be fair. I want the people who have done the work to get paid and work out a fair thing that works out for the consumer and for the label and for the producers."

Dave Jerden maintains that making money is not what drives him. "My intentions were not about making money. My intentions were about making good music and trying to have some fun. I wasn't trying to brighten some record-president's day, but brighten up some sixteen-year-old kid laying in his bed while he feels totally disenfranchised from the world. That's my job," he says. "It's not to go out and make some money off that kid. If I make him happy and he wants to pay me for it, then fair enough. But if the record company's going to try to rape him, I tell the kid go rip it off the Internet. I'd be happy for him.

"It's obvious something is wrong," Jerden continues. "Somebody has got to say that the emperor has no clothes here. If everybody pretends like everything is fine and they say that the Internet is the big problem, then they're full of shit. When you live in a fucking free-market society, if people aren't going to get what they want, they're not going to pay for it. It's as simple as that, and to try to have all these regulatory commissions and sue a thousand Internet users, that's bullshit."

Ed Cherney feels divided on the issue. "I'm not convinced that [piracy] is as big of an issue as some people would make it out to be," he says. "I always thought that people downloading something would get them more interested in an artist and make them want to go out and buy the rest of their work. But that was when people were paying $18 for a CD with fourteen, fifteen, sixteen songs on it and only one or two of the songs that they liked or that were any good. I don't blame them for going out and getting the one or two songs that they like instead of having to pay $18 for a disc that's full of bullshit."

Cherney has felt the financial ramifications of piracy, though, and it has changed the way he works. "Look, we were in the business of selling albums and CDs for a long time, and when you were a profit participant, your royalties would be reflected in sales of those albums. Now you see your royalties on the song and half the time the song is downloaded free, so it's absolutely affected everything. That's why I'm working predominantly as a mixer now, because they pay you and you spend a week or ten days or two weeks on an album, instead of three or four months. Plus, the budgets are such that you agree to some bullshit budget as a producer, on my level anyway, that you can't possibly make the record. So, you end up not seeing the back end anyway and never seeing the royalties. You give up two, three, four months of your life for something that you're never going to get paid for anyway."

Chris Vrenna points out that, though the industry has finally developed some viable pay-to-download options, such as as Apple iTunes, these services may not be the ultimate answer to the industry's financial woes. "I'd rather have somebody buying one song for a dollar from me than stealing my music or anybody's music, because it is stealing and I don't care what anybody says, but from what I understand, Apple keeps forty percent and gives the label sixty percent. So, even if you had a fifty/fifty deal with your label—and good luck getting one of those kinds of deals—that means the artist would get thirty cents, the label gets thirty cents, and Apple keeps forty cents. After the artist gets thirty cents, the manager has to be paid; that's fifteen percent, and probably a business manager at five percent, so there's twenty percent there. So, how many thirty-cent downloads would you have to sell before you can make $1,000? In L.A., that doesn't even cover rent anymore. It's weird—like, the whole paradigm shifted and it's almost impossible for anybody to make money anymore."

THE BUSINESS SIDE

Despite the well-documented demise of the music industry as we knew it, music is still being made (and even being purchased). But what happens once an album is in the can? In almost any other field of work, it's handed over and the two parties go their separate ways. In the music business, though, producers and musicians occasionally build relationships that carry on. There is a level of intimacy that develops when people create art together. Plus, the team spends a lot of time together through pre-production and recording. "It usually takes about three months for me to do a record. So, I'm definitely with the band that amount of time, and sometimes we part and that's it," says Matt Wallace. "I might talk to them every once in a while, and sometimes if things are going really well, like with Maroon 5 or Train, I'll stay in touch with them just out of the pure thrill that the record is doing well and it's exciting."

Other times the producer may begin to take an active role in the band's business, working on the marketing plan, helping get radio airplay, and continuing to cheerlead as the band hits the road. And occasionally, a sustained business relationship evolves from a difficult situation. For instance, when Chris Vrenna turned AI's debut *Artificial Intelligence* in to DreamWorks Records, the label decided to sit on it for months. In the meantime, Vrenna was approached by the band a number of times. "They came to me and asked me to help them pick singles, they came to ask me about tour plans and ideas, and I actually laid out almost an entire radio and marketing campaign for that band, because I knew where they should go. The guys just flat-out called me and I said, 'Look, I'm not a marketing guy, but here's how I would market this band. If you could time this with this and if you can do that.' I had tour ideas that I thought they'd be good for," he says. "It was crazy. I should have taken fifteen percent for all of that."

Vrenna then watched as the label released the album with no push. While it was not a strategy that he agreed with, it was one that he was familiar with; his band Tweaker had gone through the same thing with Almo Sounds. "That's what I think is wrong with these labels. You make a record that you pour months of your time into and then you get fucked," he says. "It's so sad when that happens and when the poor band has to spend a year paying legal bills out of their own pocket to just get released from a contract, that just fucks your whole career up. It took me almost a year to get out of my Almo deal when Almo folded. It's so depressing to make a record you believe in and then it doesn't even see the light of day."

Matt Wallace learned early on in his career, and the hard way, that the relationship has to end once the record gets into the company's hands. "I was very naïve, and after I made the Faith No More record at the end of 1988, I used to call the label up and say, 'Hey, what can we do? What can I do? How can we get this thing going?' At a certain point in time, I forgot who said it, one person said, 'Look, this is not your job. Don't call us.' Basically, that was it. 'The record is done and we'll do what we do. Your input is not really wanted.' At the time I took it harshly, but I understand that's their job and they have to do their thing," he says. "I was so enthusiastic and completely unaware of the protocol. Labels certainly never look to producers to figure out what to do or what singles they should release. They have their own agenda and their own experience."

"You have to let it end," Garth Richardson agrees. "The problem is that you sometimes have to let go, because if you're going to do that it would take up a lot of your time. I tend to love making records. I don't want to necessarily go into the record company and ask, 'How come this record is not being sold?' The thing that people don't understand is that the record company doesn't have any say on who is buying the records. Either [the public] gets it or they don't get it. The reason why Hootie and the Blowfish sold eight-million records and somebody else sold 2,000 had nothing to do with the record label. It just happened that the fans liked it. Tell me, how come somebody bought so many pet rocks?"

How Do Producers Measure Success?

Critical acclaim? Industry awards? Big sales numbers? Those are just a few of the ways people gauge the success of an album, for better or for worse. Yet producers look beyond the obvious to determine if they have done a good job.

"I don't put any stock in [record reviews]," says Matt Wallace. "They're nice to have and I'll keep clips and that kind of thing, but I don't really worry about that because there's nothing I can do about it at that point. First, the record's already done, so we can't change anything. Second, it's just someone's opinion about it, and that's cool. Someone's got an opinion and that's great."

J.P. Plunier is even more direct when recalling his early production work with Ben Harper. "The main reason I didn't pay attention to critics—and this is a phenomenon particular to Ben—is that not a lot of the major places paid attention to him. Most everybody else gave him positive reviews and, believe me, they never wondered who produced the albums when they thought about it. The comments of most people are so off-base anyways. You can tell that most of the people have never made any music whatsoever or witnessed the making of any music," he says. "One of the most interesting things about Ben is how he plays and sings together and the intricacy of that was almost never brought up, so musically a lot of these people don't know that much. Plus, the sort of referential aspects of it are so easy to see, because some of them are worn on the sleeve and it's kind of uninteresting to hear about them. So, there's actually very little to glean from most of the critics.

"Every once in a while I will read something and go, 'this motherfucker is on point and we fucked up on this' or 'that's a really good idea' or 'that's worth checking out, but on another kind of song,'" Plunier continues. "There is obviously stuff to be gotten. Most critics especially on the first three records were incredibly effusive and very praising, sometimes for the wrong reasons."

What equals success for Garth Richardson? "Making good records," he answers. "It doesn't matter if the band comes back or not, it doesn't matter if I win the Grammy or win the Juno. It's all about when the band leaves, they leave with something that they feel good about. The great thing is that when you finish someone's record, you know for sure that they are proud of it. If it sells, that's great. It's great to have a band come back, but it's totally their decision."

"For me the satisfaction is a job well done," says Craig Street. "Is the artist happy? That's my first thing. When I finish a project and the artist comes up to me and says, 'Man, this is it for me.'" Street ticks off a few projects where he felt satisfaction, including the soundtrack to the NBC television program *Crossing Jordan* and The Holmes Brothers' *Simple Truths* release.

In fact, the *Crossing Jordan* soundtrack was a quintessential Street release, considering he built a band and then had an assortment of singers come in and cover an eclectic array of songs. For instance, Sam Phillips covered The Beatles' "I Wanna Be Your Man," Lucinda Williams reworked the Tom Waits song, "Hang Down Your Head," and Vic Chesnutt sang on the Bob Dylan classic, "Buckets of Rain." "I got to work with people that I'd never worked with before and that I really wanted to work with, like Sam Phillips, Alison Krauss, and Richard Thompson. It was really fun stuff and I got to do whatever I wanted to do. It was like, 'Okay, we're going to pick this song and we're going to try this style.' The artists would come in and say, 'What if I did this?' then the musicians would say, 'What if I did that?'"

The Holmes Brothers recordings brought Street a different type of fulfillment. About a month after the sessions were over, he checked his mail, and, found an expression of gratitude from the group. "There was a Hallmark card from those guys and each of them had signed it," Street recalls. "They each had their own thing to say. 'Man, we just want to thank you for taking the time to work with us. We love the record and we loved working with you and the guys.' Then to see the press take off after it and then to see the record actually sell. That, to me, is perfection. These three guys that have been doing it forever, they love the record, the audiences love the record, the press loves the record, their live shows are fantastic, and they are happy and I am happy. I could care less if I ever saw a dime from that thing; to me it doesn't get any better than that.

"Somewhere down the line I came to the point where I thought, 'What really matters in the world? Love? Honesty? Does making a record really matter? I don't think so. It's really fun and it matters that there's good energy or that there's good creativity or there's something good being put into the world in a sense, so on that level it matters. But did it matter enough for me to worry about all of the things that would go down in the course of a day? Not really, so what happened is that I started to enjoy so much more and there's a sense of wonder and kind of openness to when things would fall apart. Artists might be cranky, musicians might not be having their best day, stuff in the studio is breaking down, or the A&R guy calls up ten times with some stupid request. How do you move through that?

"I started realizing that there would be a day where you feel like you didn't get anything done at all and then you'd come in the next day and there would be three gems," Street continues. "Those are the payoffs. Being in a room when somebody like k.d. [lang] or Cassandra [Wilson] is singing a vocal and you know that that's the one. Seeing somebody like Chris Whitley sitting in a tool shed in the back of his father's house, just possessed, and you realize that you are in the presence of something very special—you're in the presence of nature at its purest, you're in the presence of the divine. That's worth it to me."

Even with his long track record of releases—dating from Roxy Music in the 1970s to The Smiths in the 1980s, B.B. King in the 90s, and Los Lonely Boys in the 2000s—John Porter still gets a kick out of hearing a song that he worked on played in public. "People always say that they hate hearing their songs in elevators and supermarkets," he says with a smile. "It always stops me in my tracks if I hear something I worked on in the supermarket, and hearing stuff on the radio is great—really, anywhere where sound can be in your environment and it's unexpected. I heard one whole album in some bar in New Orleans while I was sitting there having a drink, and it was really enjoyable listening to it."

Craig Street is not alone in stating that the music business' definition of success needs to change. "Success isn't always what you think it might be," says Don Was. He recalls his experience working in Was (Not Was) on the outfit's 1998 hit song, "Walk the Dinosaur." "It was this goofy novelty record that was propelled by the video with these greased up girls," Was says. "Now, it didn't make any new fans for the band, I don't think. People bought the single. They sold a lot of singles, but not a lot of albums and [the song] alienated everybody who liked what the band was originally about. It sort of ruined the core audience without contributing to building of the core audience. It created a situation for us where the record company said, 'We need another one like "Walk the Dinosaur."' Man, you know that was an oddity. I didn't know how we did that, and we couldn't come up with another one; we didn't even know how we came up with the first one. It was not indicative to the body of our work, and it destroyed the band for years, where only now we've got our momentum back from that."

"If I used sales as the criteria [for determining success] I would be depressed all the time, because it is totally out of my control and subject to these weird flukes of nature," Was continues. "I have this little ritual where, when we finish a record, the artist and I sit in a room and play the whole thing back the day before anybody else comes in to hear it. If the artist can say to me, 'Man, that's exactly what I was hearing,' or 'That's even better than what I was hearing in my head,' then the record is a success and whatever idiotic things the marketing people do subsequently don't matter. I will not allow that to alter how I feel about the record, hence *Waymore's Blues, Part 2* [Waylon Jennings' 1994 release]. That was a big success, even though you can't find it anywhere and it sold like ten copies. Waylon loved that record. He had heard a Bob Dylan song and he wanted to do a version of it. He was talking about ambient textures and things like that, but he had no idea how to go about doing it, and he felt that I helped him to realize this thing and it was what he hoped for, but it came out even more evocative, and he told me so—that's a successful record."

AT THE END OF THE DAY

Walking out of Capitol Studios in Los Angeles, Ben Harper hangs his head in fatigue. It's somewhere around 2:30 in the morning, and he's just finished the principal recording sessions for what might be a career-defining release with the Blind Boys of Alabama. The past five days have been so thrilling that he is drained. "The challenge of working with these guys is to *not* get goose bumps, but I'm getting that feeling every day," Harper says. "Does that even happen to us once a day where we get that emotional? I don't know. It's happening to me five times a day. I'm exhausted, man. I am spending half the day in shivers."

Sylvia Massy Shivy continues to be inspired by the artists she works with and the music they make together. "The characters are so great. I just have the most fun and make new friends every time I do a new session," she says. "This is the greatest job in the world. Musicians are fun, fun people with a lot of life. The ones that take themselves too seriously aren't as fun, but most of them are light-hearted, very excited, and very willing to try new things. It's a fun environment to be in every day. It's a lot of work, still. Twelve hours a day, but it's worth it. I'd rather be here than at home. Home is fun, too," she says with a laugh, "But it's not a drag coming to work."

"It's always fun because you are inventing something every day of your life," says Walter Afanasieff. "Some people are credited with inventing one thing, or if you're lucky enough in your whole entire life to leave something behind like a legacy. How many people in the world get to write one song or do one thing that is left behind on a recording or an image, a photograph, a piece of history that people will look at, listen to, admire, or criticize at the end of the day? Most people never get to do that, and we're so lucky. I get to do it every single day. I get up in the morning and I have to go invent a song, every day. I have to write and produce, which is inventing, a three- or four-minute piece of something that's going to be left on a recording for others to listen to and hopefully enjoy.."

Even knowing everything that can, and probably will, go sideways during the making of an album, record producers continue to be excited about their chosen career. Garth Richardson once remarked in a *Mix* magazine story: "Where else can you drink, smoke, and hang out all day?"

"It's so true, isn't it?" he confirms. "I'm sitting in a 1920s barber shop chair looking at the ocean with trees everywhere. I'm a very lucky guy." He says his family has taught him to appreciate the simple things in life. "My daughter was seriously ill. She had surgery and the whole thing. She's fine now, but it was the most terrifying thing that I have ever had to go through and it put everything else into perspective," Richardson explains. "There are how many chords? There are twelve notes. There are only so many chord progressions you can write. I'm sorry, but this is not brain surgery. This whole business that we're in, people take way too seriously. Lighten up, it's only rock 'n' roll."

INDEX

Unstable (Adema), 100

V

Van Lear Rose (Loretta Lynn), 35
Vedder, Eddie, 63
Vega, Suzanne, 13
Veltrop, Rich, 191
Velvet Underground, 138
Very Proud of Ya (A.F.I.), 66
vibe, finding the right, 126–28, 131, 185–89
Vicious Rumors, 57, 92
Vincent, R. Walt, 183
Violator (Depeche Mode), 58
Virgin Records, 29, 61
Vivadixiesubmarinetransmissionplot (Mark
　Linkous), 22
"Voodoo," 37
Voodoo Lounge (Rolling Stones), 204–5
Vrenna, Chris
　on A&R reps, 70
　as artist/producer, 9, 22
　on building trust, 94–95
　career of, 19, 31–32, 33, 58–59
　on choosing radio songs, 168
　on establishing relationships, 224
　on exploring new ideas, 181–82
　on illegal downloading, 223
　on polishing arrangements, 170
　on recording budgets, 143
　on selecting songs, 161–62
　self-productions of, 47–48
Vue, 190, 193

W

Wagener, Michael, 52, 55, 62
Wainwright, Rufus, 19, 89
Wait for Me (Jubilant Sykes), 162
Waits, Tom, 15, 19, 27, 63, 119–20, 129,
　162–63, 211, 226
Walden, Narada Michael, 10, 18, 25, 52, 57
"Walk the Dinosaur," 227
Walker, Butch, 12, 178–79
　career of, 20
　on hitting problem spots, 211–12

on polishing arrangements, 171
Wall, The (Pink Floyd), 52, 209
Wallace, Andy, 214
Wallace, Matt, 1
　on A&R reps, 71–72
　on band/label disputes, 75–76
　on budget shrinkages, 4
　on building trust, 95–96
　career of, 20
　on choosing artists, 87–88
　on creating hits, 163–64
　on dealing with difficult personalities,
　　200–201
　on defining success, 225
　on establishing relationships, 224
　on getting performances, 206–7
　on illegal downloading, 222
　on letting go, 224
　on managers, 64
　on mixing process, 215–16
　on over-budget problems, 149–50
　on pre-production tasks, 157
　on recording budgets, 144–45, 146–47,
　　148
　on session players, 114
　on substance use during recording sessions,
　　196–97
　on surround sound, 216–17
　on ultimate recording goal, 33
　on using mixing engineers, 214–15
Wallflowers, the, 218
Walsh, Clint, 47–48
Wan Santo Condo, 17
Wanchic, Mike, 60
Want One (Marius deVries), 19, 89
Want Two (Marius deVries), 19, 89
Ward, Scooter, 155
Warner Bros., 4, 98, 164, 166
Waronker, Lenny, 29
Warren, Diane, 14
Warriors, the, 10
Was, Don, 169
　on artists' receptivity, 177–78
　on band chemistry, 111–12

on being the "next producer," 98
career of, 20
on changing genres, 65
on defining success, 227
on getting performances, 205–6
on knowing your strengths and weaknesses, 33
on laying down tracks, 204–5
partnership with Cherney, 12, 91, 113, 115, 121–22, 167–68
on playing on albums while producing, 49–50
on setting a vibe, 187–88
on working with Dylan, 3
Was (Not Was), 227
Water Music Studios, 127
Watts, Charlie, 112–13
Way, Gerard, 88
"Way Away," 16
Waymore's Blues, Part 2 (Waylon Jennings), 227
"We Are the Future" benefit concert, 187
Websites, setting up, 60
Weezer, 1, 155
Welcome to the Cruel World (Ben Harper), 14, 45, 172
Westerberg, Paul, 152, 158, 177–78, 200–201
Wexler, Jerry, 28
What It Is to Burn (Finch), 182–83
"What's Up?", 17, 42
Wheat, 4, 13
Where It Lands (Damnations), 213
Where You Want to Be (Taking Back Sunday), 173–74
White, Jack, 30
  as artist/producer, 35
White Stripes, the, 30, 164
Whitley, Chris, 10, 107, 162, 227
Who Am I? (Todd Sharp), 28
Will to Live, The (Ben Harper), 106, 203
Williams, Lucinda, 15, 57, 63, 146, 201–2, 226
Wilson, Brian, 38
Wilson, Cassandra, 18, 162, 181, 226
Wirt, Jim, 99

women producers, 7–8
Wood, Brad
  on A&R reps, 73–74
  on band chemistry, 112–13
  on band/label disputes, 76–77
  on building trust, 95
  career of, 20
  on choosing artists, 86
  on exploring new ideas, 183
  on majors *vs.* indies, 84, 219–20
  on owning a recording studio, 51
  on recording budgets, 145
  on selecting a studio, 127–28
"Wooly Bully," 139
World Class Fad (Paul Westerberg), 200
World Without Tears (Lucinda Williams), 15, 63, 146, 201–2
World's End Producer Management, 63

X
XTC, 24

Y
Yellowcard, 16, 179
Yoakam, Dwight, 12
Yorn, Pete, 20
Yoshimi Battles the Pink Robots (Flaming Lips), 217
"Your Side of My World," 46
"Youth of the Nation," 100, 155

Z
Zarin, Michelle, 52
Zebrahead, 11
Zirbel, Joshua, 77
Zoo (Anadivine), 79
Zooropa (U2), 180